C O L U M B I A

UNIVERSITY LIBRARY
W-STEVENS POINT

*Laurence R. Joh*

W9-BJN-553

WASHINGTON PASS
ELEV. 5477

S E L K I R K    M O U N T A I N S

I D A H O

L. Chelan

Columbia

R.

Spokane R.

**Spokane** ●

PASS
1

SS

C O L U M B I A

B A S I N

Yakima ●

Snake    River

**Richland** ●

**Walla Walla** ●

B L U E    M T S.

River

| 0 | 50 | 100 |
|---|----|----|
MILES

Map prepared by C. Ogrosky. Imagery obtained by Earth Resources
Technology Satellite (ERTS) in 570 mile orbit; image mosaic prepared
by U.S. Soil Conservation Service. Elevations in feet.

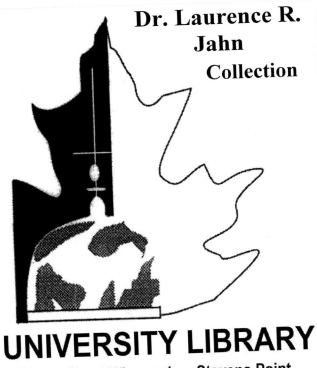

**Dr. Laurence R. Jahn**
Collection

# UNIVERSITY LIBRARY

University of Wisconsin – Stevens Point

# Coastal Resource Use

## DECISIONS ON PUGET SOUND

# COASTAL RESOURCE USE

## Decisions on Puget Sound

ROBERT L. BISH

ROBERT WARREN

LOUIS F. WESCHLER

JAMES A. CRUTCHFIELD

PETER HARRISON

*Published in cooperation with
Washington Sea Grant Program*

**University of Washington Press**   SEATTLE AND LONDON

This work is a result of research sponsored by the NOAA Office of Sea Grant, Department of Commerce, under grant numbers 1-35320, NG-1-72, and 04-3 158-42, and by the National Science Foundation under grant numbers GH-40 and GH-66 to the Washington Sea Grant Program. Publication of this book was supported by the State of Washington, Department of Ecology.

The U.S. Government is authorized to produce and distribute reprints for governmental purposes notwithstanding any copyright notation that may appear hereon.

Copyright © 1975 by the University of Washington Press
Printed in the United States of America

All rights reserved. No part of this publication may be reproduced or transmitted in any form or by any means, electronic or mechanical, including photocopying, recording, or any information storage or retrieval system, without permission in writing from the publisher.

Library of Congress Cataloging in Publication Data

Main entry under title:
Coastal resource use.

  Bibliography: p.
  Includes index.
  1. Natural resources—Puget Sound area. 2. Environmental policy—Puget Sound area. I. Bish, Robert L.
HC107.W22P84         333.7'09797'7         74-32105
ISBN 0-295-95348-9

HC
107
.W22
P84
c.2

# Preface

This study is the result of efforts by a group of faculty and students at the University of Washington to combine research, teaching, and public service. Research and student training are both improved by the active involvement of students on research projects, and research projects can be directly applicable to important public policy issues such as the future of Puget Sound.

The study was sponsored by the University of Washington Sea Grant Program directed by Stanley R. Murphy. The Sea Grant Program, begun under the National Science Foundation and now funded by the National Oceanic and Atmospheric Administration of the U.S. Department of Commerce, is designed to promote teaching, research, and public service to enhance the use of marine resources. Providing supporting services on the University of Washington campus were the Department of Economics and Institute for Economic Research.

While all authors contributed to the entire effort, research and writing of each chapter was generally the responsibility of one or two persons. Robert Warren drafted chapters 1, 6, 8, and 9 and assisted with 7. Robert Bish drafted chapters 2, 3, 4, and 5 and assisted with 6. Louis F. Weschler drafted chapter 7 and assisted with 1 and 6. Peter Harrison provided much of the research and assisted with chapters 2, 3, and 4. James A. Crutchfield was principal investigator for the project and contributed to the development of chapters 1, 3, 4, and 6.

Many persons have assisted the authors with the study. Joanne Powers undertook secretarial responsibilities throughout the effort. Students participating in the project include Steward Borland, Jon Conrad, Frank Doolittle, Susan Finney Morry, Gordon Gould, Mitchell Moss, Nancy Neubert, Martha Oliver, Wallace Spencer, Patricia Weis, and Gilbert Wright. Taylor Dennen also contributed to the research effort and undertook important responsibilities for completing the proj-

v

ect after most of the authors relocated in other areas. Charles Ogrosky of the Department of Geography merits special thanks for the cartography. His maps, figures, and designs enhance the presentation considerably.

We also appreciate the efforts devoted to review of earlier drafts of the manuscript by William Burke, Robert Coughlin, Arthur Harnish, Russel Hupe, Ruth Ittner, David Jamison, Donald Kaufman, Charles Lean, Robert Pealy, Wallace Spencer, Edward Standish, and Marvin Vaille. We appreciate the responses to our inquiries from state, local, and federal government officials and citizens concerned with the future of Puget Sound. Without their cooperation it would not have been possible to undertake this study.

Finally, we wish to thank the State of Washington Department of Ecology, which supported publication and thus permitted a lower price and wider distribution of the book than would otherwise have been possible.

This study is not just the result of a few scholars working within the university. It is the result of faculty, students, government officials, and interested citizens throughout the region who are actively concerned with the use and preservation of the natural environment around Puget Sound. We sincerely hope that this effort assists all of us to achieve a better understanding of how coastal resource use decisions on Puget Sound are made so that we can achieve continued use of this valuable resource without its destruction.

R. E. B.

# Contents

# Figures

# Coastal Resource Use

## DECISIONS ON PUGET SOUND

# CHAPTER ONE

# Introduction

PUGET Sound is a system of protected waterways without equal in the western United States in its physical setting and resource productivity. Its twenty-five hundred square miles of estuaries, inlets, bays, and passages, surrounded by rich forest lands, provide some of the most beautiful scenery and attractive recreational opportunities to be found anywhere. Two quite different but equally majestic mountain ranges, the Cascades to the east and the Olympics to the west, bracket the Sound. Many islands, large and small, dot its surface. Twelve major rivers flow into the waters of the Sound. There are stark contrasts in the extent and type of human development around its shoreline. Much of the coastal land is sparsely settled, yet two thirds of the state of Washington's population and most of its industry are located here. Puget Sound also plays an important part in defining the Pacific Northwest as a region and in linking it to Asia and Alaska through ocean commerce.

The Sound's natural resources—timber, marine life, birds, waterfowl, animals, rivers, and waters—support a wide variety of recreational and leisure activities. Boating, sports fishing, hunting, bird watching, camping, and picnicking attract not only residents of the immediate area but people from all over the West and the rest of North America. The resources of the Sound also provide a base for agricultural, commercial, and industrial activity. Shipping, commercial fishing, forestry, farming, petroleum refining, aerospace production, and power generation all make use of the lands, waters, and other resources of the Sound. The plentiful natural resources have provided a base for economic development while at the same time providing a spectacular natural environment for living and recreation. There are few places where urbanization and development are so closely tied to natural areas of water, forests, and mountains. This diversity of demands and the finite character of the resources necessarily produce conflicts among uses and users. This is not only true of the Sound but of all major coastal areas of the nation.

The growing variety, intensity, and rate of increase in demands placed upon coastal zone areas in general have created a special concern within the broader national environmental protection movement over the last decade. The land-water interface of the shoreline is one of the most biologically productive areas on earth. At the same time, it is one of the most fragile in ecological terms. These circumstances have produced a series of policy problems over the appropriate public role in coastal management.

It is clear that market transactions concerning resources use, by themselves, do not protect what has come to be viewed as the broad public interest, or one user from the negative spillover effects of another. In the case of Puget Sound, for example, there is general agreement that the aesthetic quality of the Sound should be maintained and that pulp mills should not introduce wastes into its waters that would endanger fish stocks. The implementation of these environmental concerns requires the use of public authority to absolutely constrain or encourage some types of use or favor one over another. What constitutes a politically acceptable balance between development and conservation of shoreline resources and among uses has been and still is a recurring matter of debate in the nation as a whole as well as in the state of Washington.

Apart from the question of which policies should be adopted to regulate shorelines, there is the related issue of which scale or combination of scales of government—local, regional, state, multistate, national, or international—should be utilized to exercise management authority. Puget Sound is a vast and integrated estuarine resource system and is a single entity in symbolic terms in many people's minds. In fact, however, it has a large number of quite distinctive ecological subsystems and human use patterns.

This diversity of physical, social, and economic characteristics is reflected in a variety of ways. There are few physical events which could affect the Sound as a whole or even large portions of it. The spatial distances of communities around the Sound from one another and, particularly, their great differences in population size, economic scale, and life styles have largely inhibited the emergence of any Sound-related sense of common identity among them. To a degree, the opposite has been true. The overwhelming economic and cultural dominance of the Seattle–King County area, which has half of the total population around the Sound, has contributed to conflicts between metropolitan-oriented interests and groups in other parts of the Sound over the type and rate of overall shoreline development.

There is no governmental unit that has "responsibility" for the Sound. Rather, for public management and regulatory purposes the land-water area is divided horizontally among units of local government and vertically among state and federal agencies. While the mix of jurisdictions has changed over time, the diversity has remained with conflicts over local and more centralized control providing the major tension.

## RESOURCE MANAGEMENT AND ENVIRONMENTAL POLITICS

The purpose of this study is to address issues concerning both the general question of developing shoreline management policies and the evolution and results of specific efforts to regulate Puget Sound's coastal resources. In particular, the focus is upon how governments associated with the Sound have responded to new public initiatives and have managed the shoreline resources of the Sound. All levels of the American federal system of government have some responsibilities for making public choices for the people of the region. Twelve counties, municipalities, and numerous special districts and authorities constitute the web of local government around the Sound. Several regional agencies cover portions of the region. These include the Municipality of Metropolitan Seattle, which provides sewage disposal and transportation services for the Seattle–King County area, and a voluntary intergovernmental coordinating unit, the Puget Sound Governmental Conference. The state Departments of Natural Resources, Parks and Recreation, Ecology, Game, and Fisheries are among the major units at this level with a concern for the lands and waters of the coastal zone for the state as a whole. The U.S. Army Corps of Engineers, Coast Guard, Forest Service, Bureau of Commercial Fisheries, and the Environmental Protection Agency are among the primary national agencies which affect the Sound.

Each of these units has its own functions. Although their exact range of authority has varied over time, most water-related decisions have rested with state and federal agencies and most land-related authority has been exercised by local governments. In the past decade, however, a number of public issues involving conflicts over resources use in the Sound have affected the distribution of governmental jurisdiction. In addition to the more long-term controversies over such matters as sports vs. commercial fishing, industrial and municipal waste discharges, and spillovers of logging activitites, governments have become increasingly involved in issues concerning the regulation of resource use and provision of public goods and services relating to coastal areas of the Sound.

Much of this change in focus, which treats the shoreline itself as a resource rather than simply the site where a number of resources are located, came as a response to the political activities of environmental groups. In Washington state, half a decade of "environmental politics" over coastal resource development culminated in the passage of the Shoreline Management Act of 1971 and the establishment of what amounts to a joint local-state system of coastal regulation. A good part of the impetus for the legislation was generated from conflicts over uses of the Sound's shoreline. In a number of important ways, the events producing a state-wide shoreline management system and its content provide a reflection of some of the generic issues in formulating coastal zone policy concerning the balancing of conservation and development and subarea interests and the design of governmental structures.

## ORGANIZATION OF THE STUDY

The next three chapters present the general setting of the Sound. Its major physical features are described, and the population, employment, and income patterns and trends in the twelve countries of the region are outlined. In addition, the variety and distribution of human uses of Puget Sound's resources are covered.

Chapter 5 deals with a number of general questions which arise in viewing the allocation of shoreline resources as a public policy problem. Attention is given to the interrelatedness among resource uses and the ways in which resource decisions are made. The governmental framework affecting resources management is outlined in Chapter 6. With this background, the emergence of "shoreline environmental politics" in the state and four specific conflicts over resource use are described and analyzed in Chapter 7. The evolution of these local cases into an extended legislative controversy at the state level over the passage of a shoreline management statute is discussed in Chapter 8. In the final chapter, the overall processes for making public choices in the allocation of shoreline resources are summarized and evaluated.

# CHAPTER TWO

# The Puget Sound Region

PUGET Sound is a fjordlike inland sea in the northwest corner of Washington state. Its links to the Pacific Ocean are westward between the Olympic Peninsula and Vancouver Island of British Columbia and northward through the Strait of Georgia between Vancouver Island and the mainland of British Columbia. From these straits Puget Sound's central basin and fjordlike inlets extend south a hundred miles between the Cascade and Olympic mountain ranges. The Sound and the straits within United States waters embrace an area of 2,500 square miles, close to 2,350 miles of shoreline, and more than two hundred islands.[1]

The surrounding area is called the Puget Sound region. The name "Puget's Sound" was originally given just to the inlets south of the Tacoma Narrows by Captain George Vancouver after his exploration of the region. However, as early settlers moved up along the edges of the Sound from the first settlements at Jackson Prairie and Tumwater on the Sound's southern tip, they carried the name Puget Sound with them and applied it to the waters north of the Tacoma narrows as well. Today all the water area from the southern end, north to Admiralty Inlet where the Sound enters the Strait of Juan de Fuca, is called Puget Sound. It is on this complex of inland waterways that the major urban centers of western Washington are located, and the designation of Puget Sound region is often applied to all of the areas adjacent to Puget

1. Descriptions of the Puget Sound region are available in several sources, among which are Richard Highsmith, ed., *Atlas of the Pacific Northwest: Resources and Development* (4th ed.; Corvallis: Oregon State University Press, 1968); Pacific Northwest River Basins Commission, Puget Sound Task Force, *Puget Sound and Adjacent Waters: Appendix VIII, Navigation.* An extensive bibliography of literature with special reference to the marine environment is E. E. Collias and A. C. Duxbury, *Bibliography of Literature: Puget Sound Marine Environment.*

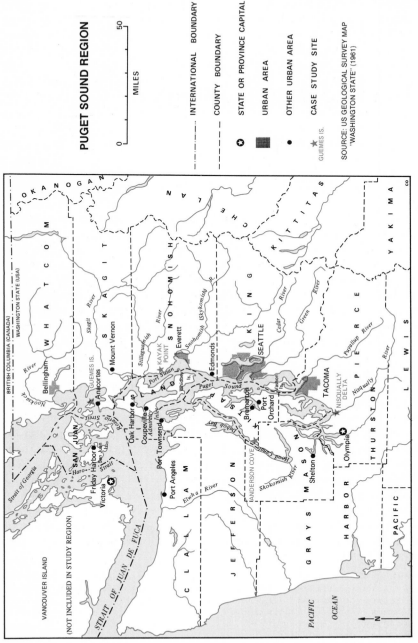

Figure 2-1

Sound and its connecting waterways. Connecting waters include Hood Canal, a fifty-mile-long arm extending south of Admiralty Inlet along the base of the Olympic Mountains on the west; the inner portions of the Strait of Juan de Fuca; Haro Strait, which connects the Strait of Juan de Fuca to the Strait of Georgia on the west side of the San Juan Islands; Rosario Strait, which connects Puget Sound and the inner Strait of Juan de Fuca to the Strait of Georgia on the eastern side of the San Juans and also forms the passage for port traffic from the Pacific to Anacortes and Bellingham; and the southernmost portions of the Strait of Georgia. Thus for the purposes of this study we have defined the Puget Sound region as consisting of the twelve counties surrounding Puget Sound and these adjacent waters.

The Puget Sound region counties are Clallam, Jefferson, and Mason on the western or Olympic Peninsula side; San Juan, consisting of 172 islands in the straits area outside of Puget Sound proper; Island, made up of several large islands within the Sound; Kitsap, consisting of most of the Kitsap Peninsula in the center of the Sound between Hood Canal and the Sound proper; Whatcom, Skagit, Snohomish, King, and Pierce on the eastern or Cascade side of the Sound; and Thurston on its southern end. Together these twelve counties contain 15,781 square miles of land. While this is slightly less than one fourth of Washington state's total, this area is almost twice as large as Massachusetts and contains approximately two thirds of Washington state's population and economic activity. The 2,350 miles of coastline along these twelve counties is also approximately equal to the entire remaining coastline of the contiguous western United States.

It is often useful to approach the study of water-related resources in terms of river basin or drainage areas.[2] While we have selected county areas for purposes of data availability and relevance to the governmental structure by which shorelines are managed, the county areas and river basins closely coincide for most of the Puget Sound region. Boundaries of the eastern counties of the region (Whatcom, Skagit, Snohomish, King, and Pierce) are at the crest of the Cascade Mountains, which divide eastern and western Washington. The land area of these counties is almost identical to that of the Nooksack-Sumas, Samish, Skagit, Stillaguamish, Snohomish, Cedar-Green, and Puyallup river basins. The southern county (Thurston) covers the Nisqually and Deschutes basins. To the south of Thurston County drainage is westward to the Pacific via the Chehalis River rather than northward into the Sound. Kitsap County in the center of Puget Sound is entirely sur-

2. For example, the *Puget Sound and Adjacent Waters* reports of the Pacific Northwest River Basins Commission use river basins as their basic framework for data collection and analysis.

rounded by other Puget Sound counties. Mason County, on the southern part of the Olympic Peninsula, includes the Skokomish and several smaller basins. Clallam and Jefferson, the two northwestern counties, extend from the Sound westward completely across the Olympic Mountains to the Pacific, thus exceeding the Elwha, Dungeness, and smaller basins feeding northern Hood Canal and the straits. However, most of the population and economic activity of Clallam and Jefferson counties is oriented toward inland waters because there are only a few small harbors along their ocean coastline. Port Angeles, for example, is within the Elwah-Dungeness basin on the straits. The remaining two counties consist entirely of islands: Island County at the northern end of Puget Sound and San Juan County at the confluence of Puget Sound, the Strait of Juan de Fuca, and the Strait of Georgia between Haro and Rosario Straits.

The coincidence of river basin and governmental county boundary definitions of the Puget Sound region provides us with a region suitable for independent study of its coastal use and management. While interdependencies with other regions, especially British Columbia to the north, do exist, the Puget Sound region is relatively isolated from external environmental effects. Its future will be primarily dependent on decision-making within the Puget Sound region.

GEOGRAPHY AND NATURAL RESOURCES

*Physical Structure*

The Puget Sound region is part of the Puget-Willamette Lowland, which lies between the Cascade Mountains on the east and the Pacific Ocean on the west.[3] It extends from the Klamath Mountains in southwest Oregon to the Fraser River Valley of British Columbia. The northern section of this lowland, the Puget Lowland, is separated from the southern section by the Chehalis and Cowlitz river basins and is bounded on the western side by the Olympic Mountains. The Puget Lowland is characterized by many estuaries, inlets, and bays. The surrounding mountains, in conjunction with proximity to the Pacific, give the region a temperate marine climate: cool and dry in summer and cool and wet in winter. The Cascade range on the east prevents either cold winter continental air or hot summer continental air from reaching the region. While a temperate marine climate prevails throughout there are climatic variations within the region, mainly with regard to rainfall. In the "rain shadow" area of the northeastern por-

3. For physical histories of the Puget Sound Region see S. N. Dicken, "Western Oregon and Washington," in O. W. Freeman and H. H. Martin, eds., *The Pacific Northwest,* pp. 54–64, and D. C. Campbell, *Introduction to Washington Geology and Resources,* pp. 8–11.

tion of the Olympic Peninsula, San Juan County, and most of Island
County precipitation is less than fifteen to twenty inches a year. In most
other lowland parts of the region precipitation ranges from thirty to
forty inches. As much as one hundred inches, much of it snow, is
common at higher elevations. Seventy-five percent of the precipitation
falls in the winter rainy season from October through March.

The intricacy of the Puget Sound water system and topography of
surrounding land was brought about by glacial expansion and retreat
combined with erosion by river systems during interglacial periods.
Actual filling of the Sound with salt water is estimated to have occurred
as the melting and retreat of the Cordilleran ice sheet of the Pleistocene
period opened the Strait of Juan de Fuca between the lowlands and
the Pacific. As a result of several periods of extensive glacial activity no
preglacial surface topography remains in the region and the land surface is covered with a mantle of glacial till and outwash sands. While
sand and gravel have economic uses, the instability of the glacial materials has presented problems for the development of urban areas. Much
of the coastline above the Sound is made up of cliffs carved into glacial
material and has remained undeveloped. Extensive urban and industrial development has been primarily limited to where rivers
flowing into the Sound have eroded cliffs to form flat estuarine areas.

*The Sound's Waters*

Puget Sound itself strongly reflects its glacial formation. Not only is it
divided into many narrow inlets but parts of it are very deep and separated from other parts of the Sound by relatively shallow sills. The
major sills occur at Admiralty Inlet (138 feet), where Puget Sound joins
the Strait of Juan de Fuca; the northern end of Hood Canal (204 feet),
where the latter joins the Sound; and at the Tacoma Narrows (156
feet), the northern boundary of what Captain Vancouver designated to
be Puget's Sound. Depths of 600 to 800 feet are common between the
Tacoma Narrows and Admiralty Inlet, with a depth of 930 feet found
off Point Jefferson. South of the Tacoma Narrows depths of 300 feet are
common. Hood Canal is shallower than the other areas.

The combination of great depths and narrow connecting sills is
important in altering the hydrologic cycles within the Sound, partially
preventing freer circulation of the more saline bottom water and partially forcing a greater mixing of the waters as tidal movements push
great quantities of water over the sills.[4] Also important in the hydrolog-

4. An expanded discussion of these characteristics of the Sound is presented in
James A. Crutchfield et al., "Socio-economic, Institutional, and Legal Considerations in
the Management of Puget Sound" (submitted to the Federal Water Pollution Control
Administration, Contract No. 14-12-420, 1969), Chap. 1.

ical cycle is the freshwater runoff from surrounding river systems. Ten major rivers, the most important of which are the Nooksack, Skagit, Stillaguamish, Snohomish, Puyallup, and Nisqually, and many smaller rivers and streams add nearly 300 million acre-feet of water to the Sound annualy. This freshwater inflow occurs primarily from lowland rivers during the rainy season from October to March, followed by spring runoffs of the snow-melt from higher elevations. This input of fresh water flows out of the Sound, primarily through Admiralty Inlet and the Strait of Juan de Fuca, to the Pacific. The addition of this much fresh water into the Sound reduces its salinity, and salinity replacement occurs through a net inflow of denser saline bottom water, also primarily through Admiralty Inlet.

Taken together, tidal patterns, seasonal variation in freshwater runoff and water exchange, the physical obstruction of the sills, variations in the depth of water, and differences in coastal topography provide the basis for an unusually varied marine environment. The northern Sound from Admiralty Inlet to the Tacoma Narrows is an extremely productive marine system because it combines some stability with a mixing of nutrient-rich saline bottom water. To a lesser extent, the southern Sound, from the Tacoma Narrows south, is also a productive region. Hood Canal, on the other hand, is relatively shallow and its sill does not force extensive mixing during tidal movements. The result is a stratification where during the spring and summer the surface water is primarily freshwater runoff unmixed with saline bottom water. This lack of mixing prevents high production of phytoplankton to support marine life and also makes the canal more vulnerable to pollution than the southern or northern sections of the Sound. In addition to the productivity of relatively open marine waters, the large numbers of rivers and streams flowing into the Sound, their mud flats and delta marshlands, and other shallow bays around the Sound provide a habitat for fish and wildlife cultures which cannot exist in the deeper, more open waters. It is also the shallow bays and estuarine areas, along with Hood Canal, that are more strongly affected by man-made changes in their environment than are the deeper waters.

*Marine Life*

As mentioned above, the Sound supports a highly diverse marine life.[5] Salmon and steelhead make extensive use of adjacent river systems during their life cycle. These anadromous species spawn in freshwater

---

5. Ibid., Chap. 3. Also see Pacific Northwest River Basins Commission, *Puget Sound and Adjacent Waters: Appendix XI, Fish and Wildlife.*

tributaries and their offspring move downriver, through the Sound and the straits to Pacific Ocean feeding grounds before returning to fresh water to spawn and complete the cycle. The open waters of the Sound are inhabited by "resident" demersal or bottom-fish species such as flounder, sole, and lingcod. Heavily dependent on the tidal areas and shallow bays are extensive communities of molluscans such as clams and oysters, and crustaceans such as crab and shrimp. All of these fishery resources are utilized by both commercial and recreational fishermen.

In addition to providing for marine species the shallow bays, tidal flats, and marshlands adjacent to the Sound are both permanent and wintering habitats for migratory waterfowl from British Columbia, the Northwest Territories, Alaska, and Eastern Russia.[6]

The habitats of both marine and waterfowl species have been altered by human activities. In addition to the simple taking of fish and shellfish for commercial and recreational use, many species have been supplemented with hatchery plantings (primarily salmon and steelhead), controlled cultivation (primarily oysters but more recently salmon aquaculture as well), and the introduction of alien species of shellfish such as the Japanese oyster. Some of the resource enhancement was necessitated by fishing itself, but much of it has been necessitated by changes in the natural environment which have reduced the capability of resident marine communities to maintain themselves. Logging, dredging, diking, the construction of dams, residential developments, and domestic and industrial effluents have all contributed to these changes in the Sound and its rivers. Overall, however, most areas of the Sound and its shoreline remain in a natural condition and continue to support marine life associated with the area.

### Land

The land surface of the Puget Sound region, like the Sound itself, contains valuable resources. The glacial deposits provide the basis for an important sand and gravel industry and the extraction of coal has been important in several areas. High quality limestone and clay deposits have also supported local Portland cement industries. By far the most important land resource, however, has been the forest vegetation. Forests of Douglas fir, cedar, and hemlock extend from the Sound's edge over foothills to the higher slopes of the Cascade and Olympic mountains. These woods form the base of an extensive lumbering and wood

6. Crutchfield et al., "Socioeconomic, Institutional, and Legal Considerations," Chap. 4, and Pacific Northwest River Basins Commission, *Puget Sound and Adjacent Waters: Appendix XI, Fish and Wildlife.*

products industry and even today over 80 percent of the land area within the region is in forests.[7]

The flood plains and lower reaches of many of the streams and rivers of the area have been cleared of their forest vegetation to provide high quality land for agriculture, especially for dairying, berry farming (strawberries, loganberries, raspberries), and root crops, primarily flower bulbs and potatoes.[8]

In addition to the rich resources of the marine and forest environment the physical configuration of the Sound provides it with several of the best natural harbors on the West Coast of the United States. This is due to both the great depths of the Sound's channels and the glacial contouring that has provided very deep water immediately adjacent to the shoreline in sheltered waters such as Elliott and Comencement bays. Excellent ports have always been important in the development of the Puget Sound region. While the first non-Indian settlers came by land up the Willamette-Puget lowland from Oregon, the greatest impetus for early growth was through water-borne trade, especially with San Francisco and Alaska. Even after the Northern Pacific Railroad across the Cascades was completed in 1881 Puget Sound development continued to be oriented toward other West Coast states and the Pacific. This outward orientation combined with heavy dependency on the natural resource base of fisheries and forestry even today gives the Puget Sound region more in common with British Columbia on the north than with eastern Washington across the Cascades.

SUBREGIONS

The Puget Sound region has in common its proximity to the Sound, its vast forests, and snow-capped mountains, and, when generally described, the region appears similar throughout. A closer look, however, reveals significant internal differences among subregions, in respect to both the natural environment and the potential for economic development. To assess properly the impact of development on the natural environment and to evaluate the uses and conflicts over uses of Puget Sound, it is first necessary to examine the major characteristics of, and distinctions among, these subregions.

*Northern Puget Sound*

Northern Puget Sound, or the main basin, extends from Admiralty Inlet in the north to the Tacoma Narrows. Its great depths, large size,

7. Land uses are summarized in Pacific Northwest River Basins Commission, *Puget Sound and Adjacent Waters: Appendix V, Water Related Land Resources,* pp. 1–14.
8. U.S. Bureau of the Census, *Census of Agriculture,* 1969, Vol. 1, part 46 (Washington, D.C.: Government Printing Office, 1972).

and the mixing of water caused by freshwater runoff and tidal movements through Admiralty Inlet make it an extremely productive marine environment for open water species. The shorelines and estuaries along the east side of the main basin also provide it with excellent harbors, especially Elliott Bay (Seattle) and Commencement Bay (Tacoma). The flat lands adjacent to these major bays—the Duwamish basin in Elliott Bay and the Puyallup off Commencement Bay—also provide extensive space for industrial and agricultural development.

The proximity of Lake Union and Lake Washington to Puget Sound has also permitted connecting those two freshwater bodies with the Sound itself through the Ballard ship canal locks. These locks opened up additional shoreline for industrial development in Seattle. The fresh water inside the locks also provides excellent moorages for fishing fleets and other saltwater ships because the fresh water kills many of the saltwater organisms which attach themselves to a ship's hull.

Within Northern Puget Sound the major developments have occurred around Seattle (population 530,860) and Tacoma (population 154,689) on the east side of the Sound. This location combines superior natural harbors with access to agricultural and forest hinterlands, and eventually with railroad connections to the east. The other significant development in this subregion is Bremerton (population 35,307) and the Bremerton Naval Shipyard. The Bremerton area, however, has not had as much growth as have east-side areas. This slower growth is a consequence of Bremerton's relative isolation from the more heavily developed Seattle-Tacoma area and its dependence almost exclusively on the naval yard for its economic base. Bremerton is the only sizable city on the western side of Puget Sound.

*Southern Puget Sound*

Southern Puget Sound extends from the Tacoma Narrows south. This area is characterized by wider tidal movements than the rest of Puget Sound. As one moves south from Admiralty Inlet the sills result in greater movement the further one goes. The daily mean tidal difference, for example, is only 7.2 feet at Port Angeles outside Admiralty Inlet on the Strait of Juan de Fuca, 11.3 feet at Seattle, and 14.45 feet at Olympia. The combination of the many small shallow inlets of its southern reaches and greater tidal movement provides the southern region with vast tidelands and mud flats. These shorelands are not as suitable for development as are the shorelands in Northern Puget Sound but they provide superior habitats for marine life, especially clams and oysters.

The only two cities of any size on Southern Puget Sound are Olympia (23,000) and Shelton (6,500), and neither has the natural harbor or urbanization of the cities on Northern Puget Sound. The best potential port on Southern Puget Sound is at the Nisqually delta, but this area remains as one of the two largest undeveloped estuarine regions of the Sound, providing a valuable marine and waterfowl habitat which has been destroyed in both the Duwamish and Puyallup basins of the urbanized Northern Puget Sound shoreline.

*Hood Canal*

Hood Canal is a relatively shallow arm of Puget Sound which lies next to the base of the Olympic Mountains on the west. It is separated from the rest of Puget Sound by the Kitsap Peninsula and its only significant harbor (Dabob Bay) is utilized primarily by the Navy.

Hood Canal waters are warmer and there are fewer mud flats than on Southern Puget Sound. It provides an excellent habitat for oysters and clams, and its development consists primarily of the construction of residences along the shoreline. Even residential development, however, is largely concentrated on the southern "toe" portion and on the west side. Most of the east side is not easily accessible by automobile and remains sparsely developed. There are no cities with a population of over 1,000 on its shorelines.

The shallowness of Hood Canal, and the stratified water system that occurs during the late spring and summer as fresh water runs off over denser salt water, make it less productive of phytoplankton for marine life and more vulnerable to pollution than the rest of the Sound. Its relative separation from the rest of the region has also contributed to its relatively undeveloped state.

*Waterways East of Whidbey Island*

The main channel of Northern Puget Sound extends northward from the Tacoma Narrows, up past Seattle, and northwest between Whidbey Island on the east and the Kitsap and Olympic peninsulas on the west to Admiralty Inlet where it joins the Strait of Juan de Fuca. To the east of Whidbey Island lies Saratoga passage which joins Rosario Strait through Deception Pass between the north end of Whidbey and Fidalgo Island. Along this passage are several large shallow bays including Port Susan and Skagit Bay. With the exception of Everett (population 53,869), which has easy access south of Whidbey Island to the main basin of Northern Puget Sound, there are no major ports on these inner passages. The water is relatively shallow, there are extensive mud flats, and the Stillaguamish and Skagit estuarine areas provide extensive natural habitats for marine life and waterfowl. Upriver from the Sound diking and draining of some land has been undertaken to enhance the rich delta land for agricultural use but in most respects these areas resemble the inlets of Southern Puget Sound more than any other area.

The major development occurring within these waterways appears to be summer home communities, especially on Whidbey and the other major island, Camano.

### The Straits and San Juans

Outside Admiralty Inlet lies the San Juan Islands where the Strait of Juan de Fuca connects to the Strait of Georgia via Haro and Rosario Straits. To the east of Rosario Strait lie Fidalgo, Guemes, Cypress, and Lummi islands, and Padilla, Samish, and Bellingham bays. Anacortes (population 7,707), the location of several oil refineries, is located on the north side of Fidalgo Island, which is connected by bridge to the mainland. Padilla and Samish bays are both shallow with extensive mud flats and undeveloped shorelines. Bellingham Bay possesses excellent port facilities and Bellingham (39,375) is larger and more developed than any of the other areas on the Sound except for Seattle, Tacoma, and Everett. Bellingham is also a major moorage location for commercial fishermen who fish the North Pacific and Alaskan waters.

North of Bellingham along the east coast of the Strait of Georgia lie several additional small bays between which there is deep water directly adjacent to the shoreline. One of these deep-water areas, Cherry Point, has been developed into a major oil refinery area. Most of the rest of the shoreline is undeveloped except for residential and recreational uses.

The San Juan Islands to the west of Bellingham Bay are surrounded by relatively deep water and possess many good natural harbors. However, their development has been limited by their separation from the mainland. At one time island citizens undertook farming but there has been a shift toward recreational development on the islands during the past two decades. Because of their relative isolation and the existence of many small harbors and bays, the San Juans provide an extremely popular location for recreational boating and summer home development. They also lie in the rain shadow area where there is more sun and less rain than in the rest of the Puget Sound region.

Development of the San Juans, especially many of the smaller islands, poses some problems not common in the rest of the Puget Sound region. Many of the islands are lacking in both underground water supply and glacial till soil. The water shortage has the potential to limit development, and the lack of a glacial till makes sewage disposal via septic tanks a serious problem near the shoreline. Because many of the islands are surrounded by deep moving channels sewage problems have thus far been limited to a few bays. Further development, however, could result in potentially serious pollution problems.

East and north of the San Juan Islands, across Haro Strait, lie the Canadian Gulf Islands and Vancouver Island. While these areas are beyond our own study area there are aspects of Puget Sound resource use which require cooperation with Canadian authorities because of their close proximity with United States waters.

To the southwest of the San Juans and west of Admiralty Inlet the Strait of Juan de Fuca extends one hundred miles to the Pacific Ocean. Its open waters can be very rough during Pacific storms and its only major port on the American side is Port Angeles (population 16,358) on the northern edge of the Olympic Peninsula.

Different parts of the Puget Sound region possess different geographic characteristics and also have developed differently. Urbanization and industrialization have occurred around the port areas at Seattle on Elliott Bay and Tacoma on Commencement Bay, with significant but lesser developments at Everett, Bellingham, Bremerton, and Olympia. Most of the region, however, especially in Southern Puget Sound, on Hood Canal, between Whidbey Island and the eastern shore, and in the San Juans remains undeveloped or development consists primarily of residences along the shoreline. Most of the western shoreline and islands within Northern Puget Sound are also only sparsely developed, primarily with summer homes.

The different natural resources, different degrees of development, different population densities, and different preferences regarding use of Puget Sound's resources in different parts of the region result in considerable diversity within the region. The extent and importance of this diversity will become even more apparent as we proceed to examine in more detail the distribution of population, urbanization, and patterns of income within the region.

# CHAPTER THREE

# Population, Urbanization, Employment, and Income

EXAMINATION of the distribution of population and differences in urbanization, income levels, and poverty rates among the citizens of the region's counties will reveal even more diversity than was indicated by the subregional differences in the natural environment studied in the preceding chapter. An awareness of the diversity within the Puget Sound region, and its implications for the lack of consensus on future uses of Puget Sound and its shorelines, is essential for understanding the extent and nature of conflicts over shoreline use.

## POPULATION AND URBANIZATION

Between 1950 and 1970 the population of Washington state grew 43.1 percent, from 2,378,963 to 3,404,169.[1] At the same time the population of the Puget Sound region grew 58.1 percent, from 1,418,424 to 2,243,069. Thus, over the twenty-year period the percentage of Washington state's population located in the Puget Sound region increased from 59.6 to 65.8 percent—a growth which reflects the increasing concentration of economic activity in the Puget Sound region.

While the Puget Sound region contains nearly two thirds of Washington state's population in less than one fourth of the state's area, the distributional differences within the Puget Sound region itself are even more extreme (see Table 3–1 and the inset map of Fig. 3–1). 1,156,633 people or 51.6 percent of the region's total population of 2,243,069 are located in a single county—King County. When population of the two counties adjacent to King County, Pierce and Snohomish, are added one observes that 1,832,896 people or 81.6 percent of the region's popu-

1. Population and employment data throughout are from the U.S. Bureau of the Census, *Census of Population 1970, General Social and Economic Characteristics,* Vol. 1, part 49, *Washington State* (Washington, D.C.: Government Printing Office, 1972).

TABLE 3-1

POPULATION IN THE COUNTIES OF THE PUGET SOUND REGION, 1950, 1960, 1970, AND PROJECTED 1980

| County | 1950 | | 1960 | | 1970 | | Projected 1980 | | % Change in Totals | | |
|---|---|---|---|---|---|---|---|---|---|---|---|
| | Number | % of PSR Total | Number | % of PSR Total | Number | % of PSR Total | Number | % of PSR Total | 1950-60 | 1960-70 | 1970-80 |
| Clallam | 26,396 | 1.9 | 30,022 | 1.7 | 34,770 | 1.6 | 36,000 | 1.5 | 13.7 | 15.8 | 3.5 |
| Island | 11,079 | 0.8 | 19,638 | 1.1 | 27,011 | 1.2 | 31,200 | 1.3 | 77.2 | 37.5 | 15.5 |
| Jefferson | 11,618 | 0.8 | 9,659 | 0.5 | 10,661 | 0.5 | 11,500 | 0.5 | −17.1 | 10.6 | 7.8 |
| King | 732,992 | 51.7 | 935,014 | 52.9 | 1,156,633 | 51.6 | 1,225,000 | 51.5 | 27.5 | 23.7 | 5.9 |
| Kitsap | 75,724 | 5.3 | 84,176 | 4.8 | 101,732 | 4.5 | 107,700 | 4.5 | 11.1 | 20.8 | 5.8 |
| Mason | 15,022 | 1.0 | 16,261 | 0.9 | 20,918 | 0.9 | 24,000 | 1.0 | 8.1 | 28.7 | 14.7 |
| Pierce | 275,876 | 19.4 | 321,590 | 18.2 | 411,027 | 18.3 | 428,800 | 18.0 | 16.5 | 27.8 | 4.3 |
| San Juan | 3,245 | 0.2 | 2,872 | 0.2 | 3,856 | 0.2 | 4,000 | 0.2 | −11.5 | 34.2 | 3.7 |
| Skagit | 43,273 | 3.1 | 51,350 | 2.9 | 52,381 | 2.3 | 54,000 | 2.3 | 18.6 | 2.0 | 3.0 |
| Snohomish | 111,580 | 7.9 | 172,199 | 9.7 | 265,236 | 11.8 | 284,000 | 11.9 | 54.2 | 54.0 | 7.0 |
| Thurston | 44,884 | 3.2 | 55,049 | 3.1 | 76,894 | 3.4 | 88,000 | 3.7 | 22.6 | 39.6 | 14.4 |
| Whatcom | 66,733 | 4.7 | 70,317 | 4.0 | 81,950 | 3.7 | 85,000 | 3.6 | 5.3 | 16.5 | 3.7 |
| PSR Total | 1,418,424 | 100.0 | 1,768,117 | 100.0 | 2,243,069 | 100.0 | 2,379,200 | 100.0 | 24.7 | 26.9 | 6.1 |
| Washington State Total | 2,378,963 | | 2,853,214 | | 3,404,169 | | 3,615,000 | | 19.9 | 19.3 | 6.2 |
| PSR as % of Washington State | 59.6 | | 61.9 | | 65.8 | | 65.8 | | | | |

Source: U.S. Bureau of the Census, *Census of Population* (1950, 1960, 1970), and Pacific Northwest Bell, *Population and Household Trends in Washington, Oregon, and Northern Idaho 1970–1985.*

lation is located in these three counties. No other county has as much as 5 percent of the region's population and the five smallest counties possess a total of only 4.1 percent of the region's population.

Diversity among counties with respect to population is also reflected by the degree of urbanization within each county. Urban residents, as defined by the census, are persons living in incorporated or unincorporated places of 2,500 or more inhabitants, incorporated places containing 100 or more houses, and the immediately adjacent built up area if population density exceeds 1,000 per square mile.

As Table 3–2 indicates, the largest counties, King, Pierce, and Snohomish, are also the most urbanized, with 92.5, 82.4, and 71.6 percent of their populations urban, respectively. At the other extreme, in the smallest counties, San Juan, Jefferson, Mason, Island, and Clallam, only 0, 49.2, 31.1, 33.9, and 47.1 percent of the population resides in an urban area.

The census definition of an urban area is very inclusive, being mainly designed to separate out "urban" from sparsely settled rural populations. When we examine the distribution of larger urban places the concentration of urbanization in the three largest counties becomes even more striking. Table 3–3 indicates the number of cities by size class in the Puget Sound region. The only city over 500,000 population, Seattle, is in King County, and the only city between 100,000 and 499,999 is Tacoma in Pierce County, with a population of 154,689. The next two largest cities are Bellevue in King County and Everett in Snohomish County. These three counties also comprise two of the three Standard Metropolitan Statistical Areas contained within Washington state.[2] Only when we reach the 25,000 to 49,999 size class do we find cities outside of the three largest counties—Bellingham in Whatcom County in the north and Bremerton in Kitsap County across the main basin of Puget Sound from Seattle. Even of the eleven cities between 10,000 and 24,999, nine are located in King, Pierce, or Snohomish counties, as are seventeen of the twenty-nine cities between 2,500 and 24,999 population size.

Figure 3–1 provides a picture of the location of the larger urban centers in the Puget Sound region. This visual representation illustrates the extent to which large, urban centers are concentrated in King, Pierce, and Snohomish counties on the west side of the main basin of

2. Standard Metropolitan Statistical Areas are composed of counties containing a city (or twin cities) of 50,000 or more inhabitants plus adjacent counties where 15 percent of the labor force in the adjacent county works in the county with the large city or 25 percent of the labor force in the adjacent county resides in the county with the large city. SMSA's in the Puget Sound region are the Seattle-Everett and Tacoma SMSA's. The third SMSA in 1970 was Spokane. Two additional areas, Richland-Kennewick and Yakima, were designated as SMSA's in 1972.

TABLE 3–2

PROPORTION OF POPULATION URBAN IN THE COUNTIES
OF THE PUGET SOUND REGION, 1950, 1960, 1970

| County | 1950 | 1960 | 1970 |
|---|---|---|---|
| Clallam | 42.6 | 42.1 | 47.1 |
| Island | 0.0 | 20.1 | 33.9 |
| Jefferson | 59.3 | 52.6 | 49.2 |
| King | 86.9 | 89.6 | 92.5 |
| Kitsap | 40.6 | 47.9 | 44.2 |
| Mason | 33.6 | 34.8 | 31.1 |
| Pierce | 66.4 | 72.7 | 82.4 |
| San Juan | 0.0 | 0.0 | 0.0 |
| Skagit | 35.7 | 44.8 | 46.3 |
| Snohomish | 42.9 | 56.0 | 71.6 |
| Thurston | 41.3 | 52.3 | 54.1 |
| Whatcom | 51.1 | 52.9 | 51.5 |
| PSR Total | 69.7 | 74.1 | 79.7 |
| Washington State Total | 63.2 | 68.1 | 72.7 |

Source: *Census of Population* (1950, 1960, 1970)

TABLE 3–3

URBAN CENTERS BY SIZE CLASS

| Population | Number of Centers |
|---|---|
| Over 500,000 | 1 |
| 100,000 to 499,999 | 1 |
| 50,000 to 99,999 | 2 |
| 25,000 to 49,999 | 5 |
| 10,000 to 24,999 | 13 |
| 2,500 to 9,999 | 35 |

Source: *Census of Population* (1970)

Puget Sound. Only three of the eighteen urban centers with populations over 10,000—Bellingham off Rosario Strait in Whatcom County, Olympia at the southern tip of Southern Puget Sound in Thurston County, and Port Angeles, on the Strait of Juan De Fuca in Clallam County—are not located within the three largest counties or on the main basin of Puget Sound.

While the population of the Puget Sound region is concentrated in King, Pierce, and Snohomish counties around the cities of Seattle, Tacoma, and Everett, the population within these counties has been becoming less concentrated in the central cities themselves. For example Seattle, which contained 63.8 percent of King County's population in 1950, contained only 45.9 percent in 1970. Seattle itself actually lost population between 1960 and 1970, falling from 557,087 to 530,860. Tacoma's share of Pierce County population fell from 52.1 percent to 37.6 percent between 1950 and 1970 and Everett's share of Snohomish

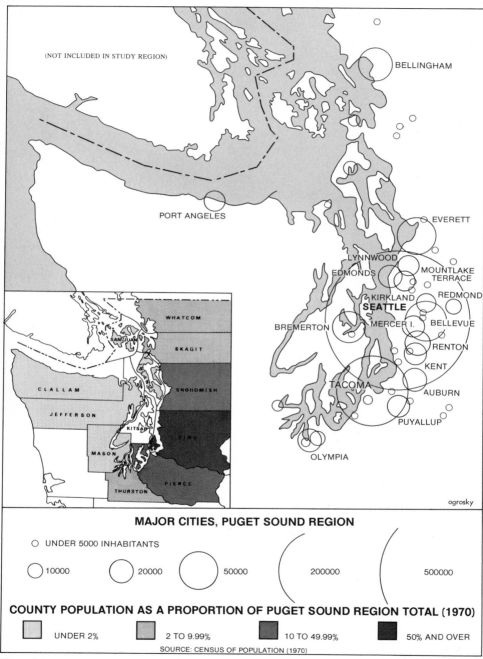

(NOT INCLUDED IN STUDY REGION)

BELLINGHAM

PORT ANGELES

EVERETT

LYNNWOOD
EDMONDS
MOUNTLAKE
TERRACE
KIRKLAND
REDMOND
SEATTLE
BREMERTON
MERCER I.
BELLEVUE
RENTON
KENT
TACOMA
AUBURN
PUYALLUP
OLYMPIA

WHATCOM
SAN JUAN
SKAGIT
CLALLAM
SNOHOMISH
JEFFERSON
KITSAP
MASON
KING
THURSTON
PIERCE

ogrosky

**MAJOR CITIES, PUGET SOUND REGION**

○ UNDER 5000 INHABITANTS

○ 10000      ◯ 20000      ◯ 50000      200000      500000

**COUNTY POPULATION AS A PROPORTION OF PUGET SOUND REGION TOTAL (1970)**

UNDER 2%          2 TO 9.99%          10 TO 49.99%          50% AND OVER

SOURCE: CENSUS OF POPULATION (1970)

Figure 3-1

County population fell from 30.3 percent to 20.3 percent during the same period. The decline of population concentration in central cities, and the absolute decline in Seattle's population between 1960 and 1970, are consistent with nationwide trends toward suburbanization as both business and residents seek less congested suburban environments to carry on their activities.

The current size and distribution of population within the Puget Sound region is easy to identify. Forecasting the future is much more difficult, especially for small county areas. Several estimates of the future population of Puget Sound region counties have been developed, including state agency forecasts and forecasts developed for the *Puget Sound and Adjacent Waters* study.[3] Neither of these studies takes into account recent changes in the local economy, migration patterns, and birth rates, and we believe their forecasts are for much larger population increases than are likely to occur on the basis of present conditions. For this reason population projections developed by Bell Telephone Company, which are based on the 1970 census and include both population dynamics and economic variables in the source model, are discussed here and presented in Table 3–1.[4]

The major difference between forecasted growth and past growth is that the Puget Sound region population is expected to increase by only 6 percent between 1970 and 1980. This low growth rate is in striking contrast to increases of 19.9 and 19.3 percent during the past two decades. The tendency for Puget Sound region population to increase relative to the state population is also expected to diminish with Puget Sound region remaining at just less than two thirds of the state's total. Within the Puget Sound region itself, the largest urbanized counties, King and Pierce, are expected to grow at lower than average rates. The difference between the lower growth rates of the largest counties and the more rapid growth of some smaller counties, especially Island, Mason, and Thurston, will not, however, be of sufficient magnitude to alter the basic distribution of population within the region. The three largest counties will still possess 81.4 percent of the region's population in 1980, and none of the twelve counties will change their relative size class as illustrated on the inset map on Figure 3–1. In conclusion, we anticipate that the Puget Sound region is not going to increase its share but will maintain its dominant position with two thirds of the popula-

3. State of Washington, Office of Program Planning and Fiscal Management, Information Services Division, *State of Washington Population Trends 1971* (Olympia, January 1972). Consulting Services Corporation, "Economic Study of Puget Sound and Adjacent Waters," published as *Appendix IV, Economic Environment,* in Pacific Northwest River Basins Commission, *Puget Sound and Adjacent Waters.*

4. Pacific Northwest Bell, Business Research Division, *Population and Household Trends in Washington, Oregon, and Northern Idaho 1970-1985* (Seattle: January 1972).

tion and economic activity within Washington state. Within the Puget Sound region the relative concentration of population will continue to be in the three large counties, although within these counties suburban population increases will continue to reduce the share of county population residing within the largest cities, Seattle, Tacoma, and Everett.

## EMPLOYMENT STRUCTURE

Historically the development of the Puget Sound region has been dependent on its rich natural resource base. Examination of the employment structure of the region in relation to that of Washington state for 1960 and 1970, as presented in Table 3-4, however, indicates that the industries where the Puget Sound region has employment concentrations considerably below the state-wide average are agriculture, forestry, and fishing; mining and quarrying; and lumber and wood products manufacturing. These natural resource based activities accounted for only 8.9 percent in 1960 and 4.6 percent in 1970 of all employment in the Puget Sound region. Thus, these activities have become relatively

TABLE 3–4

EMPLOYMENT STRUCTURE IN WASHINGTON STATE AND
THE PUGET SOUND REGION, 1960 AND 1970

| Industry | % of Total Employment, Washington State | | % of Total Employment, PSR | | PSR Employment as % of Washington State Employment | |
|---|---|---|---|---|---|---|
| | 1960 | 1970 | 1960 | 1970 | 1960 | 1970 |
| Agriculture, forestry, fishing | 6.8 | 4.1 | 4.4 | 2.0 | 30.7 | 31.4 |
| Mining and quarrying | 0.2 | 0.2 | 0.1 | 0.1 | 42.5 | 41.2 |
| Contract construction | 6.9 | 5.6 | 6.5 | 6.0 | 58.7 | 65.3 |
| Manufacturing | 25.2 | 19.9 | 27.9 | 23.2 | 68.7 | 71.5 |
| (Lumber and wood products only) | (5.3) | (3.2) | (4.4) | (2.5) | (51.1) | (48.1) |
| Transportation, communications, utilities | 7.9 | 7.0 | 8.0 | 7.6 | 62.9 | 66.7 |
| Wholesale and retail trade | 20.1 | 19.8 | 20.4 | 21.5 | 63.2 | 66.7 |
| Finance, insurance, real estate | 4.4 | 5.1 | 5.0 | 6.3 | 72.2 | 75.6 |
| Business and personal services | 22.6 | 33.2 | 22.5 | 26.9 | 61.8 | 49.6 |
| Government | 5.9 | 5.1 | 5.8 | 6.0 | 67.5 | 71.9 |
| Total | 100.0 | 100.0 | 100.0 | 100.0 | 62.3 | 61.2 |
| Total employment | 977,849 | 1,339,612 | 606,765 | 819,967 | | |

Source: *Census of Population* (1960, 1970)

TABLE 3–5

Percentage of County Employment in each Industry, 1960 and 1970

| Industry | Year | Clallam | Island | Jefferson | King | Kitsap | Mason | Pierce | San Juan | Skagit | Snohomish | Thurston | Whatcom | % of Total Employment in PSR |
|---|---|---|---|---|---|---|---|---|---|---|---|---|---|---|
| Agriculture, forestry, fishing | 1960 | 6.3 | 9.4 | 8.4 | 1.6 | 2.7 | 8.4 | 3.1 | 12.3 | 12.6 | 5.1 | 6.8 | 12.6 | 4.4 |
|  | 1970 | 3.9 | 5.5 | 5.2 | 1.0 | 1.5 | 5.3 | 2.3 | 6.4 | 7.9 | 2.3 | 4.5 | 7.9 | 2.0 |
| Mining | 1960 | 0.0 | 0.3 | 0.2 | 0.09 | 0.09 | 0.1 | 0.1 | 1.4 | 0.1 | 0.1 | 0.1 | 0.1 | 0.1 |
|  | 1970 | 0.2 | 0.0 | 0.5 | 0.1 | 0.02 | 0.1 | 0.1 | 0.0 | 0.1 | 0.1 | 0.03 | 0.2 | 0.1 |
| Contract construction | 1960 | 5.6 | 11.8 | 4.8 | 5.9 | 4.3 | 7.1 | 6.9 | 11.7 | 7.9 | 8.5 | 8.8 | 8.1 | 6.5 |
|  | 1970 | 6.5 | 6.9 | 7.8 | 5.2 | 4.4 | 5.3 | 6.5 | 17.0 | 6.5 | 8.1 | 9.7 | 6.2 | 6.0 |
| Manufacturing | 1960 | 38.5 | 11.5 | 37.0 | 28.7 | 42.4 | 40.3 | 23.2 | 11.5 | 25.3 | 29.5 | 18.5 | 19.3 | 27.9 |
|  | 1970 | 29.6 | 10.4 | 28.1 | 23.6 | 32.4 | 34.3 | 19.2 | 6.7 | 23.5 | 27.1 | 13.7 | 18.8 | 23.2 |
| (Lumber products only) | 1960 | (19.8) | (5.0) | (12.0) | (1.7) | (2.1) | (29.8) | (5.9) | (7.0) | (9.3) | (9.9) | (11.0) | (3.9) | (4.4) |
|  | 1970 | (15.8) | (1.8) | (9.6) | (1.0) | (1.3) | (21.2) | (3.9) | (2.0) | (6.2) | (4.2) | (3.9) | (3.0) | (2.5) |
| Transportation, communications, utilities | 1960 | 5.0 | 4.9 | 4.1 | 8.8 | 5.3 | 4.3 | 7.7 | 10.2 | 4.9 | 7.8 | 5.5 | 6.7 | 8.0 |
|  | 1970 | 7.2 | 7.3 | 3.1 | 8.3 | 5.2 | 3.2 | 7.4 | 6.8 | 6.1 | 7.6 | 4.6 | 6.2 | 7.6 |
| Wholesale and retail trade | 1960 | 18.2 | 19.9 | 12.0 | 21.1 | 17.3 | 16.0 | 20.5 | 16.8 | 19.3 | 20.5 | 16.4 | 20.6 | 20.4 |
|  | 1970 | 20.3 | 20.2 | 20.8 | 21.9 | 17.4 | 16.6 | 22.5 | 13.0 | 20.1 | 21.7 | 17.6 | 21.8 | 21.5 |
| Finance, insurance real estate | 1960 | 2.1 | 4.1 | 1.7 | 6.1 | 3.3 | 2.1 | 4.6 | 3.3 | 2.9 | 3.7 | 3.2 | 2.8 | 5.0 |
|  | 1970 | 3.4 | 7.9 | 2.8 | 7.1 | 4.3 | 3.7 | 5.9 | 7.0 | 3.2 | 5.8 | 4.6 | 4.1 | 6.3 |

| | | | | | | | | | | | | | |
|---|---|---|---|---|---|---|---|---|---|---|---|---|---|
| Business and personal services | 1960 | 19.3 | 20.7 | 19.6 | 22.6 | 19.9 | 17.6 | 24.3 | 25.9 | 23.4 | 20.6 | 19.8 | 25.9 | 22.5 |
| | 1970 | 23.8 | 28.6 | 21.1 | 27.7 | 22.4 | 21.7 | 28.0 | 35.0 | 27.5 | 22.9 | 25.8 | 30.3 | 26.9 |
| Government | 1960 | 4.7 | 16.9 | 11.7 | 4.7 | 4.3 | 3.8 | 9.1 | 6.4 | 4.0 | 3.8 | 20.4 | 3.6 | 5.8 |
| | 1970 | 4.8 | 12.8 | 10.5 | 4.7 | 12.1 | 10.1 | 7.6 | 7.7 | 4.8 | 4.1 | 19.1 | 4.1 | 6.0 |
| County total employment as a % of PSR total employment | 1960 | 1.6 | 0.6 | 0.5 | 57.4 | 4.2 | 0.8 | 15.4 | 0.1 | 2.8 | 9.1 | 3.1 | 3.8 | |
| | 1970 | 1.4 | 0.7 | 0.4 | 56.2 | 4.1 | 0.8 | 15.1 | 0.1 | 2.2 | 11.6 | 3.4 | 3.4 | |
| County population as a % of PSR Population | 1960 | 1.6 | 1.1 | 0.5 | 52.8 | 4.7 | 0.9 | 18.1 | 0.1 | 2.9 | 9.6 | 3.1 | 3.9 | |
| | 1970 | 1.5 | 1.2 | 0.4 | 51.5 | 4.5 | 0.9 | 18.3 | 0.1 | 2.3 | 11.8 | 3.4 | 3.6 | |
| Total county employment | 1960 | 9,839 | 3,741 | 3,095 | 348,845 | 26,059 | 5,320 | 93,965 | 856 | 17,022 | 55,678 | 18,763 | 29,582 | |
| | 1970 | 11,633 | 6,411 | 3,638 | 461,615 | 33,916 | 6,640 | 124,925 | 1,173 | 18,095 | 95,140 | 28,693 | 28,488 | |

Source: *Census of Population* (1960, 1970)

small components of the economic structure and they are declining in terms of both total employment and their relative share of employment within the region.

The major sources of employment in the Puget Sound region are business and personal services, manufacturing, and wholesale and retail trade, which together accounted for 71.6 percent of the region's employment in 1970. Finance, insurance, and real estate; transportation, communications, and utilities; construction; and government are also large emloyers, each accounting for 6 to 7.7 percent of the region's employment in 1970. Among these sources of employment, business and personal services; finance, insurance, and real estate; wholesale and retail trade; and, to a lesser extent, government, are increasing in relative importance. Manufacturing, construction, transportation, communication, and utilities appear to be of relatively declining importance within the region. These trends, especially the activities increasing in relative importance and the declining relative importance of agriculture, forestry and fishing, and manufacturing are what one expects to accompany rising incomes and increasing urbanization in an economy.

While the entire Puget Sound region exhibits trends associated with increased urbanization, such as reduced reliance on natural resource industries and increasing importance of service activities, there are differences in the degree to which these trends have affected individual counties. These differences can be identified from the data presented in Table 3–5. A comparison of the percentage of employment in a county with the percentage of employment in that industry in the region indicates whether that county is more or less oriented toward that industry than the region as a whole. A comparison of county employment as a percentage of Puget Sound region employment and county population in relation to regional population indicates whether the county has relatively more or less total employment relative to its population than the region as a whole. Comparisons of 1960 and 1970 data indicate trends in the relative importance of industries within the county's total employment pattern.

Several consistent patterns can be observed from examining the data in Table 3–5. First, agriculture, forestry, and fisheries are more important in the smaller counties than in the larger, more urban counties, but even in the smaller counties this activity is decreasing in importance. Second, business and personal services and finance, insurance, and real estate are becoming more important, while manufacturing is becoming less important, in every county; thus all counties exhibit a shift away from manufactiring toward activities which are identified to accompany urbanization in an area. It appears that the urbanization process and shift toward services is a region-wide phenomenon. Several counties, however, especially Clallam, Jefferson, Kitsap, and Mason, appear to lag behind in a shift away from natural resources and manufacturing to services. At the same time, San Juan and Island counties, two of the smallest counties, exhibit strong movements toward services while retaining above average employment in agriculture, forestry, and fishing. These two island counties appear to be skipping a period of relative importance of manufacturing generally characteristic of economic development and characteristic of the growth of all of the other counties in the region.

The only counties which have large differences between their percentage of regional population and percentage of regional employment are Island, King, Pierce, and, to a lesser extent, Kitsap. King County possessed more jobs relative to population in both 1960 and 1970, and Island, Pierce, and Kitsap counties all possessed fewer jobs relative to population than other counties. Several factors could account for these differences, one of which is population age distribution. For example, Whidbey and Camano islands in Island County contain many retired residents who may account for the low ratio of employment to population. Kitsap, Pierce, and Island counties also have residents who commute to employment in King County.

One element of the distribution of employment that should be kept in mind when thinking about the importance of different industries in different county areas is that the three largest and most urbanized counties, King, Snohomish, and Pierce, contain 82.9 percent of the total employment within the region, and there is no industry where these counties do not have a larger absolute number of employees than all of the other counties put together. Thus, the three largest counties are even slightly more dominant in their share of employment within the region than in their 81.6 percent share of the region's population.

FAMILY INCOME

Differences in urbanization and employment structure are associated with differences in family income. Census data on median family incomes for 1949, 1959, and 1969, and median income differences among counties are shown in Table 3–6 and Figure 3–2.

It is clear that during the past two decades incomes have been rising throughout the region, but between 1959 and 1969 the rate of growth was lower than the rate between 1949 and 1959 for every county except San Juan, which had exceptionally high growth during the 1959-69 decade. Accompanying general income growth, however, are continued differences within the region. Both the table and figure indicate that King County citizens continually have had the highest median incomes within the region, while citizens from the smallest counties, Is-

## TABLE 3–6

### FAMILY INCOME IN THE PUGET SOUND REGION

| County | Median Family Income | | | Percent Change | | Percentage of King County Median Family Income | | | Total Number of Families, 1969 | Poverty Families, 1969 | |
|---|---|---|---|---|---|---|---|---|---|---|---|
| | 1949 | 1959 | 1969 | 1949-59 | 1959-69 | 1949 | 1959 | 1969 | | Number | % of Total |
| Clallam | 3,426 | 5,646 | 9,213 | 64.7 | 63.1 | 89.1 | 79.7 | 77.5 | 9,198 | 790 | 8.58 |
| Island | 2,580 | 5,015 | 8,706 | 94.3 | 73.5 | 67.$ | 70.7 | 73.2 | 7,039 | 681 | 9.67 |
| Jefferson | 3,160 | 5,418 | 8,848 | 71.4 | 63.3 | 82.2 | 76.4 | 74.4 | 2,802 | 258 | 9.24 |
| King | 3,843 | 7,084 | 11,886 | 84.3 | 67.7 | 100.0 | 100.0 | 100.0 | 291,804 | 14,702 | 5.03 |
| Kitsap | 3,532 | 6,107 | 10,541 | 72.9 | 72.6 | 91.9 | 86.2 | 88.6 | 26,341 | 1,936 | 7.34 |
| Mason | 3,382 | 5,669 | 9,277 | 67.6 | 63.6 | 88.0 | 80.0 | 78.0 | 5,655 | 482 | 8.52 |
| Pierce | 3,455 | 5,950 | 9,859 | 72.2 | 65.6 | 87.9 | 83.9 | 82.9 | 99,068 | 7,972 | 8.04 |
| San Juan | 2,500 | 4,113 | 8,420 | 64.5 | 104.7 | 65.0 | 58.0 | 70.8 | 1,130 | 121 | 10.69 |
| Skagit | 3,027 | 5,717 | 9,407 | 88.8 | 64.5 | 78.7 | 80.7 | 79.1 | 13,833 | 1,189 | 8.59 |
| Snohomish | 3,190 | 6,005 | 10,897 | 88.2 | 81.4 | 83.0 | 84.7 | 91.6 | 68,065 | 4,081 | 5.99 |
| Thurston | 3,403 | 5,894 | 10,472 | 73.2 | 77.6 | 88.5 | 83.2 | 88.1 | 20,055 | 1,585 | 7.90 |
| Whatcom | 2,955 | 5,441 | 9,431 | 84.1 | 73.3 | 76.8 | 76.8 | 79.3 | 20,139 | 1,776 | 8.81 |
| | | | | | | | | | 565,129 | 35,575 | 6.20 |

Source: *Census of Population* (1950, 1960, 1970)

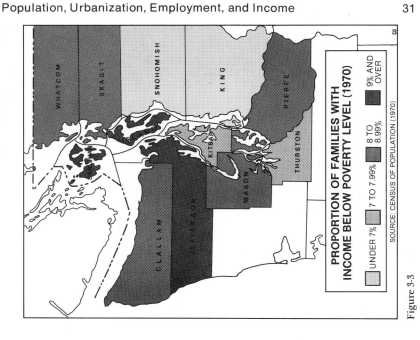

Figure 3-3

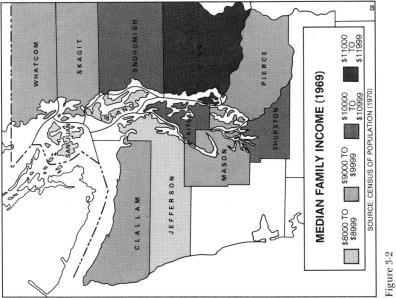

Figure 3-2

land, Jefferson, and San Juan, had the lowest income levels in 1959 and 1969. When county incomes relative to King County income are examined, two trends appear. First, four counties have consistently declining incomes relative to the King County level. Three of these counties, Clallam, Jefferson, and Mason, are above average in agriculture, forestry, and fishing, and have very high concentrations of employment in lumber products manufacturing. These economic activities are not growth areas and declining incomes reflect a dependence on them in these counties. The fourth county with declining income relative to King County is Pierce County, the second largest and second most urbanized county in the region. There is no obvious relationship between its industry mix and slow income growth.

The second trend observable from comparing county income growth with King County income growth is that the lowest income counties in the region, Island and San Juan, are realizing relative income increases. Snohomish County has also had consistent increases in income relative to King County. The remaining counties have mixed trends over the past two decades.

The data on the number and percentage of families having below poverty level incomes in Table 3-6 are also presented graphically in Figure 3–3.[5] The range among counties is from less than 6 percent in King and Snohomish counties to over 10 percent in San Juan County. When Figure 3–2 showing median incomes and Figure 3–3 showing the proportion of families with poverty level incomes are compared it is clear that the higher income counties also have lower rates of poverty, and lower income counties have higher rates of poverty. It should be noted, however, that even though lower income and smaller counties (especially San Juan, Island, and Jefferson) have higher incidences of poverty, the absolute number of poverty level families is larger in the larger counties.

SUMMARY

If we were to summarize our observations on the diversity of counties within Puget Sound region in terms of population size, urbanization, orientation toward service employment, orientation toward natural resources employment, median income, and poverty rates we would conclude that King County is largest, most urbanized, third most oriented to services, least dependent on natural resource employment, and

5. Designations of poverty are related to family size, sex of the head of the household, farm or nonfarm location and the cost of food in the area. In 1969 poverty income levels ranged from $1,569 for a single adult on a farm to $6,034 for seven persons in an urban household. Poverty level for a nonfarm family of four headed by a male was $3,745.

has the highest median incomes and the lowest poverty rates. Close to King County in these characteristics are Snohomish and Pierce counties, followed by Kitsap, Thurston, Whatcom, Clallam, Skagit, Island, Mason, Jefferson, and San Juan.[6] King, Snohomish, and Pierce are the most highly developed counties, all being located on the main basin of Puget Sound surrounding the ports of Seattle, Everett, and Tacoma. Kitsap is also on the main basin, but on the west side of the Sound surrounding Bremerton. Thurston County surrounds Olympia on Southern Puget Sound and Whatcom County is the site of Bellingham on Rosario Straits. Clallam County is the site of Port Angeles, and Skagit County is the site of the oil refineries at Anacortes. None of the other counties have major port cities.

While we observed that population growth, urbanization, and higher incomes are related to the degree to which counties have moved away from dependence upon fisheries, forrestry, and agriculture, the traditional natural resource base of the region, population, urbanization, and income growth are closely related to the availability of excellent harbors and adjacent land for industrialization and urbanization. Northern Puget Sound, or the main basin, which provides the best harbors and most suitable adjacent land, is also the site of the largest, most urbanized, and highest income counties. Lesser development has occurred at other harbor sites, namely Olympia, Bellingham, and Port Angeles, and the least development has occurred elsewhere on the Sound where harbors are not nearly as good and there are no major port cities.

6. This ranking was obtained by rank ordering each county (from 1 to 12) relative to other counties with regard to size (highest to lowest); urbanization (most urbanized to least urbanized); proportion of county employment in finance, insurance, real estate, and business and personal services (highest to lowest); proportion of county employment in agriculture, forestry, and fishing (lowest to highest); median income (highest to lowest); and poverty rates (lowest to highest). The ranks for each category were then added and a simple average calculated. The final ranking is the result of ordering the average rank of the six items considered. Average ranks are: King 1.3, Snohomish 3.5, Pierce 3.8, Kitsap 5.2, Thurston 5.2, Whatcom 6.8, Clallam 7.5, Skagit 7.9, Island 8.7, Mason 9.0, Jefferson 9.3, and San Juan 9.8.

# CHAPTER FOUR

# The Use of Puget Sound Resources

Some of the traditional activities dependent on Puget Sound's resources, such as fishing and forestry, have been declining in relative importance. At the same time, many other uses of the Sound's resources have maintained their importance or undergone rapid expansion. Among these latter activities are the many recreational uses of the Sound, including pleasure boating, sport fishing, use of shoreline parks and wildlife refuges, and the location for recreational homes. From the examination here of major uses we will be able to identify resource use interdependencies, trends, and some of the potential conflicts over alternative future uses.

## Resource Using Activities

### Ports and Industry

The Puget Sound region's ports have been its interface with the rest of the United States and world, especially during its early development. Today the ports remain an important part of the economy and the major port areas are also areas around which population growth, urbanization, and industrialization have occurred.

The location and 1972 tonnages for ports on Puget Sound are presented in Figure 4–1. Because both logs and bulk petroleum are important in port traffic, ports where logs represent over 50 percent of the port tonnage (Everett, Bellingham, Port Angeles, Port Townsend, Port Gamble, Olympia, and Shelton) are indicated as are the location of oil refineries where oil is an important part of a port's tonnages (Bellingham, Anacortes, Tacoma). General industrial zones on adjacent land and potential plant site areas for future industrial zones are also indicated.

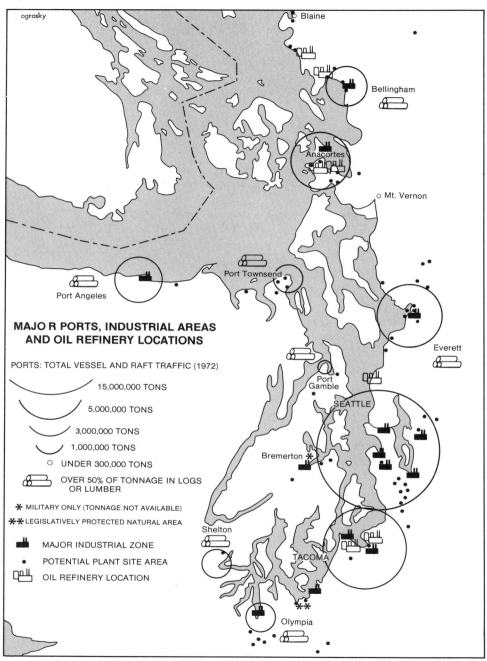

ogrosky

Blaine

Bellingham

Anacortes

o Mt. Vernon

Port Townsend

Port Angeles

**MAJOR PORTS, INDUSTRIAL AREAS
AND OIL REFINERY LOCATIONS**

PORTS: TOTAL VESSEL AND RAFT TRAFFIC (1972)

15,000,000 TONS

5,000,000 TONS

3,000,000 TONS

1,000,000 TONS

○   UNDER 300,000 TONS

OVER 50% OF TONNAGE IN LOGS
OR LUMBER

✳ MILITARY ONLY (TONNAGE NOT AVAILABLE)

✳✳ LEGISLATIVELY PROTECTED NATURAL AREA

MAJOR INDUSTRIAL ZONE

•    POTENTIAL PLANT SITE AREA

OIL REFINERY LOCATION

Everett

Port
Gamble

SEATTLE

Bremerton ✳

Shelton

TACOMA

✳✳

Olympia

Figure 4-1

If one compares the distribution of port tonnages illustrated in Figure 4–1 with the distribution of population in major cities in Figure 3–1, it is obvious that port activity is dispersed more throughout the region than is population. This dispersion is due to the large volume of timber and lumber that is shipped from smaller ports. Anacortes, a small city, has a large port tonnage because of the large quantities of oil shipped to and from oil refineries there. Seattle and Tacoma, on the other hand, are the major ports for all other goods, including the higher valued general cargos. At one time Seattle and Tacoma also shipped large volumes of logs but because logs require large land areas relative to their value these more crowded ports, especially Seattle, have reduced their log shipping so that more space is available for other products.

The largest industrial zones surround Seattle and Tacoma, with lesser development at Bellingham, Anacortes (oil refineries), Everett, Olympia, Bremerton, and Port Angeles. Sites for potential industrial development are more dispersed than current industrialization, but it is likely that the sites which are actually utilized will continue to be concentrated in the Seattle-Tacoma-Everett area.

Because ports have played such an important historical role in the development of the region, and because there has been considerable controversy over issues of port expansion (especially at Nisqually delta as analyzed in Chapter 7), an independent study of port needs was undertaken as part of this project.[1]

The study of projected port expansion from 1970 to 2000 was divided into three sections. First, projections of tonnages handled were developed on the basis of data collected in recent years by the Army Corps of Engineers.[2] Six "commodity groups" were identified by the study: general cargo, forest products, dry bulk, bulk grain, bulk petroleum, and liquid bulk. The tonnages handled by Puget Sound ports for each of these categories were analyzed to determine dominant trends in each of the individual commodity groups, and in each of the major ports. These trends provided the basis for projecting tonnages to 1980 and 2000.

The second step of the port analysis was to convert employment figures for the port areas into ratios representing the "acres per employee" currently used by eleven port industries. Projection of employment in these industries, and an estimate of the changing ratios to be expected,

1. Stewart Borland and Martha Oliver, *Port Expansion in the Puget Sound Region, 1970–2000*.

2. U.S. Army Corps of Engineers, *Waterborne Commerce of the United States: Part 4, Pacific Coast, Alaska and Hawaii* (Washington, D.C.: Government Printing Office, published annually), volumes for 1952-70 used for this study.

allowed the derivation of land requirements in each of the port areas in 1990. The third step followed the same procedure to derive the expected need for terminal facilities. In this case the ratio of the tonnages of commodities shipped to the amount of terminal land used by each commodity provided the basis of the forecast. By combining these ratios with the previously calculated tonnage projections an estimate of future terminal land requirements could be made.

The findings of this analysis are that tonnages handled in the three ports will have increased by more than one third by 1980, and will have doubled by 2000. Dry bulk traffic, which produces a greater economic spin-off effect in the local community, is expected to increase at a rate in excess of the overall average, whereas forest products and general cargo are below average. In all classes of cargo except forest products and oil there will be a shift to the three major ports (Seattle, Everett, and Tacoma), further increasing their dominance within the region.

When these traffic projections were converted into acreage required for handling all cargoes and compared with present land-holdings, it was found that Tacoma has more than enough back-up land for future requirements. Thus, proposals to develop the Nisqually Delta as a superport were not supported by a detailed independent analysis. Everett will experience some pressure for the conversion of waterfront land and some additional land development, but a need for an increase of the magnitude proposed by a previous study of the Everett waterfront is not supported by our analysis.[3] The greatest pressure for expansion will be in Seattle through conversion of already developed areas. Because Everett needs some additional land and Seattle will require more efficient use of its port area, conflicts between port activities and other water-oriented activities will tend to occur more in Everett and Seattle than elsewhere. The need to develop new areas for "superports" to cater for increasingly larger vessels seems to be nonexistent except possibly for petroleum. Adaptation of present facilities to accommodate larger vessels is a more likely occurrence than the construction of completely new ports. Thus, future port activity is likely to remain concentrated in presently developed areas.

*Transportation within the Region*

We tend to think of port shipping as primarily to and from other states or foreign ports. In fact, however, more tonnage is moved among Puget Sound posts than moves in and out of the region. Large quantities of sand and gravel and petroleum products are moved about by

3. Lawrence Halprin and Associates, "Everett: First Preliminary Report" (Everett, Wash., 1971).

barge within the region, generally from extraction or refinery locations to the larger urban centers. Logs are also rafted and towed by tug boats from smaller port and collection areas to the lumber, plywood, and pulp mills located throughout the region. The low-cost water transport of logs has been important for permitting the development of large mills because they could receive timber from such a large area.

In addition to resources and product movements, ferries and the Tacoma Narrows Bridge permit considerable passenger, automobile, and truck movement across the Sound and to Whidbey and the major San Juan Islands. The ferry traffic includes a large number of commuters (an average of nearly three thousand daily commuters, for example, arrive in downtown Seattle from Bermerton or Winslow across the Sound)[4] and thus provides access to jobs and shipping facilities in the larger cities for west-side and island residents while simultaneously providing access to recreation and seasonal homes on the less-developed west side and islands for residents of the east-side urban areas. The impact of recreational usage of ferries is illustrated by the fact that during summer months total ferry ridership is approximately 60 percent greater than during the winter months, even though the number of regular commuters remains virtually constant. On some runs, such as from Anacortes to the San Juan Islands, recreational traffic is dominant year around and summer traffic nearly three times as great as winter traffic.

Ferry routes, as well as other transportation facilities of the Puget Sound region, are illustrated in Figure 4–2. Highway and railroad transportation are both more highly developed in the Seattle-Tacoma-Everett area, and all major commercial airports are located on the east side of the Sound (Tacoma's is actually on the Kitsap Peninsula just across the Tacoma Narrows Bridge from the city). The area lacking major transportation routes is the western side of the Kitsap Peninsula (the east side of Hood Canal) and many Southern Puget Sound inlets are served only by secondary roads. There is also only limited major transportation connecting Puget Sound shoreline areas to areas away from the Sound on the Olympic Peninsula. The limited transportation network on the west side of the Sound is in striking contrast to the extensive development of major highways and rail lines on the east side which serve to connect residential, agricultural, and industrial areas with one another and with the major port areas.

*Forest Products*

The forest products industry includes activities such as logging, raft-

4. Calculated from the monthly report, "Washington State Ferries, Traffic Statistics," for January 1–31, 1973–1972 and June 1–30, 1973–1972.

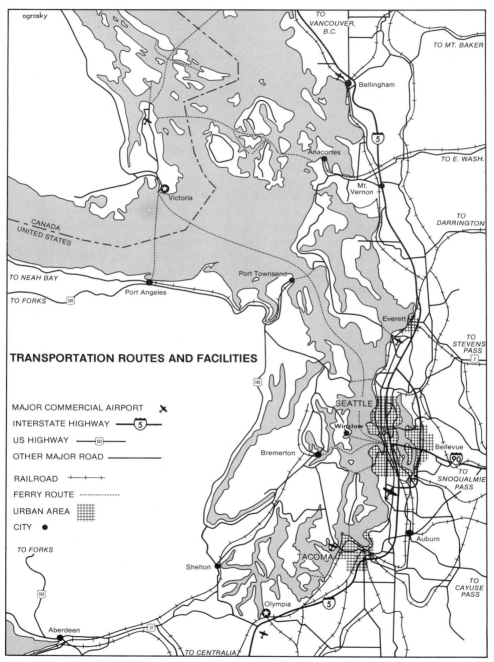

TRANSPORTATION ROUTES AND FACILITIES

MAJOR COMMERCIAL AIRPORT    ✖
INTERSTATE HIGHWAY  ──[5]──
US HIGHWAY  ──[101]──
OTHER MAJOR ROAD  ────────

RAILROAD  ┼─┼─┼
FERRY ROUTE  ────────────
URBAN AREA  ▦
CITY  ●

Figure 4-2

ing, and shipping of logs; lumber production; pulp, paper, hard-board; plywood and veneer production; and the manufacture of finished wood products. We have previously noted that logging or direct forestry employment is small and has been declining. However, when all forest products, most of which are classified as manufacturing, are considered together they constitute a much larger share of the economy. Total forest products related employment may be as much as 8 percent of total regional employment and, like logging and shipping of logs, it is relatively more important in the smaller counties than in King or Pierce. For example, the two counties most dependent on forest products, Mason and Clallam, have over 20 percent of all employment in those activities.

The forest products industry, while based on a land resource, is also closely related to Puget Sound's water resources. Over 80 percent of the Puget Sound watershed is in forests, and logging is potentially one of the most disruptive uses of forest land.[5] The construction of access roads and removal of vegetation leads to soil erosion, stream sedementation, and accumulation of debris in channels. This in turn inhibits salmon spawning and reduces the Sound's fisheries resources. The forest products industry is also a large user of fresh water from Puget Sound rivers and streams. Over 70 percent of all industrial water use in the region is in this industry, and the pulp and paper products manufacture is especially dependent on the availability of large quantities of pure water. In addition, the effluents released by lumber mills, plywood plants, and especially pulp and paper manufacturers have historically been major sources of water pollution in the region, affecting anadromous fish runs, shellfish, and nearby residents. Fortunately with the adoption and acceptance of recent federal and state water and air quality standards, the forest products industry is undergoing rapid cleanup. It should be a much less destructive user of Puget Sound's resources in the future than it has been in the past.

*Fisheries*

Fisheries in Puget Sound waters include both sport and commercial fisheries for salmon, for demersal or bottom-fish species, and for the collecting of clams, oysters, crab, and shrimp. Steelhead trout also support a major recreational fishery. There are several aquaculture projects where salmon are reared in pens for commercial sale and many hatcheries for supplementing resident salmon populations important to anglers.

5. A good discussion of the impacts of logging on water resources is contained in Pacific Northwest River Basins Commission, *Puget Sound and Adjacent Waters: Appendix V, Water Related Land Resources,* Part III.

The salmon fishery is the most important fishery, accounting for approximately 80 percent of the value of Puget Sound landings.[6] Even so, this fishery probably results in employment of no more than ten thousand fishermen, many of whom are part time. There is additional employment in related areas of processing and marketing. Thus, while Puget Sound residents tend to think of salmon fishing as big business it provides a relatively small part of the employment in the Puget Sound region: no more than 1 or 2 percent. On the other hand, the high and increasing unit price of the canned, fresh, and frozen salmon makes it a more significant factor in the dollar value of regional exports.

Sport salmon fishing is one of the most popular recreational activities in the state. Approximately five hundred thousand people or nearly 15 percent of Washington's citizens fish for salmon, and salmon fishermen are a rather constant proportion of population throughout the state.[7] Thus, sport salmon fishing is a state-wide activity, not limited to Puget Sound area residents. Most sport salmon fishermen, however, are from Washington state (82 percent) with another 8 percent from Oregon. Contrary to general opinion sport salmon fishing does not appear to be an important tourist attraction.[8]

Commercial fishermen fish for all five species of salmon (coho, chinook, sockeye, pink, and chum) which pass through the Strait of Juan De Fuca on their way to spawn in freshwater rivers and streams each year while sportsmen take a large proportion of coho and chinook runs and a much smaller share of pinks. In terms of total value the sockeye, most of which are of Fraser River, British Columbia, origin, are the most important. Pink, chum, coho, and chinook salmon spawn throughout the rivers and streams of the Puget Sound region, but the pinks unlike the others run only in odd-numbered years. Commercial fishing is quite limited within Puget Sound proper, although some fishing takes place in Skagit Bay, Port Susan, and in the Seattle area. The major effort is centered off the coast (by trollers only) and along the western and northern boundaries of Puget Sound and the Strait of Juan de Fuca by gill netters, purse seiners, and reef netters. The importance of Puget Sound to the overall salmon fishery is enhanced by two linkages: first, the ocean and straits catches include salmon spawned in Puget Sound rivers; and second, a large number of fishermen utilize commercial fishing moorages and deliver their catches to canneries and

6. Relative values of commercial fisheries based in Puget Sound are discussed in James Crutchfield et al., "Socioeconomic, Institutional, and Legal Considerations in the Management of Puget Sound," p. 60.

7. State of Washington, *1973 Annual Report, Natural Resources and Recreation Agencies,* p. 25.

8. Crutchfield et al., "Socioeconomic, Institutional, and Legal Considerations in the Management of Puget Sound," p. 123.

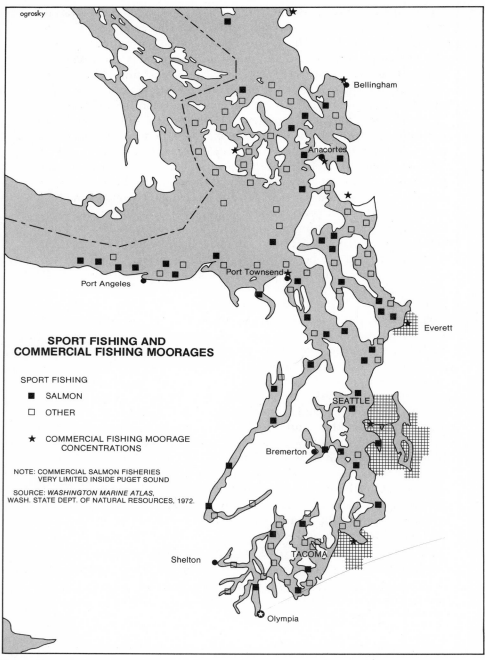

ogrosky

SPORT FISHING AND
COMMERCIAL FISHING MOORAGES

SPORT FISHING

■   SALMON

□   OTHER

★   COMMERCIAL FISHING MOORAGE
     CONCENTRATIONS

NOTE: COMMERCIAL SALMON FISHERIES
      VERY LIMITED INSIDE PUGET SOUND

SOURCE: *WASHINGTON MARINE ATLAS*,
WASH. STATE DEPT. OF NATURAL RESOURCES, 1972.

Bellingham

Anacortes

Port Townsend

Port Angeles

Everett

SEATTLE

Bremerton

TACOMA

Shelton

Olympia

Figure 4-3

marketing firms in Puget Sound ports. The location of commercial fishing moorage concentrations are indicated in Figure 4–3.

Popular salmon sport fishing locations are also indicated in Figure 4–3. Sport fishing for salmon is carried on throughout the region. While salmon sport fishing on the Sound remains widespread, there has been a decline in the number of angler days devoted to this activity over the past decade. This decline does not appear to be due to either a decline in fishing interest or a decline in salmon catches, but rather to the opening and expansion of more productive ocean sport fisheries off Ilwaco, Westport, and La Push on the Pacific Ocean coast. Access to the ocean fisheries, however, takes more time and is more expensive than fishing on the Sound, so after the initial development pull of the ocean fisheries ceases it is estimated that the number of angler days spent fishing for salmon on Puget Sound will again begin to increase.

Neither sport nor commercial fishing for demersal species such as sole or rockfish is a major activity on Puget Sound. Of more than one hundred fishing boats based on Puget Sound that fish for these species, it is estimated that no more than half a dozen regularly fish the Sound's waters.[9] Commercial demersal species account for only about 3 percent of the value of Puget Sound landings. The low effort devoted to bottom-fish inside the Sound reflects the relatively low market prices fishermen can obtain because of the lower cost of production by foreign fisheries which provide for most of the American market in these species. Puget Sound trawlers fishing for bottom-fish must operate in more distant waters, particularly the Strait of Georgia, where catch rates are much higher. A small, specialized fishery for English sole does operate, interestingly, in the immediate vicinity of the outfall for the largest Everett pulp mill.

It is difficult to estimate the extent of sport fishing for demersals. Effort is much less than in sport salmon fishing, but angler interest in demersals is increasing, especially around the San Juans where the success ratio for salmon is very low. As one can note from Figure 4–3, areas of good fishing for demersals are widespread throughout the Puget Sound region.

Shellfish (primarily oysters, crabs, and clams) account for about 17 percent of the value of Puget Sound region commercial fisheries and also support a popular recreational activity.[10] No licenses are required for sport shellfish gathering and many of the suitable shellfish beaches are either private or adjacent to private land. Shellfish gathering also requires virtually no expenditure and chances of success approach 100

9. Ibid., Chaps. 3 and 4.
10. Ibid., p. 60.

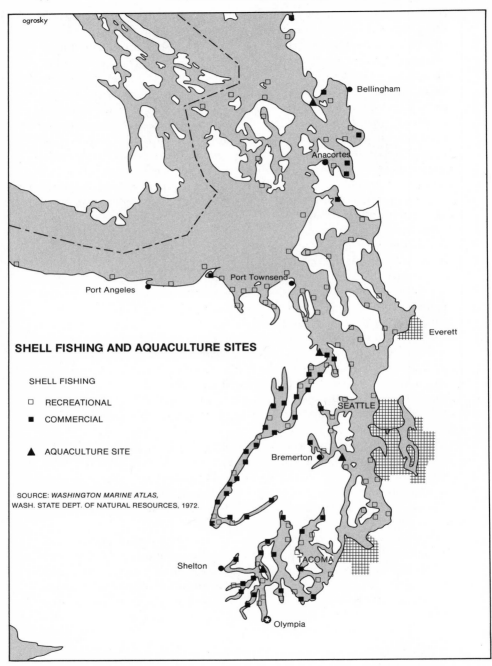

Figure 4-4

percent for butter clams or oysters. In 1972 the state Department of Fisheries estimated that approximately five hundred thousand persons participated in shellfishing.[11]

Commercial and sport shellfishing sites are indicated on Figure 4–4. The concentrations on Hood Canal and on the inlets of Southern Puget Sound are primarily for clams and oysters, while the sites in the northern areas are primarily for crab. The warmer waters of Hood Canal and shallow inlets with high tidal differences in Southern Puget Sound provide excellent shellfish habitat. Sport shellfish gathering is spread throughout the Puget Sound region, including many areas where habitats are not good enough to support commercial cultivation.

Also shown on Figure 4–4 are four aquaculture sites where salmon are being raised in pens for commercial sales. Shellfish, particularly oysters, have long been cultivated in fixed locations, but pen rearing of salmon on the Sound is relatively new. The state Department of Natural Resources is encouraging aquaculture developments and anticipates ten to fifteen additional projects over the next decade. The department and private firms are also experimenting with rearing oysters and clams on trays suspended in deeper water where commercial production would not take up relatively scarce beach space and would also be safer from natural predators and the poaching of sport collectors in private commercial beds.

An important fishery closely related to Puget Sound is the sport fishery for steelhead trout. Steelhead fishing takes place in Puget Sound rivers during steelhead migration upstream. It is estimated that 250,000 to 300,000 of Washington's citizens fish for these sea-going rainbow trout an average of over ten times a year. The most popular steelhead rivers include the Skagit, Green, Puyallup, Skykomish, and Stillaguamish, but almost all streams entering Puget Sound and the straits have runs of these great game fish.[12]

All of the higher valued fisheries resources—salmon, shellfish, and steelhead—are vulnerable to water pollution. All require relatively clean water for survival. While some shellfish can survive in moderately polluted water, they may collect contaminants and become inedible. Because of their sensitivity both anadromous fish and shellfish have been adversely affected by the development of the Puget Sound region. Salmon and steelhead have been especially damaged by the silting of spawning areas in smaller tributaries as a result of logging and urban development. The damming of some rivers has also reduced salmon

11. State of Washington, *1973 Annual Report, Natural Resources and Recreation Agencies*, p. 24.
12. Crutchfield et al., "Socioeconomic, Institutional, and Legal Considerations in the Management of Puget Sound," Chap. 4.

runs. The native Olympia oyster has almost disappeared from the region, in part because of pollution, primarily from the pulp and paper industry.

To offset reductions in natural production of salmon and steelhead the state Departments of Game and of Fisheries have developed fish hatcheries, fish farms, stream clearance programs, and other techniques for enhancement of natural runs. Pacific oysters from Japan have also been introduced into the region and have long since supplanted the native Olympia in both commercial and sport harvests. It is currently anticipated that sport and commercial fisheries for salmon, steelhead, and shellfish can be maintained at about their current level through hatchery supplementation if care is taken to avoid much more damage to salmon spawning streams and to protect water quality in critical areas. This should enable salmon and shellfish gathering to remain a very important part of life in the Puget Sound region. It is expected, however, that recreational fishing will continue to grow in importance relative to commercial fishing in the area.

*Pleasure Boating*

Pleasure boating is a popular pastime in the Puget Sound region. Per capita boat ownership is nearly two and one half times the national average, providing nearly one hundred boats for each thousand individuals.[13] Approximately 34 percent of the citizens in the region engage in pleasure boating each year, and one third of boat owners use their craft year around.

The sheltered yet extensive waters of the Sound are suitable for both large and small pleasure boats. The largest single type of boat in the region is the outboard motorboat, averaging 15.8 feet in length, which make up 50.7 percent of the total. Next most numerous are small rowboats, dingies, and canoes (35.3 percent), followed by inboard motorboats (9.8 percent) averaging 25.3 feet in length, sailboats with less than 10 h.p. auxiliaries (3.4 percent), and sailboats with auxiliary power over 10 h.p. averaging 29.8 feet (0.8 percent). Over 90 percent of the boats on the Sound each year are owned by Puget Sound area residents.

Boat ownership, like population, is concentrated in the urban counties of King, Pierce, Snohomish, and the east or main basin side of Kitsap. However, while 81 percent of the boats are owned by persons in this area, per capita boat ownership at 88 per 1,000 citizens is less in

13. Extensive data on pleasure boating are contained in Seattle District, U.S. Army Corps of Engineers; and Pacific Northwest Region, Bureau of Outdoor Recreation, *Pleasure Boating Study: Puget Sound and Adjacent Waters* (Olympia: Washington State Parks and Recreation Commission, November 1968).

this region than in other parts of the Sound. In Southern Puget Sound and on Hood Canal, for example, boat ownership is 155 per 1,000 population, and outside of Puget Sound proper in Island, San Juan, Whatcom, and Skagit counties boat ownership is 109 per 1,000.

There are also relatively more moorages in rural areas. The urban area counties, with 81 percent of the boat ownership, contain only 77.1 percent of the moorages. Southern Puget Sound, Hood Canal, and Olympic Peninsula residents own 10 percent of the boats but possess 11.2 percent of the moorages and citizens of the islands and northern area outside Puget Sound proper possess 9 percent of the boats and 11.1 percent of the moorages. This indicates that many boat owners in the urban area keep their boats in other areas, especially the northern and island areas where they have better access to more pleasant and less developed waters.

The distribution of marinas, state marine parks, and boating rendezvous areas is indicated on Figure 4–5. Marinas are distributed throughout the region with large concentrations in Seattle and Tacoma and lessor concentrations in Southern Puget Sound and in the San Juan Islands. Their distribution reflects both the population concentration of boat owners and location of the most desirable cruising waters. Boating rendezvous areas pinpoint desirable, sheltered areas where cruising pleasure boats often anchor overnight. Their location also reflects the attractiveness of immediately adjacent waters for pleasure cruising. Rendezvous areas are heavily concentrated in the San Juan Islands, on the less developed west side of Northern Puget Sound, and in the inlets of Southern Puget Sound. The pattern of these rendezvous areas indicates that boat owners from the urban areas make extensive use of cruising waters in other areas of the Sound. One lesser developed area noticeably lacking in boating rendezvous areas is Hood Canal. The entrance to Hood Canal is a relatively long distance from moorage concentrations and there are few facilities such as marinas or marine parks along its fifty-mile length.

The state marine parks indicated in Figure 4–5 are heavily concentrated in the San Juan Islands and northern Whidbey Island area. There are lesser numbers on Southern Puget Sound and only one in the populous main basin. State marine parks are specifically oriented to boaters, and many have no nonwater access. They may provide moorages, beaches for swimming and claming or oyster gathering, and picnic and camping areas on shore. Their distribution, like the distribution of boating rendezvous areas, reflects the desire of pleasure boaters to cruise the San Juan Islands and Southern Puget Sound waters. During 1973 nearly one half million persons visited water-access-only marine parks in

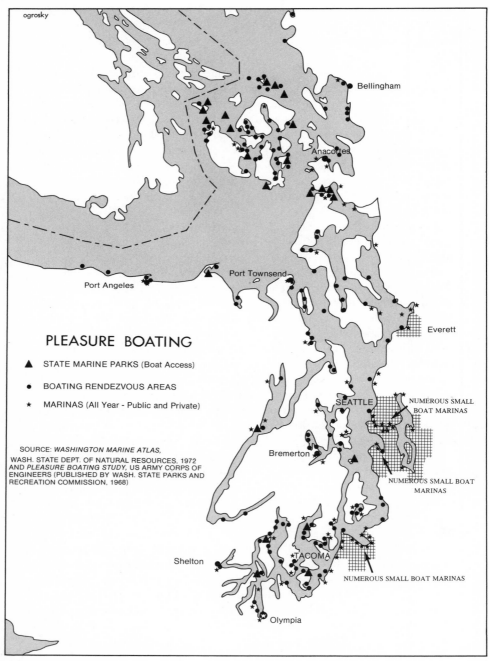

ogrosky

Bellingham

Anacortes

Port Townsend

Port Angeles

Everett

# PLEASURE BOATING

▲ STATE MARINE PARKS (Boat Access)

● BOATING RENDEZVOUS AREAS

★ MARINAS (All Year - Public and Private)

SOURCE: *WASHINGTON MARINE ATLAS*,
WASH. STATE DEPT. OF NATURAL RESOURCES, 1972
AND *PLEASURE BOATING STUDY*, US ARMY CORPS OF
ENGINEERS (PUBLISHED BY WASH. STATE PARKS AND
RECREATION COMMISSION, 1968)

SEATTLE

NUMEROUS SMALL
BOAT MARINAS

Bremerton

NUMEROUS SMALL BOAT
MARINAS

Shelton

TACOMA

NUMEROUS SMALL BOAT MARINAS

Olympia

Figure 4-5

the region. Many of the parks already face the same crowded conditions as other shoreline parks, and if pleasure boating increases as rapidly as expected they will be still more crowded in the future.

*Parks and Wildlife Refuges*

Figure 4–6 indicates the distribution of national, state, major urban, and underwater parks and wildlife refuges in the area surrounding Puget Sound. A striking feature of the location of these parks is that they are virtually all located on water, and predominantly along Puget Sound's shorelines even though they are oriented toward users arriving by automobile instead of boat as are the marine parks pictured in Figure 4–5. The state and major urban parks are also distributed widely throughout the region, not concentrated in areas of especially attractive cruising waters. In fact there is a noticeable lack of parks for non–boat owners in the San Juan Islands. The relatively even geographic distribution, instead of concentration in urban areas, also leads one to believe that urban users prefer their parks in more rural areas of the region.

This park system provides the same access to beaches as is enjoyed by the many persons who reside along Puget Sound waters, albeit under more crowded and congested conditions. On busy weekends or holidays most state shoreline parks are filled to capacity and many potential users are turned away. In spite of crowded conditions, however, state parks on Puget Sound were visited by over 4.6 million persons in 1973.[14]

A relatively new feature on Puget Sound is the creation of underwater parks for scuba divers to observe marine life. Areas for this purpose were not usable until the development of wet suits which permit longer immersion in Puget Sound's relatively cold waters. This activity, while small, is rapidly growing in popularity.

The wildlife refuges indicated in Figure 4–6 are considered with parks because in addition to providing relatively natural habitats for wildlife (predominantly waterfowl) they are extremely popular as less developed recreation areas.

*Recreational Homes*

In 1970, 42,593 families, or just over 6 percent of the residents in the Puget Sound region, owned second homes.[15] Second home ownership, like population, is concentrated in King, Pierce, and Snohomish coun-

14. Washington State Parks and Recreation Commission, *State Park Calandar Year Attendance 1973* (Olympia: 1974).
15. U.S. Bureau of the Census, *Census of Housing 1970, Housing Characteristics for States, Cities, and Counties*, Vol. 1, Part 49, *Washington State* (Washington, D.C.: Government Printing Office), Table 63.

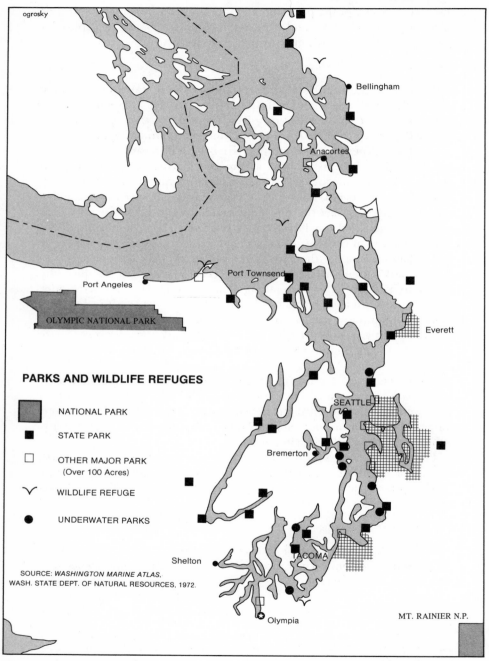

ogrosky

Bellingham

Anacortes

Port Townsend

Port Angeles

OLYMPIC NATIONAL PARK

Everett

**PARKS AND WILDLIFE REFUGES**

SEATTLE

NATIONAL PARK

STATE PARK

OTHER MAJOR PARK
(Over 100 Acres)

WILDLIFE REFUGE

UNDERWATER PARKS

Bremerton

SOURCE: *WASHINGTON MARINE ATLAS*,
WASH. STATE DEPT. OF NATURAL RESOURCES, 1972.

Shelton

TACOMA

MT. RAINIER N.P.

Olympia

Figure 4-6

ties, which together account for 81.5 percent of second home ownership within the region. Second home ownership rates, however, are not higher in the urban counties; the ownership concentration simply reflects population concentration in the urban areas. While census information on the location of recreational homes owned by residents of the three urban counties is lacking, other data on travel time, location preferences, site availability, and recreational home developments indicate that a great majority of the homes are within the Puget Sound region, either on or adjacent to the shoreline of Puget Sound.

In an attempt to identify patterns of second home developments more closely, the Interagency Commission on Outdoor Recreation undertook a survey of second home developments and second home lot purchasers which was published in 1971.[16] They observed that, as in the rest of the United States, there was a large increase in recreational home developments during the 1960s. While only four recreational developments were identified as having begun before 1960, between 1960 and 1970, 160 new developments were started in Washington state. Ninety-four of these were in the Puget Sound region. Within the Puget Sound region, one third of the developments were either on the shoreline or possessed easy access to the shoreline in Island and San Juan counties, and another 14 percent were on Puget Sound's shorelines on Hood Canal or Southern Puget Sound. Not all of the ninety-four developments within the region are located on the Sound; several, especially in Whatcom, Skagit, Snohomish, King, and Pierce counties, were located in the Cascade Mountains, usually on rivers tributary to the Sound. Still others, such as several in Mason County, are oriented toward small lakes. The number of developments in each county is presented in Table 4–1.

TABLE 4–1

RECREATIONAL HOME DEVELOPMENTS—1970

| County | Developments | County | Developments |
|--------|--------------|--------|--------------|
| San Juan | 7 | Pierce | 8 |
| Island | 23 | Thurston | 9 |
| Whatcom | 6 | Mason | 15 |
| Skagit | 5 | Kitsap | 5 |
| Snohomish | 2 | Jefferson | 6 |
| King | 2 | Clallam | 8 |

Source: Interagency Committee for Outdoor Recreation, *Second Homes in Washington*, p. 9.

16. Data for this section are from Interagency Committee for Outdoor Recreation, *Second Homes in Washington* (Pullman: Cooperative Extension Service, Washington State University, July 1971).

One observation that can be made from the county locations of second home developments is that in spite of the attractiveness of mountain locations in the Cascades, most of the second home developments are in the smaller and less urbanized counties that do not contain mountainous areas. Furthermore, of the three most urbanized counties only Pierce county has many developments, and those are primarily in the Nisqually River Valley on the route between Tacoma and Mount Rainier National Park. Populous King and Snohomish counties have the fewest number of developments of any of the counties—two each.

A survey of second home lot purchasers in these developments indicates that purchasers come primarily from the urban counties.[17] For example, for all developments state-wide, 84 percent of all purchasers were from Washington state, 38 percent of the purchasers were Seattle residents, and another 11 percent were from the Tacoma area. Because this survey was for developments all across the state it is likely that citizens from Seattle and Tacoma are even more heavily represented in developments within the Puget Sound region. While precise data are not available, when we consider total recreational home ownership in the three urban counties (34,700 homes and over 110,000 family members) and patterns of older recreational homes and new developments in the region, it is very likely that more people in the three largest counties own second homes oriented toward Puget Sound's shorelines than the total populations of San Juan, Island, Mason, Jefferson, and Clallam counties added together.

It is difficult to estimate the extent to which second home developments will continue as they did in the 1960s. The economic downturn of the late 1960s and early 1970s will undoubtedly retard development for a time, but as incomes and the amount of leisure time increase and public parks become even more crowded, the demand for recreational homes in environmentally attractive areas of the Puget Sound region by residents from the urbanized areas will continue to increase.

*Utilities*

The major utilities—water supply, power production, and waste disposal—all make use of Puget Sound's water related resources.

Water supply for both industrial and domestic use is drawn primarily from rivers which enter Puget Sound. Most intakes are upriver from the urban developments themselves to obtain higher-quality water than would be possible to obtain further downstream. Some municipalities, such as Seattle and Tacoma, also own and carefully regulate large forest watershed areas to help assure higher water quality for their

17. Ibid., p. 21.

usage. Smaller cities and suburban water districts often rely on pumping from groundwaters instead of river intakes for their smaller requirement. In general, there is no shortage of water in the Puget Sound region because of its adequate levels of rainfall and the large area drained into Puget Sound.

Water bodies are also convenient, and sometimes efficient, places for disposal of wastes. As long as the oxygen demand of organic wastes does not exceed the dissolved oxygen in the water, organic wastes can be harmlessly assimilated. Puget Sound, with its deep channels and mixing of waters through its narrow sills, can assimilate large quantities of organic wastes without being damaged. Not all domestic and industrial wastes are as easily dissipated, however. Coliform bacteria from domestic waste and chemicals—such as sulfite liquors from pulp mills—can cause considerable problems for human and marine organisms coming into contact with contaminated water. Problems are also caused by the discharge of human and oily wastes from pleasure and merchant craft into the Sound's waters. There has been a concern over water pollution since the 1930s—beginning with the concern shown by sport and commercial fishermen for the damage done by sulfite liquor discharges from pulp mills.[18] Many shellfishermen are convinced that it was pulp mill waste that led to the virtual demise of the native Olympia oyster in the Sound. Today pulp mill wastes along with municipal industrial and domestic wastes still cause the greatest problems, but the problems are confined to the immediate area of the discharges. Problem areas—Bellingham Bay, Anacortes, Port Angeles, Everett, Elliott Bay and the lower Duwamish, Commencement Bay and the lower Puyallup, Bremerton, Olympia—are the most populated and/or the location of large pulp mills. Except for these relatively small areas the Sound is actually a very clean body of water, and as current regulations are implemented and improvements in effluent treatment are installed, the quality of water in these areas too should improve.

The production of power has a long history of reliance on water in the Pacific Northwest.[19] The Puget Sound region was one of the first regions to develop extensive hydroelectric capacity by the damming of, or installation of power houses on, rivers feeding Puget Sound. Today, with the development of even greater hydroelectric capacity on the Columbia River, the Puget Sound region has become a net importer of electric power, importing over two thirds of its needs.

It is unlikely that further extensive development of hydroelectric power will be undertaken on Puget Sound's rivers. This is not because

18. Pacific Northwest River Basins Commission, *Puget Sound and Adjacent Waters: Appendix XIII, Water Quality Control,* Chap. 1.
19. Ibid., *Appendix IX, Power.*

their potential has been exhausted, but because developments in electricity production have made much larger hydro and thermal plants than could be supported by Puget Sound's rivers relatively more efficient, and because Puget Sound's rivers have other valuable uses, such as for fisheries production.

New developments in power production are likely to involve large nuclear or coal fired thermal plants. If coal fired plants are developed, however, it is likely that they will be located near coal deposits in western Washington, probably south of the Puget Sound region itself. Nuclear plants, however, because of their need for large quantities of water for cooling, have been and are likely to continue to be proposed for siting on the shorelands of Puget Sound. The major potential problem with nuclear power plants is their discharge of large quantities of heated water. This thermal pollution can harm marine life in the vicinity and could reduce the productivity of Puget Sound's waters if it formed a warmer top layer of water that reduced the mixing of nutrient-rich saline bottom water with the surface layer. Because of the size and diversity of the Sound there are no doubt locations where nuclear power plants could be sited with minimal disruption of the natural environment. It is also possible that sites could be identified where the warming of adjacent waters could contribute to shellfish culture and recreational usage.[20]

There is no question that in the past the use of Puget Sound's resources for waste disposal and the production of hydroelectric power has altered the natural environment and damaged marine species. Hatchery plantings of salmon and steelhead are making up for much of the damage to salmon and steelhead runs caused by restricting upstream migration, and the introduction of the Pacific oyster has done much to make up for the loss of the native Olympia. While problems of waste disposal do remain, and problems of thermal pollution associated with nuculear production of power are still to be encountered, most Puget Sound waters remain in a near natural state. With reasonably careful regulation, further deterioration can be prevented, and some improvements achieved as recent water quality regulations are implemented and enforced.

TRENDS IN THE USE OF PUGET SOUND RESOURCES

For most of the uses of Puget Sound resources we have been able to provide some indication of recent and expected trends. The *Puget Sound and Adjacent Waters* studies also provide detailed forecasts

20. Some of the potential impacts of thermal pollution on Puget Sound are discussed in Crutchfield et al., "Socioeconomic, Institutional, and Legal Considerations in the Management of Puget Sound," pp. 26, 200-2.

of most uses of Puget Sound resources. Most forecasts, however, confine themselves to a single resource use with little attempt to identify the growth or decline of different activities in relation to one another. As part of this project we undertook two studies designed to reveal relative changes in the growth of different resource-using activities. It was our feeling that by knowing what uses are tending to increase more rapidly we can also provide some indication of what kinds of resource use conflicts are likely to occur in the future.

*Relative Usage Trends*

In our first study the objective was to forecast relative resource use changes for activities which directly use Puget Sound's resources.[21] For each activity the closest variable reflecting the use of Puget Sound's resources for which there were time-series data was identified. For example, angler trips were used for sports fishing activity, pleasure boats registered for pleasure boating, board feet of timber harvested for forest products production, and tonnage handled for port facilities. Because these diverse physical-measure variables are not directly comparable, each was converted into an index with 1962 as the base year. Forecasts of the deviation of the index for each activity from the index average for all activities were made for 1980 using data from 1955 to 1970. The result was an index number representing each activity's level relative to other activities and its activity level relative to 1962, for which the index values were all 100. The results of the analysis are presented in Table 4–2.

What the result of this relative-activity-level forecast tells us is that activities with higher index numbers have been and will be increasing more rapidly than activities with lower index numbers. For example, visitor days to wildlife refuges and parks and the amount of electricity used in the region are increasing very rapidly, while all other activities are increasingly more slowly. Activities whose index numbers are less than 100 are forecast, on the basis of past trends, to be at lower levels in 1980 than they were in 1962, the base year of 100. It must be emphasized that the size of the index number does not indicate the absolute level of the activity or the importance of the activity to the region. The index can be interpreted only in relation to relative rates of change in activity levels from 1962 to 1980. If an activity was very small in 1962, such as wildlife refuge visits, moderate increases could give it a large index number in 1980. For example, even though there are more angler days spent salmon fishing and the increase in the number of angler days

21. Peter Harrison, "The Land Water Interface in an Urban Region: A Spatial and Temporal Analysis of the Nature and Significances of Conflicts between Coastal Uses" (Ph.D. diss., University of Washington, 1973), Chap. 6.

TABLE 4–2
INDEX OF RELATIVE ACTIVITY LEVELS, 1980

| Activity | Variable Used | Index Number |
|---|---|---|
| Wildlife refuges | Visitor days | 326 |
| Parks | User days–state parks | 325 |
| Utilities | Kilowatt hours sold | 306 |
| Forest products | Board feet of timber cut | 207 |
| Manufacturing | Number of employees | 162 |
| Pleasure boating | Boats registered | 156 |
| Sports fishing | Angler trips for salmon fishing | 152 |
| Port facilities | Tonnage–6 largest ports | 138 |
| Residential construction | New units | 115 |
| Commercial shipping | Outbound movements–6 ports | 98 |
| Commercial fishing | Pounds of fish landed | 77 |
| Commercial shell fishing | Pounds of shellfish harvested | 65 |

spent salmon fishing is greater than the increase in the number of visits to wildlife refuges, because there were more angler days in the base year, 1962, salmon fishing has been increasing at a slower *rate* and thus shows a smaller index number than wildlife refuge visits for 1980. The same observation, however, would not hold for state parks visits; state parks attracted more visitors and had greater absolute and percentage increases than sport salmon fishing during the entire period under analysis.

Our interpretation of these relative increase trends is that recreation activities such a wildlife refuge visits and state park visits are going to continue to increase very rapidly. Pleasure boating and sport fishing will also enjoy increases, but not at such high rates. Among other activities, it looks as if there will be continued increases in the demand for more electric power and hence additional nuclear or thermal power stations will be needed. Timber harvests are also on an upward trend, although this kind of analysis does not indicate whether or not the trend will be halted by supply constraints before higher levels are achieved. Manufacturing should enjoy continued expansion, as will to a lesser degree the tonnages moved in major ports. Our interpretation of the difference between port tonnage forecasts and vessel movements is that on the average, vessel size will be larger than in the past so that more tons can be moved in fewer ships.

Of all the activities, commercial salmon and shellfish cultivation are the only ones showing absolute declines. Both of these activities, however, show wide variations from year to year and confidence in the forecasts is lower than for other activities. Thus, while commercial salmon fishing and shellfish cultivation may not decline, we can still reasonably conclude that they are unlikely to increase along with the other activities using Puget Sound's resources.

*Shoreline Property Values*

In addition to obtaining an indication of overall relative activity increases we are particularly concerned with what is happening directly on Puget Sound's shorelines, especially those outside the most heavily urbanized areas. Unfortunately, neither good current nor historical data on actual use of the 2,350 miles of shoreline in the Puget Sound region exist (although upon completion of shoreline inventories required under the Shoreline Management Act better current data will be available).

To obtain some understanding of trends in the use of Puget Sound's shoreline, a study of price changes for waterfront land used for different purposes was undertaken.[22] If prices were increasing more rapidly for one kind of use than another, we could then conclude that demands for the use with the higher price increases were increasing more rapidly than demands for alternative uses. Over time, we would also expect more land to be shifted to the higher demand use.

Because of information and sample-size limits we divided shoreline usage into only two categories: final consumption and intermediate production. The former use is one where the benefit to the shoreline user is the final-consumption benefit, as when summer home residents enjoy their shoreline location or visitors to a marine park enjoy the use of the shoreline for clamming, picnicking, or camping. Final-consumption uses of shoreline include sport shellfish beaches, parks, wildlife refuges, and sites for summer homes. In general, final-consumption uses tend to be recreational or residential. In contrast, intermediate-production uses occur when the shoreline location is used to produce a product that is consumed away from the shoreline. The shoreline location is *intermediate* to the consumption of the final product, as when an oil refinery uses a shoreline location for its production, but consumption of the product, oil, takes place away from the shoreline it-

22. Ibid., Chap. 8.

self. Intermediate-production uses include manufacturing and port facilities, but the commercial cultivation of shellfish is also an intermediate use because the shellfish are finally consumed on people's dinner tables far from where commercial shellfish cultivation was undertaken.

Our decision to divide shoreline uses into final-consumption uses or intermediate-production uses was based on two major considerations. First, conflicts between individuals preferring to use the shoreline directly, especially for recreational and residential purposes, and individuals desiring to use the shoreline for intermediate production such as oil refineries or other industrial uses have been important on Puget Sound. And, second, as incomes and leisure time increase, people have more rapidly increasing demands for recreational and high-amenity residential locations which shorelines provide, than for most manufactured products. Thus, to test whether or not prices for waterfront lands are increasing more rapidly for final-consumption than for intermediate uses also indicates whether rising demands for recreational and residential use of Puget Sound's shorelines are occurring as would be predicted from increases in income in the region.

To determine the changes in price paid for shoreline land in different uses a random sample of coastal points outside of existing harbor areas was drawn. Waterfront lots used or to be used for a final-consumption and an intermediate activity nearest to each point, which had changed ownership at least twice since 1951, were identified. The classification of use was based on pictures or descriptions in county assessors' files. The amount paid for the lot at each transaction was obtained from the auditor's office of the respective county.

The data collected were then standardized by setting the value of the property in 1956, as derived from the selling price data, equal to 100. Using 100 for 1956 as the base year value, an index of the average annual increase in value between the two times the lot changed ownership was calculated. The index numbers of annual increase in value for final-consumption and intermediate-production lots were then averaged separately for each year. The results are presented in Table 4–3 and illustrated in Figure 4–7. The figure and table indicate that a typical lot used for a final-consumption use selling for $100 in 1956 had an average annual increase in value of $54.10 and sold for $911.40 in 1971, while a typical intermediate-production lot selling for $100 in 1956 had an average annual increase in value of $27.70 and sold for $515.60 in 1971. Our data indicate that the value of shoreline property for direct consumption uses has been increasing nearly twice as fast as value of shoreline property for intermediate-production uses.

While this comparison of the increases in prices of shoreland for

TABLE 4–3
INDEX OF ANNUAL CHANGE IN THE PRICE
PAID FOR WATERFRONT LOCATION

|  | Intermediate-Production | | Final-Consumption | |
|---|---|---|---|---|
|  | Annual Increase | Cumulative Increase | Annual Increase | Cumulative Increase |
| 1956 | . . . | 100.0 | . . . | 100.0 |
| 1957 | 45.5 | 145.5 | 76.1 | 176.1 |
| 1958 | 36.6 | 182.1 | 69.4 | 245.5 |
| 1959 | 33.4 | 215.5 | 71.7 | 317.2 |
| 1960 | 31.9 | 247.4 | 60.0 | 377.2 |
| 1961 | 26.8 | 274.2 | 57.2 | 434.4 |
| 1962 | 26.9 | 301.1 | 54.5 | 488.8 |
| 1963 | 25.1 | 326.2 | 48.7 | 537.5 |
| 1964 | 20.7 | 346.9 | 51.3 | 588.8 |
| 1965 | 21.9 | 368.8 | 55.1 | 643.9 |
| 1966 | 25.2 | 394.0 | 55.9 | 699.8 |
| 1967 | 36.6 | 430.6 | 47.3 | 747.1 |
| 1968 | 20.7 | 541.3 | 47.9 | 795.0 |
| 1969 | 22.1 | 473.4 | 45.9 | 840.9 |
| 1970 | 21.4 | 494.8 | 33.2 | 874.1 |
| 1971 | 20.8 | 515.6 | 37.3 | 911.4 |
| Average | 27.7 |  | 54.1 |  |

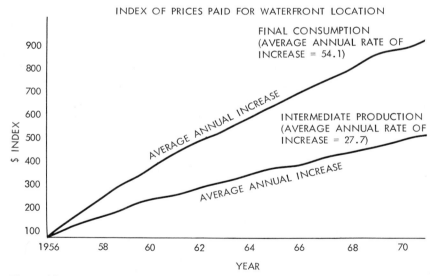

INDEX OF PRICES PAID FOR WATERFRONT LOCATION

FINAL CONSUMPTION
(AVERAGE ANNUAL RATE OF INCREASE = 54.1)

INTERMEDIATE PRODUCTION
(AVERAGE ANNUAL RATE OF INCREASE = 27.7)

AVERAGE ANNUAL INCREASE

AVERAGE ANNUAL INCREASE

$ INDEX

900
800
700
600
500
400
300
200
100

1956    58    60    62    64    66    68    70

YEAR

Figure 4-7

final-consumption and intermediate-production uses does not permit us to say anything about the absolute level of prices for either land use, we can conclude that demands for final-consumption uses of shorelines are increasing more rapidly than demands for intermediate-production uses. This conclusion is consistent with our previous observations that recreational housing developments have undergone tremendous expansion and that the use of parks and wildlife refuges has been increasing more rapidly than other marine related activities during the past decade. If these trends continue we can anticipate relatively greater demands for uses of Puget Sound's resources and shorelines for recreational and other final-consumption uses. These demands may also make it increasingly difficult for industrial or other intermediate-production users to locate in areas that are currently undeveloped or used primarily for final-consumption uses, thus confining future industrial expansion primarily to already developed port and harbor areas.

CONFLICTS OVER THE USE OF PUGET SOUND RESOURCES

Many uses of Puget Sound resources either damage or prevent other potential uses and users from undertaking their preferred activities. As large as it is, there is simply not enough of "Puget Sound" for every potential user to use the Sound to the extent that he would prefer. Too many users will "get in each other's way" and conflicts are the likely result.

Puget Sound has not been free from conflict in the past. Use of Puget Sound waters for effluent disposal has made the pulp and paper industry, food processors, and many municipalities very unpopular with sport and commercial salmon- and shellfishermen. At the same time the sport and commercial fishermen have had considerable disagreement over the division of the Sound's fishery between them, while at the same time both groups are willing to cooperate to encourage greater fish hatchery production for them to share. More recently, it has been recognized that upstream logging and urban development may have actually done more damage to salmon fish runs by silting salmon spawning areas than the direct water polluters fishermen have confronted in the past. Now, of course, fishermen have a new worry with the potential introduction of Alaskan oil into the Sound's waters.

In the past fishermen have been highly visible in most major conflicts, both over dividing the fish catch among themselves and in attempting to prevent damage to the fishery by water pollution or other adverse uses. The sensitivity of salmon and shellfish to pollution forced fishermen to defend Puget Sound's waters against destruction of the natural environment if they were to be able to continue their own activities.

Conflicts over the use of Puget Sound resources, however, are changing. Decisions on shoreline use are becoming increasingly important. Increasing numbers of summer-home owners, park visitors, and wildlife refuge visitors view the Sound as a place where the natural environment should be preserved, not developed for industrial uses that would reduce the value of the Sound for recreational purposes. Thus, competition for limited shoreline space and efforts to preserve areas not yet developed appear to many to be as important as the earlier efforts of fishermen to keep the waters clean and the salmon running. These controversies such as over the proposed aluminum reduction plant at Guemes Island, the proposed oil refinery on Port Susan Bay, or the development of Nisqually Delta, are all examples of competition and conflict over the use of scarce shoreline space. Not all controversies are between industry and recreation or the natural environment, however. Residents of Puget Sound shorelines also contest denser recreational-residential developments like the Boise-Cascades proposed marina and new town on Hood Canal at Anderson Cove, and local summer-home owners resist development of nearby parks for nonresident recreational use, much as sport and commercial fishermen contested the division of salmon not destroyed by still other uses.

Current demographic and urban patterns and forecasts presented in the last two chapters indicate a potential for conflict among citizens from different subregions of the Puget Sound area with regard to the uses of the Sound's shorelines and other resources. We have predicted a continued concentration of population, urbanization, port activity, and industrial activity around the major ports in the presently developed urban counties. We have also predicted relative increases in demands for shoreline parks, wildlife refuges, pleasure boating, and residential recreation developments, all of which are activities for which the lesser developed subregions such as Southern Puget Sound, Hood Canal, the waterways east of Whidbey Island, and the San Juan Islands are especially well suited. At the same time, however, residents of the less developed subregions have lower incomes and higher poverty rates than citizens of the urban counties, and many residents of the smaller counties would welcome economic development which would permit less reliance on the wood products industry and provide higher incomes and more jobs.

Thus, we have a paradox. Should the lesser developed areas of the Sound be preserved in a near natural state, primarily for the benefit of wealthier urban residents who wish to undertake recreational activities there, or should greater development of smaller counties be encouraged to provide more jobs and higher incomes to their residents even if that would reduce the "naturalness" of the environment in these areas? We do not believe the answer of preservation or development of lesser developed areas of the Sound is an "all or nothing" question. However, we should not be surprised if residents of urban counties desire continued concentration of industrialization and development in their own areas. This would contribute to raising their own incomes while preserving the rest of the region for their recreational use. We should also not be surprised if many citizens in smaller counties welcome new industry to provide employment and higher incomes for themselves, even if this caused some reduction in the value of their area for recreational use. After all, to the urbanite who resides in a congested area the region seems crowded and overdeveloped, while to the rural county resident the Sound's resources still appear only sparsely utilized.

While conflict among potential users of Puget Sound's resources has been intense in the past, it is likely to be even more intense in the future as more people with higher incomes impose their demands on a natural resource with limited capacity. Everyone cannot have everything he wants from Puget Sound. The outcomes of these conflicts will determine the future of Puget Sound, as well as whose preferences for resource uses are best met. The market and political decision-making processes through which these conflicts will be resolved is the focus of the next chapter and the rest of the study.

# CHAPTER FIVE

# Resource Allocation and Political Organization

In Chapter 4 we described the major uses of Puget Sound's resources. We also indicated some conflicts that have occurred and can be expected to occur between and among different uses. These descriptions, however, were undertaken with no explicit consideration of the decision-making framework within which resource uses are determined and conflicts resolved. The resource uses and trends are the outcomes of many decisions concerning resource allocation on Puget Sound. If different resource allocation patterns are desired the decision-making framework may have to be changed. Before it can be changed with some assurance that the consequences of the change will be those desired, the processes by which decisions are made and conflicts resolved must be understood.

In this chapter we will take a closer look at the nature of interdependencies between and among the uses and users of Puget Sound resources and between Puget Sound resources and other resource uses in the economy. Because Puget Sound is a geographically defined resource we will pay special attention to the geographic area over which uses of the Sound have direct effects. Following an examination of resource interdependencies we will indicate how resources are allocated through market transactions, where market transactions fail to achieve desired resource allocation patterns, and some major characteristics of political decision-making processes. This analysis will provide a framework for the more detailed analysis of government and resource use decision-making on Puget Sound in following chapters.

PUGET SOUND RESOURCE INTERDEPENDENCIES

In Chapter 4 we observed that for some uses the final consumer or beneficiary of the use was himself the direct user of the Sound's resources. For other uses the user played an intermediate-production role and produced a service or product for a consumer who did not use the Sound's resources directly. For example sport fishermen and shoreline summer home residents are both users of the Sound's resources and final consumers of the services provided by the Sound. On the other hand, the operator of a shoreline refinery is the user of the Sound's shoreline but the final consumer is the user of the refined petroleum product; similarly, the commercial fisherman is the user of the Sound, but the final consumers are the individuals who enjoy the salmon on their dinner tables.

In addition to each use being related to a final consumer who may not use the Sound himself, each use is related to complementary activities, competitive activities, incomes of other people, and other uses of the Sound as transmitted through impacts on the natural environment. Each of these relationships is an important aspect of Puget Sound's resource use interdependencies with other uses and users. *Complementary* activities are those which accompany and enhance the resource's use. For example, the manufacture, shipping, sale, and rental of fishing tackle, boats, and motors are complementary to fishing, as the drilling of oil, manufacture of super tankers, shipping of oil, and manufacture of oil refining equipment are complementary to undertaking oil refining on Puget Sound shorelines. *Competitive* activities are options the user or final consumer may choose in place of the activity using Puget Sound resources. Other kinds of recreation such as fishing on inland lakes and streams, camping, and mountain climbing are all competitive options for fishermen. Choosing to refine petroleum in British Coumbia oil fields for pipeline shipment to Puget Sound also represents a competitive alternative to refining petroleum on Puget Sound's shoreline.

*Income effects* from uses of Puget Sound are the changes in income that result from changes in direct spending by users and the respending of income derived from users by other people in the community. Income effects occur when incomes are earned by selling a locally produced product outside an area or when people from outside the area come into it and make purchases.[1] Most of the intermediate-production uses of Puget Sound are activities which ship and sell products outside the region. The income generated from these sales is used by employees of the exporting activities to purchase local goods and services, and hence enhances the income of local grocers, shoe store owners, and so on. Many of the final-consumption uses require the purchase of com-

1. For an analysis of income effects of public and private expenditures see Charles Tiebout, *The Community Economic Base Study* (New York: Committee for Economic Development, 1962).

plementary goods at the site of direct consumption, as when a sports fisherman rents a boat or a summer home owner hires a local builder. Thus final-consumption activities also generate incomes for local residents.

The different income levels and poverty rates in different counties surrounding Puget Sound[2] lead us to believe that some residents would be much more concerned with income effects than others. Lower incomes and higher poverty rates are found in rural counties, with higher incomes and lower poverty rates found in the urban counties, especially King and Snohomish. These different incomes and poverty rates also indicate that the economy of the Puget Sound region may not be fully integrated. This means that income effects generated in one part of the region do not affect the entire region, but instead remain concentrated where created, or contribute to income growth in the urban core.

In addition to being related to complementary activities, competitive options, and income effects, many uses of Puget Sound's resources have effects on the natural environment which in turn affect other uses of the Sound. For example, sport fishing may affect commercial fishing by reducing the stock of fish available, or pollution from a municipal sewage plant may affect sport and commercial fishing by killing off a fish run. Similarly, thermal pollution may warm waters near swimming beaches and raise their level of use for recreation. Finally, many other activities, perhaps occurring far away from Puget Sound itself, may affect the uses of the Sound because the Sound's resource use activities are complementary, competitive, or affected by others' incomes. For example, if the Department of Game suddenly increases the stock of giant trout on inland lakes, sport fishing on Puget Sound would be expected to decline. This decline in sport fishing would be followed by a decline in the incomes of sport fishing suppliers and their communities. Similarly, if new technology reduces the costs of boats and motors, sport fishing on the Sound might increase and the incomes of sport fishing suppliers might increase. To get a better idea of the nature of these interrelationships let us look at two examples of uses of Puget Sound.

In 1966 an aluminum reduction plant was proposed for Guemes Island. The user of the site would be the company operating the plant on Puget Sound. The final consumers of the product, however, would be the purchasers of aluminum products, located primarily in the rest of the United States. Complementary activities include mining bauxite (primarily abroad), shipping ore, the production of machinery used in the plant, electrical power production, and finishing of aluminum products for consumers. All of these activities except power production

---

2. County incomes and poverty and unemployment rates were presented in Chapt. 3.

take place primarily outside of Washington state. Competitive activities include alumina processing in other locations, and the manufacturing of substitute products including wood, steel, other alloys, and plastics. Income effects occur because the aluminum reduction plant would pay incomes to employees who in turn would spend that income in their local community. Stockholders in the company operating the plant, who may live anywhere, also hope for higher incomes. Finally, effects transmitted through the natural environment include potential air and water pollution in the area of the plant. From identification of these effects we can conclude that the production of aluminum is a part of the mining industry, part of manufacturing industry, one of many potential financial investments, and a part of the income base of a local community as well as a part of the resource allocation system utilizing Puget Sound's resources.

Another example of use of Puget Sound is a hypothetical terminal for transferring oil from ships to pipelines. Such a terminal would have as users the terminal operators. The final consumers are the users of oil, located perhaps in the Midwest. Complementary activities include oil drilling and production, oil shipping, pipeline construction and operation, oil refining, and petrochemical operations. Competitive activities include alternative terminals and pipeline operations at different locations and production of coal, natural gas, or other fuels. Income effects are incomes resulting from employee and company spending in the local community and accruing to terminal company owners. Effects on Puget Sound include navigation congestion and potential pollution.

We could go through each use of Puget Sound's resources and identify the users or undertakers of the activity, the final consumers, complementary activities, competitive activities, income effects, and effects transmitted through Puget Sound's natural environment. We would discover that each activity is related to many other activities in many different geographic locations. We would also find that no simple decision-making system could account for all interdependencies and result in efficient resource allocation patterns.

Most of the relationships among activities related to the use of Puget Sound take place through market transactions, or with reference to potential market transactions. Sports fishermen purchase or rent complementary goods such as boats, motors, and tackle. Sports fishermen may not actually undertake competitive activities, but the availability of options influences the terms upon which sports fishing will be undertaken. Income effects are also transmitted through series of market transactions. The only major aspect of sports fishing coming under political management is the management of the fishery resource. Political management is undertaken by setting limits and gear restrictions and adding to fish stocks through operating hatcheries for supplemental planting.

All of the effects of the aluminum plant except control of potential air and water pollution also take place through market transactions. Complementary goods are purchased and aluminum sold. The purchase of aluminum is influenced by availability of competing products, and income effects are transmitted through markets. Activities related to an oil transfer terminus would also occur primarily through market transactions. Complementary inputs would be purchased and oil products sold. Prices and quantities sold would depend on availability of alternative products. Income effects would occur through markets. The major nonmarket relationships would occur with regulation of potential oil pollution and regulation of oil shipping. If we followed an oil terminal's relationships further we would find it related to other governmental activity, including determination of national energy policy, regulation of foreign oil imports, the foreign policy of other countries, and regulation of oil drilling because oil pools themselves are common pools where regulation of pumping increases their yield.

Our major concern is not with all the relationships of all the activities undertaken on Puget Sound. It is primarily with important interdependencies of Puget Sound's resource uses that require more specific recognition in resource use decision-making, perhaps through government policies or programs. In order to narrow our focus to problem areas it is necessary first to understand how existing resource allocation decision-making takes place.

RESOURCE ALLOCATION IN MARKETS

Private exchanges among individuals and firms, within a governmentally provided legal framework, are the major processes by which resources are allocated in the United States, and Puget Sound's resources are no exception. All of the intermediate production uses depend on market demands and the ability of producers to purchase inputs such as labor and raw materials to meet those demands at competitive prices with a Puget Sound location. The final consumption activities are also dependent on markets—but often for complementary goods rather than the use of the Sound itself. For example, to undertake sports fishing or pleasure boating, fishing equipment, boats, motors, and launching or moorage facilities must be available—and market provision of reasonably sized and priced outboard motors and fiberglass boats has greatly expanded the opportunities for fishing and boating on Puget Sound. Likewise, the use of shoreline parks has been encouraged by widespread ownership of automobiles, camping equipment, travel-trailers, and boats. The use of shoreline land for housing is also directly dependent on the market provision of dwelling units—even if it is market provision of lumber and nails for people who build their own cabins. To a very large extent it is the market provision of complementary goods which has facilitated and encouraged increased use of Puget Sound, and the increased need for paying closer attention to resource allocation problems where reliance on market decision-making leads to undesired rather than desired results.

An important characteristic of market resource allocation is that under certain conditions individuals trading among themselves voluntarily will exchange goods and services until the gain from additional units of a good equals the sacrifice of whatever has to be given up to acquire the good. When this situation is achieved no further incentives for trade exist and an efficient allocation of scarce resources, without any control, overall planning, or direction has been achieved.[3]

The fact that individuals making agreements among themselves can bring about an efficient and mutually beneficial allocation of scarce resources is an extremely important observation, and in one form or another underlies most of the arguments for free markets and a voluntary exchange economy. Efficient resource use from decentralized decision-making is a consequence of the information and incentives individuals respond to, which lead them to "correct" behavior.[4] Prices of goods and services are the basic bits of information individuals see. For example, suppose a large number of individuals decide that they prefer sailboats to travel-trailers. They then go to the boat salesman and place orders for boats instead of for trailers. The boat salesman orders more boats from the builder, who in turn must buy more fiberglass, lumber, boat hardware, sails, etc., and hire more men to build boats. The boat builder will be willing to pay higher prices for his inputs than before because he has a greater demand for his product. The producers of fiberglass, lumber, hardware, and sails in turn purchase increased amounts of inputs for their products by bidding them away from alternative users. At the same time, travel-trailer salesmen are ordering fewer trailers, trailer makers are hiring fewer employees and buying less aluminum, hardware, steel, and other inputs. Makers of aluminum, hardware, and steel buy fewer inputs for their products, and so on. Eventually, the economy adjusts to reflect the change in consumers' preferences away from travel-trailers toward sailboats—all without any

3. An efficient allocation of resources is one where trade has taken place until no one can be made better off without making someone else worse off. Up to that point it is possible to make someone better off without harming anyone, and thus there are net gains to be achieved through further trade.

4. F. A. Hayek, "The Use of Knowledge in Society," *American Economic Review*, 35 (September 1945): 519-30.

central direction or plan—as a consequence of each individual dealing only with other individuals he either buys something from or sells something to. As long as the only individuals affected by the series of transactions are those involved in them, the resulting equilibrium will be stable until there is a change of consumer or producer preferences or a more efficient technology invented.

Market economies are commonly called "competitive" systems. It is important to recognize, however, that market transactions are also co-operative; when parties make an exchange they both gain from it. A competitive element is present because sellers compete among them-selves to satisfy potential buyers, and buyers compete among themselves to purchase from sellers. Thus, every market transaction involves simul-taneously cooperation among transactors and competition among sets of people or firms wishing to enter into transactions with others. The in-centives inherent in this cooperative-competitive interaction are for buyers and sellers to try to do the most for the individuals they do busi-ness with. This does not preclude them, however, from adversely af-fecting third parties, as occurs when a refiner can sell oil at a lower price to customers or offer investors a higher rate of return for their in-vestment by not installing pollution-control equipment. The normative acceptance of market systems for allocating resources is based on the ethical position that individuals are the best judge of their own inter-ests and that voluntariness should be the primary criterion for interac-tions among individuals. This criterion also implies that affected third parties should have a say in actions affecting them.

The price system or voluntary exchange economy does not work by itself and it does not work perfectly. Men must agree on rules of owner-ship, exchange, and competition, their enforcement, and the general provision of a legal system. Thus men must consciously or uncon-sciously create the institutional structure in which a market economy will lead to efficient resource use. If proper rules and institutions are missing, monopolization, coercion, chaos, or the destruction of resources may result. We have good understanding of how a market economy functions. It is only recently, however, that considerable attention has been devoted to understanding specifically how the legal structure and governmental organization affects resource use—especially where effi-cient resource use does not result from individuals pursuing their own interests via voluntary exchange. It is on these aspects of resource alloca-tion that a study of land and water resource use must focus.

WHERE MARKETS WILL NOT WORK

In Chapter 4 we referred to conflicts among uses of Puget Sound. We used "conflict" simply to indicate that one use had a negative effect on another use and that the relationships between the uses needed to be taken into account in resource allocation decisions. Simple knowledge of incompatibilities among different uses, however, does not take us very far in understanding the relevance of conflicts for resource allocation decisions. Thus, for analyzing resource use interaction we will use a framework derived from the study of markets and market failures, of which conflict resolution among incompatible resource uses is but one part.

In the discussion of markets it was indicated that under some conditions market exchanges would result in mutual benefits and that all transactions together would lead to a situation where resources were allocated efficiently and no further mutual gains were possible. When third parties are damaged by transactions, or potential gains are not realized because of constraints of one kind or another, efficient resource allocation is not achieved and market failure occurs.[5] In this context, third party effects are analogous to our use of the term conflict in Chapter 4. Our concern, however, is not as much with conflict among *uses* as it is with conflicts that prevent achievement of the greatest mutual benefit to *users*. Thus, we wish to identify whether or not decision-making structures facilitate individuals adjusting their activities so that the greatest net benefits are achieved. Decision-making frameworks facilitating mutual gains will reduce conflicts among users, even if conflicts or incompatibilities among different uses of Puget Sound remain, as they always will when resources are scarce.

In addition to third party, or external, effects, three other types of market failures are of special relevance to Puget Sound and other multiple-use natural resources. One is the undertaking of investments or providing of services to enhance resource usefulness which benefit everyone whether or not they contribute to the expenditure. Unless processes other than voluntary exchange are used, these investments and services are likely to be underprovided in a market system. A second problem is that natural resources may be destroyed through overuse, and market systems may possess incentives which exacerbate rather than ameliorate this problem. The third problem is the difficulty of clearly defining and enforcing property rights to different uses of natural resources. Unless firm enforceable property rights exist, market systems cannot function efficiently. Each of these problems will be described in turn and the implications for collective or politically or-

5. It is common to refer to external effects, public goods problems, and common pool overuse as "market failures." It is more accurate, however, to consider external effects, public goods insufficiency, and common pool overuse as "legal system" failures because problems with them are a consequence of inadequate specification and enforcement of property rights, a prerequisite to market resource allocation.

ganized action to resolve them indicated.[6]    As will be indicated, the three problems are closely related and solving one may reduce or eliminate the others. While this discussion may initially appear abstract, it is precisely these problems which must be resolved to use the resources of Puget Sound efficiently without destroying them.

*External Effects*

External effects or spillovers are effects of an action which accrue to parties not directly involved in the action. The effects may be either beneficial, referred to as positive externalities or spillovers, or harmful, referred to as negative externalities or spillovers. An example of a positive externality accruing to an individual is his pleasure resulting from large tracts of undeveloped land near his summer home. Examples of negative externalities include the fouling of one's beach from an oil spill by a passing barge or the reduction in fish catches because other fishermen catch too many fish. The basic problem with external effects is that there are no prices or incentives which accrue to the generator that would encourage him to take into account costs or benefits generated externally in adjusting levels of his activities to where he is best off. To achieve efficient resource allocation *all* benefits and costs of the activity must be taken into account. Externalities are prevalent in uses of natural resources such as Puget Sound, where many of the potential uses do affect other potential users.

Not all external effects are worth worrying about. We are all affected by the actions of others; the question is, are we affected strongly enough so that if the person generating the externality has a legal right to carry on that activity would we be willing to compensate him to reduce activities generating negative externalities (or conversely would we be willing to pay him to keep producing positive externalities).[7] In terms of Chapter 4, conflicts among different uses are caused by external effects of one use on another. By limiting our analysis to those externalities where the users are affected strongly enough to be willing to give up something to get a change, externalities are "valued" the same as all other goods in the economy. This also permits us to compare the values accruing to the externality generator from carrying on his

6. Our focus on these particular problems of resource allocation does not imply that markets do not have other problems as well. Monopolization and antitrust regulations; discrimination and equal opportunity laws; and unemployment, inflation, and stabilization policies are just three of many other areas where market problems have been analyzed and governmental solutions attempted.

7. For a more detailed analysis of externalities see Robert L. Bish, *The Public Economy of Metropolitan Areas,* Chap. 2; J. M. Buchanan and W. C. Stubblebine, "Externality," *Economica,* 29 (November 1962): 371-84; and R. H. Coase, "The Problem of Social Cost," *Journal of Law and Economics,* 3 (October 1960): 1-44.

activity with the values of those affected to see if there are net benefits to both parties considered together from a change in the level or nature of the externality generating activity. For example, if a group of summer home owners valued the benefits of adjacent undeveloped property more than the benefits the owner of the property could obtain from developing it, there would be an opportunity to make both parties better off if homeowners paid the property owner not to develop his property (perhaps purchasing it for a park). On the other hand, if a shoreline property owner is permitted to let his trees grow so tall as to block the views of residents behind him, and residents whose views are blocked value their views more highly than the shoreline owner values tall trees, both parties would be better off if the residents whose views were blocked got together and paid the shoreline owner to have his trees trimmed. Our major concern with external effects is where opportunities for net gains from cooperation exist, but for some reason are not being taken advantage of. The problems of property rights, that is, rights to undertake activities which generate negative externalities, or rights to be compensated for damages caused by the activities of others, are treated later in the chapter.

*Public Goods*

Public goods are goods or services that can be used or consumed by many people simultaneously and for which exclusion of users is not feasible. For example, an unfenced beach preserved in its natural state can be used by many people simultaneously and it is difficult to prevent people from using it. Another public good is a lighthouse; once it is provided all boaters in its area benefit from it. Other examples of public goods include provision of flood control, the legal structure, or the odor from a pulp mill (the last often referred to as a "public bad"). One should be careful to note that the term "public" relates only to the form of use or consumption of the good and has nothing to do with the nature of the producer, whether government or a private firm.

Public goods tend to be underprovided or not provided at all in a purely market economy.[8] This is because if a single individual chooses to pay for provision of the good, other individuals can use it simultaneously without paying. Thus, from the perspective of any single individual it is better to "let George do it," and then use the good, rather

8. Terminology of authors for public goods varies. The terms "social goods" and "collective goods" also are used to describe "public goods" as defined here. The basic analyses of public goods are found in: Mancur Olson, Jr., *The Logic of Collective Action: Public Goods and the Theory of Groups;* Paul A. Samuelson, "The Pure Theory of Public Expenditure," *Review of Economics and Statistics,* 36 (November 1954): 387-89; and Samuelson, "Diagramatic Exposition of the Theory of Public Expenditure," *Review of Economics and Statistics,* 37 (November 1955): 350-56.

than pay for it themselves. The reluctance of individuals to contribute voluntarily to the provision of public goods is called the "free-rider" problem. If everyone else contributes, the noncontributor can use the good for free.

While all public goods are simultaneously consumable and not subject to exclusion, some public goods are more equally available for consumption than others. The services of a lighthouse or clean air are equally available to anybody *in the area* who wishes to use the services they provide, but not available at all to persons in other areas. Public beaches are also available (since the principle of exclusion does not apply) but some individuals will find them much more accessible than others. Different public goods are provided over different geographic areas; very few are like national defense which benefits everyone in the entire country.

Some public goods also provide the individual with a choice between use and nonuse while others do not. All individuals in a flood plain will be protected from floods and all individuals are protected by national defense. Local parks, however, are available to everyone but one can choose whether or not he wants to use them. An important case of public goods where free choice is important is called "option demand."[9] This is a demand to have a good available in case the individual decides he wants to use it in the future. Option demand is important only for all-or-none decisions, where potential users are willing to pay to maintain wilderness areas or public beaches in case they want to use them some day and do not want them developed in the meantime.

Very few goods are pure types, as between private or public or as between equal availability or unequal availability or no choice versus complete choice. Also, public goods provided in an area (say municipality) may generate externalities for individuals in other areas. The concepts of externalities and public goods are closely related, and indeed, the same good can be both an externality and a public good. For example, any externality accruing to a large number of people may be accruing like a "public" good or bad. The odor of a pulp mill may be an externality (it accrues to individuals who do not participate in transactions concerning the pulp mill's production) and the odor may accrue as a public bad (anyone in the area will be affected by it without detracting from the effects on someone else). Likewise the provision of a large free park by a municipality will be not only a public good for its residents, but it is likely to provide external benefits, also available as a public good, to individuals residing outside the municipality's boundaries.

9. Burton A. Wiesbrod, "Collective-Consumption Services of Individual-Consumption Goods," *Quarterly Journal of Economics,* 78 (August 1964): 471-77.

There are many boundary problems related to public goods and externalities. Different kinds of public goods have different spatial boundaries (for instance, the divergent areas served by a neighborhood park and by national defense), and the difference is important for determining the kind of organization able to provide the good most efficiently. Solutions to the free-rider problem to get public goods provided and the issues surrounding selection of the proper scale over which the goods are to be provided are treated later in this chapter.

*Common Pool Resources*

Common pool resources possess characteristics of both externalities and public goods.[10] A common pool resource is one that is available for everyone's use, where exclusion of users or limitations of use is not feasible or legal, but where one person's use directly reduces the use of the common pool by others. A common pool is like a public good where congestion or crowding has set in so that each person's use generates a negative externality for other users. Two examples of common pool resources are groundwater basins, where pumping by each user lowers the water table and raises the cost of pumping to other users, and fishing grounds, where each fisherman's catch reduces the number of fish remaining and hence raises the cost of catching fish to other fishermen. Other examples include oil pools, lakes, wilderness areas, wild animals and birds for hunting, the atmosphere for waste disposal, and areas such as Puget Sound. Some common pool resources are also called "fugitive" resources. Resources such as oil, fish, or wild animals are fugitive because they become usable only upon capture. Common pool resources are also called common property resources. However, common "property" is somewhat of a misnomer because common pools are not property in the usual sense, where some individual owns the resource and can prevent others from utilizing it. In fact one reason why some resources are common pools is that the costs of appropriating and defending exclusive use rights, that is, making into appropriable property, are higher than the added returns which more efficient use of the common pool might bring.

The economic efficiency problem with common pool resources is just the opposite of that with public goods. Public goods tend to be undersupplied because individuals find it rational to avoid paying their share of production costs. Common pools tend to be overutilized because it is in each individual's interest to use the resource until his additional costs

10. A classic analysis of common pool resources is H. Scott Gordon, "The Economic Theory of a Common-Property Resource: The Fishery," *Journal of Political Economy*, 62 (April 1954): 124-42; for an analysis of fisheries regulation see James A. Crutchfield and Giulio Pontecorvo, *The Pacific Salmon Fisheries: A Study of Irrational Conservation*.

equal his additional benefits—neglecting to take into account the external costs he generates for others. Thus at the individually selected use level, total additional costs (costs to the user plus external costs) are greater than additional benefits (to the user) and gains could be made by all individuals agreeing to curtail their use simultaneously. In addition, the fugitive nature of the resources makes it irrational for any single individual to reduce present use to save some of the resource for the future because it is likely that any resource he leaves unutilized will be immediately captured by someone else. For example, all fishermen or clam diggers would find it rational to leave sufficient fish and clams to insure their continued availability, but unless all individuals curtail fishing and clamming any single individual who reduced his own consumption would not be guaranteed that there would be any increase in fish or clams for the future.

Excessive use because of the failure to take into account externalities, and rapid use because individuals cannot save the resource for their own use in the future, may lead to destruction of the common pool. A fish run may be eliminated by overfishing; a river which can harmlessly assimilate and destroy a limited quantity of waste gets so much waste in it that the biological oxygen demand is exceeded and it loses its capacity to destroy any waste material at all.

There are two major approaches to the management of common pools. One is to make it into appropriable property that an individual can own and then have an incentive for careful, efficient use of the resource. The second is to institute some collective (i.e., government) management program. The two approaches can also be mixed.

A classic example of resolving common pool resource problems through creating private property is the Enclosure Movement of medieval Europe. The common was available for all individuals to pasture their animals. However, while each individual found it in his interest to put additional animals there, the large number of animals there at once had the potential for destroying ground cover, permitting erosion, and thus destroying the common as a grazing area. The Enclosure Movement resulted in pasture becoming private property, which the owner then had the incentive to use efficiently and preserve for the future by limiting the number of animals grazing upon it.

Examples of the regulation of common pools by management include oil pumping regulations and fisheries regulation. However, the general conclusion by economists for both of these cases is that while regulation is preventing too rapid a depletion of oil and the destruction of fish stocks it is extremely inefficient.[11] Both industries use too much capital

11. Stephen L. McDonald, *Federal Tax Treatment of Income from Oil and Gas*

because individuals still face the problem of "getting there first." With oil drilling, regulation limits the amount of oil to be pumped per well (with the result being many more wells than necessary), and fisheries regulation usually limits both the efficiency of the gear permitted and the fishing time. This leads to many more fishermen and boats than would be necessary to utilize fisheries resources efficiently. It also appears that the regulation of oil pumping on the basis of "conservation" has permitted the regulatory agencies, under the domination of the major oil companies, to act as a monopolist and keep prices much higher than would otherwise be the case. The imposition of monopoly pricing via regulation has not occurred in the much more decentralized fishing industry. Monopoly pricing via regulation is less likely to occur when different common pools (different fishing ground or different oil basins) are regulated by different agencies so that no single one's actions affect the market price of the product. If regulation of all common pools of a single type is by the same agency it will automatically function as a monopolist and may use monopoly pricing to obtain extra profits for its clientele.

Many of the most pressing environmental problems—air and water pollution and the destruction of beaches or wilderness areas through overuse—are common pool resource problems. Efficient, nondestructive use of these resources is extremely difficult if not impossible without either the introduction of new property rights or direct management of some type.

*Group Size*

The number of people affected by an externality, benefiting from the provision of a public good, or using a common pool resource, is an extremely important determinant of solutions to these resource allocation problems.[12] If very few people are involved there is a good chance that they will recognize their interdependency and enter into direct negotiation to take into account external effects, to agree to contribute to the provision of a public good, or to limit use of a common resource to its sustained yield. However, if large numbers of individuals are involved it is unlikely that externalities, public goods, or common pools will be dealt with efficiently.

There are two reasons why large numbers of individuals may fail to deal with resource allocation problems successfully in purely voluntary arrangements: first, the group may be so large that individuals do not

---

(Washington, D.C.: Brookings, 1963), p. 81, and Crutchfield and Pontecorvo, *The Pacific Salmon Fisheries*.

12. For an extended analysis of the problems of group size see Olson, *Logic of Collective Action*.

really sense their interdependence, and second, even if interdependence is recognized, each individual may not find it in his interest to take the time and trouble of promoting cooperative action among such a large group. Groups that are so large that a single individual's contribution makes no perceptible difference to the burden or benefit of other members of the group or to his own consumption of a public good are called latent groups. In latent groups each individual feels that his actions are insignificant in relation to everyone else's actions—and thus being a free-rider is the rational action for him to take. One would predict that unless some incentive or sanction is offered in addition to the public good or benefits from preserving a common pool, latent group members will not be provided with public goods or preserve common pool resources. Will a large group of homeowners get together and voluntarily contribute to purchase land for a park to keep it undeveloped or will fishermen voluntarily restrict their fishing to preserve fish stocks?

*Property Rights*

The importance of enforceable property rights for efficient resource allocation reappears continually in areas of the economy where the market does not function efficiently. In general it appears that everyone's property is no one's property: "Wealth that is free for all is valued by none because he who is foolhardy enough to wait for its proper time of use will only find that it has been taken by another."[13] A public good is unlikely to be provided voluntarily because once produced it is available for everyone to consume; a common pool is destroyed because no one has the incentive to save it for future use because he can not prevent rapid current exploitation by others. Over time it appears that property rights to most easily appropriable items where costs of enforcement are relatively low have evolved to permit the functioning of a broad-based market economy. Areas where property rights to valuable resources are unclearly defined are also areas where enforcement of property rights may be relatively expensive. However, even though appropriation and enforcement of property rights may be relatively costly in common pool management areas, the value of many common pool resources is rapidly increasing so that efficient management is more and more important and it is increasingly becoming necessary to institutionalize management of these resources.[14]

There are many popular biases against converting public common pool resources into private property. However, some type of rationing,

13. Gordon, "Economic Theory of a Common-Property Resource," p. 135.
14. For an analysis of the importance of property rights see S. N. S. Cheung, "The Structure of a Contract and the Theory of a Nonexclusive Resource," *Journal of Law and Economics,* 13 (April 1970): 49-70.

either through creating private property or through government licensing of use (which, like privatization, must have the effect of restricting unlimited public use if the common pool resources are to be preserved) is necessary. The Enclosure Movement was a conflict-ridden process. Perhaps we can do better with today's common pool resources, but conflict and controversy are likely to accompany any creation of institutions which limit individuals' use of formerly free resources.[15] Without limitations common pool resources may be destroyed so that no one benefits from their use—an even more undesirable situation than restricting their use through private property or licensing arrangements. A diagnosis of a market failure does not imply that there is a ready political solution to the problem. Political systems have their own problems and failures as well as potentials for enhancing cooperation among individuals.

POLITICAL ORGANIZATIONS

Problems with externalities, public goods, and common pools are related to high costs of decision-making among large voluntary groups.[16] Obtaining agreement among two or more individuals to do something takes time, effort, and resources in a bargaining process. Such costs are likely to increase with the size of the group and the potential for holdouts to prevent agreement. Increased costs attributable to group size are simply the result of having to obtain agreement among larger and larger numbers of people. Decision-making costs within latent groups, for instance, are likely to be especially high because each individual sees the cost to him of contributing to group aims without seeing that his individual contribution has any effect on provision of the public good. Increased opportunities for holdouts to prevent an agreement are also likely to raise decision-making costs. When an individual is in a position to hold back his support and demand a relatively large share of any benefits before he will participate in the group decision, high decision-making costs and stalemates may occur. Stalemates may contribute to the destruction of common pool resources if excessive use cannot be curtailed through users' agreement. By the time all pollu-

15. A common suggestion is that users can be taxed and the proceeds given to those excluded or used for general government expenditures.
16. Decision-making costs, also called bargaining costs, are all of the costs borne by individuals in reaching an agreement regarding the allocation or exchange of resources. They include the value of time and effort engaged in bargaining as well as any direct outlays. If bargaining costs are zero, in economic analysis it is generally assumed that individuals will continue to bargain until all gains from economic exchange have been exhausted and a Pareto optimal allocation of resources is achieved.

ters agree to stop polluting, the water body may be irreversibly damaged.

It appears obvious that the way to deal with holdouts and free-riders is "legally" to require them to cooperate. However, "legally required cooperation" may also generate costs.[17] Earlier in the chapter, negative externalities were defined as costs imposed on an individual as a by-product of someone else's action. Political-externality costs are costs imposed by actions of others, but these occur when an individual is coerced by a political organization or law into participating in an action with which he does not agree. For example, if the county government decides to increase spending for beach parks through an increase in local taxes, all residents of the county will bear the costs whether or not they agreed with the decision; individuals who voted against the Shoreline Management Act because they wanted to undertake a now forbidden use on shorelands they own bear costs from the majority-approved act.

In general, political-externality costs will decrease as the proportion of the members of the political unit required to agree before action by the unit is taken increases. For example, if 10 percent of a group could commit the entire group to action, each random individual member of the unit could potentially be forced to bear very high political-externality costs. If 51 percent of the group were required to agree before action by the unit could be taken, potential political-externality costs would be lower but still positive, because random members would have a 51-49 chance of belonging to the half of the group agreeing on the action. If 90 percent of the group were required to agree, political externalities would diminish because of the high probability that any member would be part of the motivating majority. Political-externality costs would be zero if unanimity were required for group action, in which case political action would be identical with voluntary group action.

Potential political-externality costs depend on the issues the political unit has authority to decide, as well as on the proportion of members required to commit the group to action. For example, when a political unit is limited to relatively low-expenditure decisions and can impose only very low taxes, potential costs to an individual will be relatively low even if he does not benefit from the tax-financed action. On the other hand, if the political unit is empowered to undertake actions which could potentially deprive an individual of all his property, political externalities are potentially high.

17. This analysis draws heavily on James M. Buchanan and Gordon Tullock, *The Calculus of Consent: The Logical Foundations of Constitutional Democracy.*

To determine the least costly decision-making rule for a group of in-dividuals it is necessary for the individuals to compare the expected decision-making costs with potential political-externality costs. In general, rule changes which lower decision-making costs will raise potential political-externality costs and vice versa. For many functions, especially for providing public goods or managing common pools, it is possible to reduce the total costs of group decision-making by forming groups where some fraction, perhaps 51 percent of the members, can decide policy even though individuals will be dissatisfied with policy from time to time. Groups where decisions binding on all members can be made with less than unanimous consent are called political groups. Most actual governmental units have the capacity, through a decision-making rule of less than unanimity, to commit members of the unit (citizens) to some action. The formation of political groups and the relaxing of voluntary consent as a condition of exchange are justified for many functions strictly on a basis of economic efficiency; political units are necessary complements of private markets for efficiently allocating some resources, especially public goods and common pools. Governments are not the only organizations within which a proportion of a group determines organization policy. For example, clubs, lodges, unions, professional associations, and so on, are private, but many of their programs or actions are undertaken on the basis of majority vote rather than unanimity.

Whenever organizations provide a framework within which a subset of members or citizens can make policy which directly affects other members or citizens, the rules of citizenship or membership, internal decision-making rules, and scope of activities the organization may deal with are extremely important for determining whose preferences will be met most closely and who will bear the costs of organization policy. Thus we expect greater dispute over changing rules regulating decision-making and creating new political organizations than occurs over day-to-day decisions within organizations because new rules or new organizations will influence "who gets what" for a long time to come.

Major problems can arise in obtaining agreement on decision-making rules among individuals when they have radically different perceptions of their likelihood of being in the subgroup making decisions for the entire group or when they are affected differently by group decisions. For example, one would expect civic leaders, lawyers, and perhaps local business leaders to expect to be in a governmental decision-making subgroup a disproportionate share of the time and thus have a tendency to favor relatively low decision-making rules. On the other hand, ethnic minorities and individuals with no informal access to government officials would prefer relatively high or restrictive decision-making rules under the expectation that they are unlikely to be in a decision-making subgroup very often and may bear costs of decisions made by others. Where individuals are affected differently by the group's decisions similar divergencies appear. For example, the potential costs of having a waterway closed to boats for certain times a day are likely to be much higher to individuals engaged in water transportation than to occasional pleasure boaters. Thus, individuals in water transportation would be especially concerned that rules permitting waterway closures take their interests into account.

These problems of individuals' likelihood of being in the decision-making subgroup, or differently affected by the group's actions, make it extremely difficult to get agreement on decision-making rules for natural resource management because of the diverse interests of the many users and uses to which resources are put. For example, the Shoreline Management Act represented a change in the decision-making rules for the use of Puget Sound's resources. Because the rules are so important for those who wish to utilize Puget Sound's resources, organizations and individuals concerned with shoreline use devoted considerable effort toward influencing the content of the act in directions which would make it easier for their preferences to be met. The difficulty of making major rule changes with which all strong groups would be satisfied was a major reason why passage of the act took a relatively long time and was not accomplished within the legislative process alone.

Let us look more closely at some characteristics of political organizations which determine whose or what kinds of preferences are likely to be met most closely and those which are likely to be neglected.

### The Size and Scope of Political Units

The rationale for political organizations in a market economy, as derived from the existence of external effects, public goods, and common pool resources, is quite clear.[18] The actual design of political systems is a complex task, especially when multiple-use common pool resources are involved.

Each political unit must be defined in terms of functions it may undertake, the geographic area it operates in (which in turn defines citizens by residential location), and its decision-making structure. The functions political units undertake range from single narrow functions, such as collecting and processing sewage or controlling mosquitos, to a large number of broad functions, such as those undertaken by national, state, county, and city governments. From the perspective of the individ-

18. Gordon Tullock, "Federalism: Problems of Scale," *Public Choice*, 6 (Spring 1969): 26.

ual, the fewer the functions of a political unit the more precisely he may indicate his preferences, but the more political units he will have to pay attention to. Direct voting on a bond issue for sewage facilities permits a relatively precise indication as to whether higher levels of sewage treatment are desired. On the other hand it is hard to tell just what a vote for mayor, governor or president means with regard to specific programs or policies. The problem of having to let a single vote express preferences on a large number of issues is called the menu or joint-product problem; à la carte selection is not permitted.[19]

Production interdpendencies are also important for determining functions of political units. It may be efficient to combine regulation of commercial fisheries with operating hatcheries to increase fish stocks because the biological knowledge required for the two activities is similar and the activities themselves closely related. It may also be efficient to combine provisions of elementary, secondary, and community college education or provision of water supply and sewage collection and disposal.

Geographic size is also important for determining political unit boundaries. The smaller the size the more impact any single voter can expect to have, and, more important, the more likely the policies pursued are to meet his preferences. People with similar tastes tend to reside in proximity to one another, and thus the smaller the area the more homogeneous the preferences of citizens are likely to be.[20] Also in homogeneous groups both decision-making costs and political-externality costs are expected to be lower.[21]

While considerations of preference indication may make relatively small political units desirable, many external effects, public goods, and common pools cannot be handled on a small geographic scale. External effects from pollution may affect entire river basins—which in the case of the Mississippi is the entire Midwest. Public goods also serve citizens in different sized areas: national defense must be provided on a nationwide scale, highway networks are provided at different scales from nationwide to local subdivisions, waterfront parks may serve citizens from within a few miles or from an entire region. The earlier discussion of resource interdependencies of complementary activities, competitive alternatives, and income effects indicated that individuals over the en-

19. These issues are also treated in Bish, *The Public Economy of Metropolitan Areas*, Chap. 3.

20. Kent P. Schwirian, ed., *Comparative Urban Structure: Studies in the Ecology of Cities* (Lexington, Mass.: D.C. Heath, 1974), especially Parts II, VI, and VII.

21. For an analysis of voting and public goods outputs, see Gordon Tullock, *Toward a Mathematics of Politics* (Ann Arbor: University of Michigan Press, 1967), Chaps. 3 and 4; also see Anthony Downs, *An Economic Theory of Democracy* (New York: Harper and Row, 1957), pp. 260-76.

tire United States may be affected by resource use decisions on Puget Sound. Where can we draw a line on who should or should not be included in a political decision-making group?

The geographic boundaries of common pool resources are crucial in determining the geographic scope for regulation. If regulation does not encompass the entire common pool, effects of regulation may be negated by individuals using the pool beyond the area of regulation. For example, if salmon fishing were regulated on Puget Sound only, salmon would soon be eliminated by river fishing and fishing in the North Pacific; or if air pollution were regulated in King County, but not Snohomish County, King County residents could still get polluted air because both counties are in the same air shed. While common pool regulation needs to include the entire common pool, there are also problems associated with having areas much larger than the common pool for regulatory purposes. Organizations covering large areas are unlikely to pay particular attention to internal differences or unique local circumstances which may be of extreme importance to a few people in a very small area.

The need to account for topography in common pool regulation, however, does not necessarily mean that political units themselves must be the same size as the common pools boundaries. Regulation can occur through intergovernmental agreements among different independent units. For example, the division of Fraser River fish stocks is governed by a treaty between the United States and Canada, and regulation of the North Pacific fishery is by treaty among the United States, Canada, Japan, and the USSR.

While some issues of political organization boundaries are related directly to functions or geographic size, others are related to political unit organization size per se, whether size is a consequence of many functions, large geographic scale, or both. These considerations relate to the use of information in organizations, problems of managing large bureaucracies, the decision-making structure, and the potential problem of a single interest obtaining a monopoly over some important function or resource.

The ability of organizations to collect, analyze, and use information varies with organization size. Within limits, the larger an organization the better able it will be to undertake research to produce scientific data such as physical laws of tidal movement or the long-run effects of different uses of Puget Sound. Smaller organizations, however, are usually better able to process and use time and place information in decision-making.[22] For example, local government may know much

22. Hayek, "The Use of Knowledge in Society."

more about developers silting a salmon spawning stream than the state departments of Ecology, Game, or Fisheries who are supposed to regulate such actions. Local sportsmen's clubs may know where ducks and geese are at any given time, even though the United States Bureau of Sports Fisheries and Wildlife understands their migration patterns better. In order to respond to time and place information large organizations often decentralize; decentralization, however, may complicate the problem of control by responsible officials and move more of the decision-making to bargaining among the strongest interests.

The difficulty of managing an organization also increases with size. This is especially true with many public organizations because their outputs are not easily measured or evaluated. Thus, public officials cannot manage an organization by looking at output measures such as profits and losses and concentrate efforts in problem areas. They must instead try to regulate the behavior of employees in hopes that behavior according to rules will produce outputs desired by the manager. When outputs are not easily measurable and organizations are so large that employee behavior is not easily regulated, it is not clear that employees have any incentives to be efficient and productive. Employees are unlikely to be rewarded for especially productive behavior, and may even receive sanctions if especially productive behavior deviates from the rules.[23] It should be remembered that these management problems are not due to the organization being public rather than private. They are due to the intangible nature of many public goods and common pool regulations.

The problems of citizens indicating their preferences to public officials are also affected by organization size. Relatively simple and direct citizen–public official decision-making structures are adequate only for small organizations. As size of political units increases citizens are less likely to vote on specific programs and more likely to vote for representatives who in turn delegate important decisions to subcommittees and employees in government agencies. As size increases individual votes for public officials mean less relative to direct contacts. Testifying at hearings, lobbying, writing letters, assisting with elections, and providing "free" information all may become relatively more important than voting. Citizens with particular interests will also find it efficient to coordinate their own efforts through private associations, representatives of which have a much stronger voice than individual citizens when bargaining or lobbying with government officials. No one is surprised that organizations of commercial fishermen play a more promi-

23. These issues are analyzed in Gordon Tullock, *The Politics of Bureaucracy,* and Marie R. Haug and Marvin B. Sussman, "Professional Autonomy and the Revolt of the Client," *Social Problems,* 17 (Fall 1969): 153-61.

nent role than voters in state Department of Fisheries policies, that real estate developers' associations pay special attention to laws affecting land use, or that associations of port officials are active whenever legislation affecting ports appears. The interests likely to be neglected in such a system are those of large latent groups, where no individual has a strong enough interest to organize the latent group into action to participate in the bargaining that determines the political unit's policies. In general, the larger the political structure the more we can expect interest group politics to predominate and unorganized individuals to have less impact on public policies.

Two constraints exist on strong special interests in political bargaining situations. One is the existence of other, often competing, special interests so that a variety of interests usually have to be taken into account as any group pursues its own interest. The second constraint is that elected officials do have to stand for election—and rivals for the offices have incentives to expose any special group favors which adversely affect others. The rivals, as well as incumbents, also have incentives to look out for latent groups in exchange for their votes. In spite of these constraints, however, relatively well-organized interests do better in influencing large political units than do less well-organized or latent groups.[24]

One final issue that is related to size per se is whether the public sector should be organized with relatively few large organizations or many small organizations. The traditional wisdom has been that relatively few large organizations are superior. However, the problems of citizen preference indication, domination by special interests, information, and management do not go away. The decisions are simply worked out within the organization away from public scrutiny. When there are many smaller political organizations many more decisions have to be made between and among political units. This may require higher decision-making costs but it also exposes information and agreements to greater scrutiny by a larger number of interests, and elected officials may have to pay more attention to the interests of unorganized voters. The requirement of agreement among independent units may also lead to solutions with broader mutual benefits than solutions arbitrated within a single unit, where the stronger faction can impose its preferences on others.[25]

24. For an analysis of these issues see Charles Lindblom, *The Intelligence of Democracy: Decision-Making through Mutual Adjustment.*
25. Robert L. Bish and Robert Warren, "Scale and Monopoly Problems in Urban Government Services," *Urban Affairs Quarterly*, 8 (September 1972): 97-122; and Vincent Ostrom, *The Intellectual Crisis in Public Administration.*

*Boundaries for the Management of Puget Sound?*

Are there any obvious boundaries, either functional or geographic, for political institutions to assist with the allocation of Puget Sound's resources? In the beginning of this chapter we indicated the range of interdependencies among the uses of Puget Sound's resources and other activities in the economy and society. We observed that final consumers of products produced with the aid of Puget Sound resources could be located anywhere; further, when we went on to consider complementary activities, competitive activities, income effects, and the effects of uses transmitted through the natural environment, we observed that the use of Puget Sound's resources are interdependent with many functional areas of economic activity and that interdependencies extend over many different geographic scales. We also observed that most interdependencies are handled through market transactions, but that the existence of external effects, the need for public goods, and the need to prevent destruction of common pool resources require the design of political institutions to improve the use of the resources. Finally we observed that the geographic scale, functional responsibilities, and decision-making rules and size of political organizations will have direct consequences for whose preferences are met most closely and who will bear the costs of political decisions. The resource uses of Puget Sound are parts of many complex systems and in spite of the fact that Puget Sound is a geographically defined entity, the geographic boundaries for political units to account for external effects, provide public goods, and regulate its common pool nature are not obvious.

If we cannot relate all resources to a set of appropriate boundaries can we at least designate boundaries for identifying consequences of resource uses transmitted through the natural environment? Can a focus on the natural environment itself, which would be consistent with a focus on preserving Puget Sound in a relatively natural state, help us define boundaries for management purposes more precisely?

For some purposes environmental and resource use interdependencies can be viewed as world-wide; for most purposes, however, a much smaller scope can be used to analyze the impact of man's uses on the natural environment. If we look again at the uses of Puget Sound we observe that probably no instance of moderate activity would have environmental effects throughout the Puget Sound region—but that many uses generate environmental effects for nearby uses. The Sound itself, however, is large and diverse and the environment of some parts, such as Hood Canal, could be affected significantly by any large disturbance of the natural environment. There are other parts of the Sound such as North Puget Sound where there is sufficient water movement and mixing to disperse the environmental consequences of relatively large man-made changes—including the development of Elliott Bay and the Duwamish Basin in Seattle for areas outside Elliott Bay itself.

While the environmental effects of any single use are not usually Sound-wide, particular uses generate effects over different areas. For example, construction of low-density summer homes along shorelines will have minimal environmental effects unless significant wildlife habitats are destroyed or extensive bulkheading is undertaken. On the other hand, a large pulp liquor spill during a salmon run may affect fish runs, not only in Puget Sound but in the North Pacific. The effects of many uses may also be cumulative. Dredging and filling shallow tidal lands where a single river enters may not have widespread impact beyond that particular estuary, but if all estuarine areas were filled and dredged marine life cycles would be significantly altered because organisms unable to live in deeper water would lose their natural habitats. Thus, some uses of Puget Sound may be related not only to immediate adjacent consequences of that use, but to long-run and spatially distant effects as well.

Puget Sound is a relatively large body of water, much larger than estuaries in the East or in San Francisco Bay, and thus much less subject to disturbance throughout from even intense human activity at particular locations. Puget Sound is also relatively clean, with much of its shoreline still in a near natural state.[26] While Puget Sound waters are hydrologically related it is not necessary that Puget Sound be treated as a comprehensive whole in evaluation of all activities, only some of which have Sound-wide consequences. Special attention, however, must be given to spatially distant and cumulative effects of resource use that may not be readily apparent.

The existence of cumulative environmental effects, especially those that are spatially distant, makes the development of information on consequences of water and land uses costly and difficult to obtain. Long-run base-line studies and the research required to identify the extent and magnitude of physical and biological interdependencies among potential uses is far more costly than any single individual or organization can or is willing to afford. In fact, knowledge of cumulative and distant consequences of any particular use may well be considered a public good; that is, when the knowledge is obtained it is available for everyone to use, but it is too costly for any single user to attempt to produce for himself. Unless information on effects of uses, especially cumulative and spatially distant effects, is produced coopera-

---

26. Crutchfield et al., "Socioeconomic, Institutional, and Legal Considerations in the Management of Puget Sound," pp. 192-200.

tively it is unlikely to be produced at all, and the lack of knowledge of direct and indirect consequences among uses and on the natural environment makes it difficult to evaluate the efficiency with which Puget Sound's resources are used.

We must conclude at this time that there is no obvious geographic scale for identifying the consequences of man's uses of Puget Sound's resources on the natural environment. Different uses will require different scales of analysis.

CONCLUSIONS

The discussion in this chapter provides an introduction to the complexity of resource allocation decision-making for large multiple-use natural resources such as Puget Sound. While we define Puget Sound geographically, there is no obvious set of geographic boundaries for analyzing resource use interdependencies or effects of its uses on the natural environment. The issues of resource allocation are still more complicated when we recognize how decisions made on Puget Sound effect other activities within the economy.

It is now time to begin a closer examination of just how decisions on the use of Puget Sound's resources are made.

# CHAPTER SIX

# Governments in the Puget Sound Region

Puget Sound is a dominant factor in linking the people around its boundaries. Its physical presence and image have strongly influenced how residents of the region have organized themselves geographically and economically. Similarly, the Sound provides a symbol of identity and invites life styles which interrelate land and marine environments in ways that are probably unique in the United States. Numerous governmental actions are demanded and, in some cases, taken in the name of using, protecting, enhancing, or developing the Sound and its resources. In light of this, the Sound would appear to be a logical focus for efforts by environmental groups to establish a regulatory body which is charged with the planning and management of this complex resources system. This has not, however, been the case. On the one hand, the very size and diversity of the region also has produced substantial social, economic, and political differences in the metropolitan, suburban, and rural communities that ring the Sound. This has inhibited the development of a common perception of the area as a unified region for governing purposes. On the other hand, as previously discussed, the scale effects of various resource uses differ and no single set of boundaries could internalize the consequences of all major uses.

A look at the boundaries of the public organizations which are relevant to the Sound indicates that they are either considerably smaller or larger than the Sound itself. The region is divided vertically and horizontally for both representative and administrative purposes. Numerous cities and counties and many special districts independently exercise authority over subareas of the Sound. They make decisions concerning land use, local public investment in shoreline development, and the way in which the coastal areas relate to the inland territory and population for which these units also are responsible. In addition, a number of state and federal agencies all overlap the Sound but are largely autonomous of one another in their activities.

Puget Sound, quite literally, represents a microcosm of the complex and interleaved system of public authority that characterizes the American federal system.[1] Elected officials, administrators, citizens, and interest groups contest resource use policies within their own local units of government as well as attempt to act through other public arenas to resolve conflicts or mobilize support to implement programs. As will be seen in Chapters 7 and 8, substantial conflict can arise at either the local or state level over the use of shoreline areas. Further, the material reflects the ability of interest groups to pursue goals concurrently in some cases, and sequentially in others, before county officials, the state legislature, the electorate, and the courts.

Governmental structure and decision-making processes provide a framework for the type of policy actions that are central to this study. The rules and rights that govern the utilization of resources arise from a series of statutes, ordinances, administrative regulations, and legal precedents. These grow out of legislative and administrative decisions at three levels of government, state and federal court cases, and the common law. Recent environmental issues dealing with the law relating to land and water utilization and shoreline resources regulation reflect a *de facto* concurrent jurisdiction among federal, state, and local governments.[2] Consequently, environmental policies concerning the shoreline have been structured by, and aimed at changing, the present distribution of governmental authority and law dealing with resources allocation. This chapter will review the governmental arrangements, legal provisions, and political processes which provide the framework for shoreline policy-making.

### THE STRUCTURE OF GOVERNMENT AND DECISION-MAKING

Just as there is no government for Puget Sound, there is no summary public policy for the use of its resources. There are a variety of policies made at the local, state, and national levels. These change over time and at different rates. The formal organization of governments and their rules for making decisions provide the structure and opportunities

1. The 1972 Census of Governments enumerated 78,269 independent units of government in the nation, with the overwhelming proportion at the local level.

2. Two useful discussions of the workings of the federal system are contained in Morton Grodzins, "The Federal System," in The American Assembly, *Goals for Americans* (Englewood Cliffs, N.J.: Prentice-Hall, 1960), pp. 265-82; and Vincent Ostrom, "Operatonal Federalism: Organization for the Provision of Public Services in the American Federal System," *Public Choice*, 6 (Spring 1969): 1-18.

for interested parties, public as well as private, to seek to maintain or change the distribution, rate, and type of resource use. How the opportunities are utilized depends upon the initiatives governments and groups are willing to undertake and their number and influence on a particular policy question. The electoral process, lobbying, interagency bargaining, and recourse to the judicial system all may be involved in determining a specific policy. It will be useful at this point to outline the governmental units with responsibilities for providing public goods and services relating to Puget Sound's waters and shoreline and consider the role of political parties, interest groups, and the courts in decision-making.

*The Federal Government*

Over 2.8 million personnel are employed by the federal government. National programs expend well over $200 billion a year. The operational boundaries of agencies vary from the world-wide activities of the Department of State to administrative subunits of the Department of Interior which may cover only part of one state. In no case is there a federal resources-related agency that is organized on the scale of the Sound. All have larger boundaries. There is no "national policy" for the Sound in terms of resource use. While some efforts have been made to coordinate programs, which will be discussed below, this is more common with counterpart agencies below the national level than with other federal units.

A mixture of functions is performed by federal agencies with increasing emphasis being put upon environmental protection and enhancement. The Army Corps of Engineers carries out multiple roles and has been active in the Sound's development since statehood and even before. The Corps's long run involvement has related to the funding and construction of river and harbor improvement. It has been closely associated with port development in the Sound as well as small-boat marinas. The Corps also is responsible for regulating all uses of navigable waters and has the authority to grant or withhold permits for any filing, dredging, or construction on, over, or under water that affects navigable waters. Until quite recently, this permit-granting authority was used to deal only with questions of the obstruction of movement over water. Now, however, the permit process has become a focal point for raising environmental issues in general and particularly in Washington state.

The role of the Department of Defense, the Corps's parent organization, is more limited and segmental but can be dramatic in terms of direct impact. The department's decisions to maintain or eliminate a naval facility, for example, can have far-reaching consequences for the economy of the immediately involved community. In other cases, there may be local demands for an installation, such as a fort, with an urban shoreline location to be turned over to civilian use but with conflicts over which use would be the most appropriate. Finally, a decision to establish a new defense facility may produce substantial opposition from environmentally concerned interest groups.

Environmental considerations also have affected the traditional role of the Coast Guard, now a unit within the Department of Transportation. The Coast Guard has had the responsibility for allocating navigational space for the movement of vessels on the Sound. More recently, it has become the principal federal unit for policing and responding to oil spills. There are both state and federal statutes concerning oil spillage and the Coast Guard has assumed a central role in receiving reports of spills, transmitting the information to relevant state agencies, and taking the lead in organizing the response.

The Bureau of Sport Fisheries and Wildlife of the Department of Interior cooperates with the Washington State Department of Game to regulate and enhance sports fisheries and waterfowl production. On the whole, the national bureau is more engaged in monitoring wildlife and environmental conditions, especially for migratory waterfowl, while the state undertakes most of the direct regulation and resource enhancement. The National Marine Fisheries Service of the Department of Commerce and the State Department of Fisheries interact on a similar basis for commercial fisheries.

A more generalized federal responsibility for research and information production on environmental conditions of water and air resources rests with the National Oceanic and Atmospheric Agency of the Department of Commerce. This agency's functions, if systematically coordinated, could make it a key point in the federal-state interface on matters relating to the Sound. Its activities include the management of the Weather Service, the National Ocean Survey, the National Marine Fisheries Service, and the Sea Grant Program. It also has been assigned the responsibility for implementation of the 1972 Coastal Zone Management Act.

Other national agencies with authority that affects the Sound include the Department of State, which through its role in negotiating international treaties concerning fishing can have a substantial consequence for the Sound's fisheries; the Forest Service of the Department of Agriculture which manages 32 percent of the Puget Sound watershed which is located on federal land; and the Public Health Service of the Department of Health, Education, and Welfare which undertakes research and supervision of shellfish beds and shellfish processing plants.

Several other line agencies have some but lesser importance in terms of affecting the region's resources. These include the Bureaus of Reclamation and Land Management (Department of Interior) and Public Roads (Department of Transportation). The federal government is also involved in the management of seven military installations and two national parks located on the shoreline and is a party to ten treaties that govern Indian reservations on the Sound's waters.

In addition to these agencies, a number of independent federal units have environmental responsibilities. The Atomic Energy Commission controls the siting and operation of nuclear power plants and the disposal of radioactive waste. Production of hydroelectric power is regulated by the Federal Power Commission. The Environmental Protection Agency plays a major role in setting general federal environmental control policies. In turn, the Council on Environmental Quality reviews Environmental Impact Statements which must be submitted by federal agencies and others utilizing federal funds or operating under federal permits in activities which affect the environment.

As noted above, no formal federal policy toward the Sound exists, but attempts have been made to interrelate project planning of federal as well as state agencies with regard to their programs within the region. In 1964 the Columbia Basin Inter-Agency Committee, composed of the governors of Washington, Idaho, Oregon, Montana, Utah, Nevada, and Wyoming, established a Puget Sound Task Force to make a detailed resource study of the region. The Task Force was charged with development of the regional water and related land resources. (The Inter-Agency Committee was subsequently replaced by the Pacific Northwest River Basins Commission, which is responsible to the National Water Resources Council.)

The Task Force was originally composed of nine members, representing the State of Washington and the U.S. Departments of Agriculture; Army; Commerce; Health, Education, and Welfare; Interior; Labor; and the Federal Power Commission. Later, the Departments of Transportation and Housing and Urban Development were also represented. The Task Force has produced three main volumes, including a summary and two studies of the river basins in the Sound region and fifteen appendixes dealing with individual functional areas such as navigation, power, recreation, fish and wildlife, and water quality control.[3]

These studies have provided a substantial amount of information relating to specific projects and produced considerable interaction among members of different federal and state agencies involved with activities

3. These studies were published by the Pacific Northwest River Basins Commission, Vancouver, Washington, in July 1970.

affecting the Sound. However, the Task Force did not produce a set of reports or interaction procedures which constitute or can lead to an integrated or coordinated federal or federal-state policy toward resources utilization in the Puget Sound region. Vertical functional interaction concerning the Sound between individual federal and state agencies is still far more prevalent than horizontal coordination within the national or state levels.

Puget Sound is not only a location for the activities of federal administrative and regulatory agencies. Five of the seven members of the state's delegation in the House of Representatives come from districts which are entirely or partially within the twelve-county Sound region. Because the Puget Sound area contains two thirds of the registered voters in Washington, the two U.S. senators are usually from that region.

### State Government

Washington State is the governmental unit which is most immediately responsible for the content and administration of public policies concerning the Sound as a whole.[4] Not only do a number of its programs have direct impacts on the Sound, but local jurisdictions—cities, counties, and special districts which substantially affect the shoreline— are generally subordinate to the state and subject to policies adopted by the legislature.

Two of the nine elected state officials have the authority and visibility to raise issues and play key roles in policy determinations that may affect the Sound: the governor and the commissioner of public lands.[5] The successful enactment of any environmental initiatives in the legislature and administration of the resulting programs is highly dependent upon the active backing of the governor. The involvement of the governor in general environmental questions has increased substantially over the last decade. The same is true of the legislature, which, with the governor, is the primary source of environmental policy in the state. It is in the legislature, particularly, that conflicts and accommodations over any major shift in the law concerning resource use takes place. The Sound region is divided by the boundaries of a number of legislative districts for the state House of Representatives and Senate. Nineteen of the state's forty-nine legislative districts (each of which has

4. For a general description of state governmental organization in Washington, see Mary W. Avery, *Government of Washington State* (rev. ed.; Seattle: University of Washington Press, 1973); and Washington State Research Council, *The Research Council's Handbook* (Olympia, 1973).

5. The nine state-wide elected officials are: governor; lieutenant governor; attorney general; secretary of state; treasurer; auditor; commissioner of public lands; superintendent of public instruction; and commissioner of insurance.

one senator and two representatives) contain land directly on the Sound and thirty-two are wholly within or include part of the twelve-county area. Thus, 39 percent of the total membership of each chamber has a district abutting the Sound and 65 percent come from within the Puget Sound region.

In addition to the governor, the commissioner of public lands is also directly involved with Puget Sound, in this case, more from an administrative perspective. The commissioner is elected every four years and serves as director of the Department of Natural Resources (DNR). In this position, the incumbent acts as "proprietor" for the management, leasing, or sale of state-owned land, which includes thirteen hundred miles of tidelands and two thousand square miles of marine beds under navigable waters. The commissioner's control of these resources around the Sound has placed the office in a significant policy role concerned with decisions on public development of state tidelands in the Sound or leasing them for private development.

The Department of Ecology (DOE) is the most important state agency, in terms of resource allocation, that is directly responsible to the governor.[6] It was established in 1970 as part of the governor's "package" of environmental bills that was submitted to a special session of the legislature that year. This agency comes as close as has been politically possible to centralizing the state's environmental regulatory activities. The DOE administers water and air pollution-control programs, including oil spillage regulations. It is also responsible for the Shoreline Management Act. While many of its activities directly concern Puget Sound, the agency is not organized administratively or territorially to focus or coordinate its programs in relation to the region.

Two other major agencies are involved with common pool problems associated with fisheries and wildlife. The Departments of Fisheries and Game both are engaged in conservation through regulation of the taking of fish, fowl, and animals and enhancement through increasing or introducing new stocks. While these departments are responsible for the state as a whole, a substantial number of their activities, particularly those of the Department of Fisheries, relates to the Sound and adjacent waters. Fisheries is concerned with commercial and saltwater fishing and anadromous salmon stocks. Game deals with freshwater fish, steelhead, waterfowl, and animals. There is extensive interaction between these units and other state and federal agencies. Both play a

6. Elizabeth H. Haskell and Victoria S. Price, *State Environmental Management* (New York: Praeger, 1973), pp. 69-108, discusses the organization and operations of the Department of Ecology. For a review of the programs of DOE and other state agencies reviewed in this section, see State of Washington, *1972 Annual Report, Natural Resources and Recreation Agencies*.

role in approving any change in water that would affect fisheries.

In addition to regulating fishing through setting catch limits, seasons, and gear restrictions, Fisheries and Game cooperate with DOE in controlling adverse effects of other activities. Special concern is given to regulations on minimum stream flows and such things as silting which effect stream beds or food for migratory fish. To supplement stocks both Fisheries and Game undertake research and the raising and planting of hatchery fish. The departments operate over fifty hatcheries throughout the state and Fisheries alone planted more than seventy-six million fish in Puget Sound tributary waters in 1971. The planting of salmon and steelhead trout (by the Department of Game) has substantially increased the supply of fish available to sport and commercial fishermen. Some of the state's research on enhancement of fisheries is funded by the federal government. Other related research and development is undertaken by the Bureau of Sports Fisheries and Wildlife and the National Marine Fisheries Service.

Aquaculture, the raising of fish and shellfish for food in pens or specific areas, has received increasing attention in the Sound, largely through activities of the DNR and private entrepreneurs. Several private businesses and two Indian tribe organizations have leased sites on the Sound for aquaculture projects.

The Department of Game has the state responsibility for the regulation of waterfowl in the Sound region. Migratory waterfowl are jointly managed by the Bureau of Sports Fisheries and Wildlife. Puget Sound is in major flyways for these birds and many from Canada, Alaska, and eastern Russia winter in the region. The DNR has designated some sixty sites in areas it manages in the Puget Sound region for waterfowl use.

The state Department of Parks and Recreation maintains eighty-nine state parks and monuments on Puget Sound, fifty-one of them in San Juan County alone.[7] This agency also has pioneered in establishing a number of marine and underwater park areas for scuba and skin divers and students of marine life and anticipates expanding its activity. Facilities on the Sound and the state in general for camping, boating, picnicking, hiking, diving, and other forms of recreation represent one of the fastest-growing demand areas in the public sector. In addition to the department, county, city, and special park districts, DNR, U.S. Forest Service, and National Park Service are all involved in providing these services in the Sound region. An agency has been created to coordinate state-wide acquisition of state park lands and to provide grants on a cost-sharing basis to local governments for parks. The

7. Wallace H. Spencer, *Environmental Management for Puget Sound*, pp. 45, 46.

Interagency Committee on Outdoor Recreation is composed of the directors of the Departments of Game, Natural Resources, Fisheries, Highways, Commerce and Economic Development, and Ecology. The overwhelming portion of funds allocated by the IAC since its establishment in 1964 have gone to acquire park sites in counties in the Puget Sound region. Over one half (158) of the 286 local projects approved by the IAC between 1965 and 1972 were located in King, Pierce, and Snohomish counties.[8]

One other state agency has a major impact on the Sound. Virtually all facilities for cross-Sound passenger and auto travel are administered by the Department of Highways through the Washington Toll Bridge Authority. The latter body was created in 1937 and is responsible for the construction and maintenance of several bridges which span various portions of the Sound. In 1951 the Authority purchased what is now known as the Washington State Ferry System. Since then the state has become increasingly committed to expanding and improving the quality of the system. In 1970 over six million passengers moved on the Sound over nine domestic and one international route between eighteen terminals.[9]

The Thermal Power Plant Site Location Council is a particular example of a response by the state to an environmental and development policy conflict which overlapped the authority or interests of a number of governmental units.[10] The council was formed as a mechanism to require a number of state agencies to collectively treat an environmental problem and facilitate their interaction. The council was established by the legislature in 1970 to provide statutory authority for a unit that had been set up by executive order of the governor in 1969 to advise him on the environmental consequences of any proposed nuclear power plants. Its charge was also expanded to cover all thermal plants. The council's authority is state-wide for reviewing and recommending to the governor on the site and design of proposed thermal power plants. But decisions concerning locations on or adjacent to the Sound will be among the potentially most volatile policy issues in the future. The council's decisions are only recommendations to the governor. But it administers an application procedure which is organized to provide the information necessary to make an environmental evaluation of the proposed site.

8. State of Washington, *1972 Annual Report, Resources and Recreation,* p. 55.

9. Washington State Research Council, *The Research Council's Handbook,* p. 455.

10. Several articles in "Symposium: The Location of Electricity-Generating Facilities," deal with the origin and structure of the Thermal Power Plant Site Location Council, in *Washington Law Review,* vol. 47, no. 1, 1971.

Members of the council include the heads or their designees of the following state agencies: Departments of Agriculture; Civil Defense; Commerce and Economic Development; Ecology; Fisheries; Game; Natural Resources; Social and Health Services; the Interagency Committee for Outdoor Recreation; Office of Program Planning and Fiscal Management; Planning and Community Affairs; Washington State Parks and Recreation Commission; and Washington Utilities and Transportation Commission. In addition there is a chairperson appointed by the governor and a representative selected by the county commissioners of the county in which the proposed site is located.

A final state agency of concern here was established with the specific mandate to promote, develop, and advise on oceanography in general and to promote national interest in Puget Sound as a base for national oceanographic programs. The Oceanographic Commission of Washington was created by the legislature in 1967. It also administers the Oceanographic Institute of Washington, a nonprofit research and educational corporation. Both the commission and institute work closely with the University of Washington Sea Grant program which is funded by NOAA and involves a substantial research and public service program related to coastal and shoreline areas.

### Local Governments

Major responsibility for decisions concerning the nature and rate of development on the shoreline and land immediately adjacent to the Sound traditionally has rested with a multiplicity of units of local government.[11] Cities and counties, with the exceptions of federally and state owned lands and Indian reservations, divide all of the Sound region into areas which are governed independently of one another. The twelve Puget Sound county governments, particularly those with urbanized populations, exercise most of the same powers as cities over unincorporated territory—portions not included within cities.

Special districts and authorities constitute the third component of local government. Districts are commonly authorized to perform one function and are governed by an elected commission. Initially these units were used for water-related purposes such as irrigation, drainage, and diking. They were a mechanism which allowed public authority to be utilized for performing single functions and relating cost to benefit through assessments. As the population of the region increased and suburban trends set in toward the middle of this century, newer types of districts were authorized to provide municipal services—fire, water, sewer, parks, libraries—to urbanizing areas outside the boundaries of

11. Avery, *Government of Washington State*, pp. 254-90.

cities. Thus, an unincorporated shoreline area on the periphery of Seattle, Tacoma, or Bremerton might be served by a combination of fire, water, and sewer districts and obtain law enforcement, land use control, and other types of municipal services directly from the county.

Port districts are of particular interest. They are authorized to acquire, construct, maintain, and operate all forms of transfer and terminal facilities for land, water, and air transportation. Their boundaries may cover all or a portion of a county. In addition, ports may establish industrial development districts within their boundaries. Port commissions are elected and have taxing authority and may issue general obligation and revenue bonds to support port and industrial development district operations. These districts, then, are politically and financially independent of other local units. Consequently, the policies of major districts located on the Sound, the Ports of Seattle, Tacoma, Everett, Bellingham, Bremerton, and Olympia, can have a substantial impact on the development of the region's shoreline and on-water activities.

More recently, special districts have been used to organize certain environmentally related services on a scale larger than single cities and, at times, counties. The Municipality of Metropolitan Seattle was formed in 1958 to respond to a water pollution crisis in Lake Washington and the Sound.[12] It initially provided sewage collection and disposal services for the Greater Seattle area. Since then its boundaries have been extended to cover all of King County and it has assumed responsibility for public mass transportation. Air pollution control districts in Washington may contain a number of counties: the Puget Sound Air Pollution Control Agency covers King, Pierce, Snohomish, and Kitsap counties. One subregional planning agency has been established. The Puget Sound Governmental Conference includes King, Pierce, Snohomish, and Kitsap counties and is composed of representatives of each county government as well as a number of municipalities within their boundaries.[13] It is a voluntary organization without power to enforce its decisions but has taken the lead in proposing and developing advisory land use and functional plans for the four county area. It has also been designated as a regional clearing house agency for federal grants to local governments within its boundaries.

A primary difference between these local jurisdictions and the federal and state agencies discussed above concerns the relationship between the residents of the Puget Sound region and the public officials who

12. The formation of the Municipality of Metropolitan Seattle is recounted in Roscoe C. Martin, *Metropolis in Transition* (Washington, D.C.: Housing and Home Finance Agency, 1963), pp. 75-87.

13. Puget Sound Governmental Conference, *1971-72 Annual Report.*

make and administer decisions for the counties, cities, and special districts. In all cases, their territory is completely within the region and is smaller than the area as a whole. Consequently, the elected officials are directly selected by and responsible only to citizens or individual governmental units within the twelve county region. In contrast, the Sound is a small subunit of the boundaries of the state and federal governments and the officials selected by Sound residents constitute only a portion of the legislative bodies of which they are part.

## Political Parties and Interest Groups

The two major political parties in Washington, Democratic and Republican, are not strong as organizations and to a large extent vie with interest groups for control of the decision-making process.[14] They do not command unwavering loyalty on the part of voters or exercise discipline over officials elected to public office at the state or federal level under the party label. The citizens of Washington are frequently described as viewing themselves as political independents rather than firm party adherents. In addition to and perhaps because of this state of mind, there are also several election rules which make it difficult for parties to strengthen their positions.

All elections at the local level are conducted with nonpartisan ballots with the exception of those at the county level. The party affiliation of candidates is not listed on the ballot and persons running for office are barred from soliciting or accepting the support of political parties. With rare exceptions, political parties play little part in local elections and are organized only to effectively contest for state and federal offices.

In the partisan county, state, and federal races another set of election rules substantially reduce the ability of either major party to control who gains the party nomination in a primary election and runs under its banner in the general election. Washington's "blanket primary" is unique in the nation. Citizens are not required to identify themselves as members of any political party when registering to vote. Nor are they required to do so when voting in a primary election to select party nominees. Rather, a person is given a ballot which lists all candidates who are seeking the nomination of any party holding a primary. Voters not only can withhold a decision on whether to participate in the primary of one party or another until they receive the blanket ballot but they can vote in the primary of more than one party in the same elec-

14. Hugh A. Bone, "Washington State: Free Style Politics," in Frank H. Jonas, ed., *Politics in the American West* (Salt Lake City: University of Utah Press, 1969), pp. 380-415. Also see Neal R. Peirce, *The Pacific States of America* (New York: Norton, 1972), pp. 222-63; and Robert Warren and James J. Best, "The 1968 Election in Washington," *Western Political Quarterly,* 22 (September 1969): 536-45.

tion. Under this system, for example, a citizen could choose among the candidates seeking the Democratic nomination for a seat in the state legislature; indicate a preference among these running for the Republican endorsement for governor; and move back to the Democratic primary to support a person as the party nominee for the United States Senate. Political observers have long viewed the blanket primary as an important factor in inhibiting the development of strong party organization in the state.

Candidates for legislative, state-wide, and federal offices run for nominations in the primaries largely on the basis of their own personal campaign organizations. While the party label is often of critical importance in determining the outcome of a general election, it is captured by the nominee rather than bestowed or withheld by the party. This individual style of politics usually carries over into the general election. Personalized campaign organizations, little identification with other party nominees, and picking and choosing among the planks in the party platform are more common than not.

Within the policy-making process in Washington state this has meant that a governor may be committed to programs that are not subscribed to by all members of his party in the legislature or that the opposite party has control of one or both houses. It further means that highly controversial issues in the legislature are not likely to produce party-line votes and that bipartisan coalitions and interest group pressures and lobbying will play substantial roles in determining policy.

There are also opportunities to remove decision-making authority from the legislature and delegate it directly to the people through constitutional provisions for initiative and referendum by petition. The initiative allows citizens to draft a proposed statute and then, if the necessary petition requirements are met, have the proposal submitted to either the voters of the state or the legislature. If an initiative is addressed to the legislature, the matter will still be placed on the ballot if it is not approved as written by that body. In either case, petition signatures of qualified voters must equal at least 8 percent of the total votes cast in the last election for governor. An approved initiative cannot be repealed by the legislature until it has been in effect for two years. It can be amended only by a two thirds vote of each house during this period.

The petition referendum provides citizens with the opportunity to veto legislative action. In this instance, a referendum measure—asking voters to approve or reject a bill enacted by the legislature—can be placed on the ballot if its sponsors are able to obtain the signatures of qualified voters at least equal in number to 4 percent of the votes cast in the most recent election for governor. Substantial use of both of these provisions, particularly the initiative, has been made by citizens in Washington state. Voters have been asked by initiative petition to act on a number of major policy questions since these constitutional provisions were enacted in 1912, including alternative arrangements for establishing a shoreline management system for the state. Similar provisions are available to citizens in the charters of a number of cities and King County in the Puget Sound region.

These election rules and the style of politics in Washington have made special interest group activities a critical part of the process of initiating, supporting, or opposing proposals before legislative and administrative bodies or taking issues directly to the voters. This is even more true at the local level where political parties play almost no role. Under these circumstances, interest groups have usually been the catalysts for raising public policy questions concerning the environment and highly influential in determining both the arenas in which decisions are made and the outcomes.

Sportsmen's councils, for example, play a major part in shaping the policies of the state Departments of Game and Fisheries. Real estate associations and land developers pay careful attention to any proposed state legislation affecting planning laws and land use regulations or zoning changes at the local level. Heavy industries carefully monitor air or water pollution legislation, frequently initiated and backed by environmental interest groups, in local or state legislative bodies.

Not all special interest that enter into bargaining and lobbying are "private" groups. The Association of Washington Cities and the Washington Association of Counties are active in Olympia during each legislative session, as are port districts. State agencies such as the Department of Natural Resources are active on environmental issues.

There is no single source which identifies all nongovernmental groups which attempt to influence or participate in decisions relating to the allocation of Puget Sound's resources. Further, in most cases, environmental policy conflicts at the state level concern general rules or regulations that may substantially affect the Sound but are not specifically directed at or limited to the Sound. During the 1971 regular and extraordinary legislative session when the Shoreline Management Act was passed, there were 366 lobbyists registered with the legislature as required by law.[15] The vast majority represented are private firms and

15. Secretary of State, "List of Lobbyist Filings: 1971 Regular and Extraordinary Sessions."

Under the Washington Constitution, the legislature meets every two years for thirty days. However, special sessions may be called by the governor, and in recent times it has become the custom to call a special session to begin immediately after the regular biennial meeting in order to deal with the growing volume of state business. A number

associations, voluntary organizations, and local governmental units. It is not possible to identify how many of these organizations were directly involved in the negotiations concerning the Shoreline Management Act or were potentially affected by it, but eighty-four of the registered lobbyists represented groups which expressed direct interest in the legislation.

An additional source of information about relevant interest groups is the *Directory of Environmental Organizations for Alaska, Idaho, Oregon, Washington, and British Columbia,* published by the Environmental Protection Agency in 1973. It lists eighty-six organizations in the state of Washington, many of which have several chapters within the state. These groups range from the Citizens for Clean Water and the twelve-thousand-member National Federation of Fishermen to the Washington Envionmental Council, which includes a large number of other organizations among its membership. There is an intricate network of voluntary special interest groups in the state concerned with environmental issues and their role in recent decisions affecting the allocation of shoreline resources will be considered in subsequent chapters.

*The Courts*

Studies seeking to describe and analyze policy formation frequently fail to consider the judiciary as an integral part of the process. Yet, in many cases, the final step in a particular decision-making cycle is a court ruling.[16] Court action or the threat of it also are used as strategic weapons by parties to a conflict. Further, a judicial ruling in one case may have substantial consequences for other issues and parties not directly involved in the adjudication. There is no area of public policy in which all of these roles of the court are more significant than in environmental questions.

The courts provide a last resort for citizens or groups when they feel they have failed to receive fair or legal treatment in legislative or administrative proceedings. The possibility of having either a governmental or private action concerning resource allocation taken to court normally encourages decision makers to take divergent interests into account. Bargaining for agreement with active opponents is often perceived as less costly than judicial proceedings and the chance of losing a case altogether.

Environmental interest groups in Washington have been particularly

---

of efforts to amend the constitution to allow annual sessions have failed, and now short special sessions in even-numbered years are growing in use.

16. Robert Warren, Robert L. Bish, Lyle C. Craine, and Mitchell Moss, "Allocating Coastal Resources: Trade-off and Rationing Processes," in Bostwick Ketchum, ed., *The Water's Edge,* pp. 239, 240.

successful in overturning specific decisions of local officials as well as in using precedents in these decisions to affect the behavior of governmental agencies in subsequent controversies. One of the most important incentives in producing a completely revised state policy on shoreline control in Washington grew out of court case which, at the time it was initiated, had no relationship to the protracted conflict that it helped to resolve. A controversy between private parties regarding the right of one to fill a portion of an inland lake entered the courts nearly a decade before the passage of the Shoreline Management Act of 1971. But the ruling in the case in 1969 by the state supreme court became a major factor in changing a political contest over whether there would or would not be a state-wide shoreline regulation to a question of what form the new legislation should take.[17]

Both a state and federal judicial system operate concurrently in Washington and one or both may be important in environmental matters. The state courts of primary importance are the superior courts; at the county level, the intermediate court of appeals and the supreme court. The United States district courts, courts of appeal, and Supreme Court represent a parallel structure. A case dealing with substantial environmental issues will commonly wind up in the U.S. Supreme Court whether it is initiatied in the federal courts or appealed from a decision of the Washington Supreme Court.

It should be noted that while the courts often play a decisive part in public policy making, there are biases in who has access to adjudication. The initiation of a suit requires knowledge of the option and the financial resources for legal expertise and court expenses. Further, litigation can be protracted and if appeals are necessary within the federal or state court systems or from the latter to the U.S. Supreme Court substantial amounts of money are needed. Thus, well-organized interest groups, large enterprises, and governmental agencies utilizing public funds tend to be the most aware of their legal options and the most capable of absorbing the time and money costs.

As can be seen, policy formation and specific decisions concerning resource allocation take place within a system that provides a wide range of entry points and options to make strategic moves from one level and arena to another. Public organizations as well as private interest groups are participants in the electoral process, legislative decision-making and lobbying, administrative policy and rule making, interorganizational bargaining and adjudication. In order for these processes to function there must be a set of commonly accepted legal rules which distribute

17. Wilbour v. Gallagher, 77 Wash. Dec. 2d. 307 (1969). This case is discussed in detail in Chapter 8.

rights and authority within and between the public and private sectors. A look at the broad set of land and water laws and regulations which affect the shoreline will make this point more clear and allow further elaboration of jurisdictional interrelationships.

## LAND AND WATER REGULATION

This body of law and precedent provides the general framework for negotiation among private interests and for public policy making in Puget Sound. Rights, ownership, jurisdiction, responsibilities, and procedures are established in federal, state, and local law. Constitutional provisions, statutes, ordinances, administrative orders, practices, and court decisions all contribute to the structure of public and private options in resources policy. Consequently, any situation which makes significant use of coastal resources will likely involve a combination of decisions, laws, and precedents from all three levels of government.

In the federal system, most authority to regulate land use rests with the states, and by delegation, with local governments. Control of land use in Washington traditionally has been the province of cities and counties. City and town councils and county legislative bodies and their local planning boards have been the primary focus of politics relating to land use.[18] Parties interested in land use policies necessarily have directed their attention to local officials, as the case materials in Chapter 7 illustrate. As will be seen, recent environmental controversies have placed the state government in a more active role in land use. However, local governments continue to be the major arenas for day-to-day decision-making.

By contrast with land regulation, federal and state governments exercise the primary control over water-related policies. The federal government has authority over navigable waters. The national government also has assumed jurisdiction over water quality and has set federally determined guidelines which must be met by the states and localities. But the states have been delegated authority to enact their own standards, provided that they meet the guidelines. Looking further at the position of the states, however, a number of ambiguities emerge in the distribution of authority over the shoreline within the federal system.

The states hold ownership of lands underlying navigable waters and of tidelands (unless they have been sold to private parties). State property law also governs out of channel uses of fresh water, and the division of control between state and federal law is not clear in this area. The combination of state land law, delegated to the local level, federal

18. For a general review of municipal zoning practices and policies, see Richard F. Babcock, *The Zoning Game* (Madison: University of Wisconsin Press, 1969).

water law, and state ownership of bottom lands has created a situation where any significant use of the land-water interface involves federal, state, and local government decision makers and administrators. This overlapping of jurisdiction and authority coupled with the extensive intersection of land and water on Puget Sound has resulted in a legal framework that is equally as complex as the governmental structure which grows out of it. The following sections seek to outline relevant land and water law provisions and the governmental units which administer them.

*Land Use Regulation*

Land law performs two important functions. First, it establishes rights of private ownership and use; and second, it sets up the conditions for public ownership, use, and regulation. Rights of ownership are specified in law and permit private individuals to hold and make use of land as private property. Public rights to access and use are specified as are the conditions of public regulation of land use. The first permits many land use decisions to be made in the market and the second provides for collective authority over decisions not relegated to the private market.

The provisions for public use and regulation of private use of land are our major consideration here. As indicated in the previous chapter, public action is needed under conditions in which private rights are unclear and in which important externalities may pertain. Both of these conditions are inherent in the use of the coastal lands of Puget Sound. Many land uses have major externalities and land law is sufficiently mixed and ambiguous to require public intervention.

Three areas of land law that are especially important for shoreline lands are the common law tradition that private ownership ends at the highwater mark; the law of easements; and the rights of riparian owners (owners of land adjacent to water). The tradition that private ownership ends at the highwater mark exists in both common and Roman law, although some states, including Washington, have sold tidelands and beaches to private owners. Thus, in Washington, not all tidelands and beaches on Puget Sound are in public ownership. The law of easements is important because where individuals habitually cross private land to obtain access to public beaches and tidelands, the rights to use those easements become established in law. This common law tradition has led both to provisions for public access to beaches, and to private owners rigidly enforcing no-trespassing laws to prevent the public from obtaining easements across their property.

In common law, riparian owners have special rights to water and shoreline use. These generally include access to water, the right to make improvements to facilitate access to water (i.e., construct piers), the right to fish or draw water, and rights to aesthetic considerations (i.e., preventing obstruction of views). One reason for the relatively high prices of riparian lands is the value of accompanying rights to utilize the adjacent waters for a variety of purposes.

While there are common law traditions governing shorelands, the law is quite ambiguous as to what uses an owner can make of his land in relation to water uses and submerged land uses. The lack of well-defined property rights, complicated by the fact that external effects of use of shoreland may be transmitted via water, makes it difficult, if not impossible, for an efficient allocation of resources to occur through the market mechanism alone.

Rights to use land are regulated in Washington through zoning and the exercise of police powers to protect public welfare. Under both state constitutional and statutory provisions counties and cities can regulate the use of land in the best interest of the community. This is usually accomplished by establishing zones for different land use activities. If a decision is made to undertake zoning, the procedures designated by state legislation must be followed by counties and cities of populations less than twenty thousand. First class cities (those with populations exceeding twenty thousand) may zone under constitutional police powers and may set their own procedures for zoning as long as they are "fair."

The basic processes for zoning by either a county or city are:[19]

1. Preparation of a master plan. The master plan is prepared by either a consulting firm or the local government planning commission staff. The planning commission must hold public hearings before the master plan is recommended to the local government governing body (city council, county commissioners, or county council).

2. Adoption of the master plan. The governing body must also hold hearings prior to adopting the master plan.

3. Preparation of zoning ordinances. Following adoption of the master plan, zoning ordinances consistent with the master plan are prepared by the planning commission. The planning commission must hold hearings prior to recommending the zoning ordinances to the governing body.

4. Adoption of zoning ordinances. The governing body may adopt the zoning ordinances at a public hearing. An additional hearing is required prior to adoption if the planning commission recommendations are changed by the governing body.

19. A summary of Washington planning and zoning law and municipal authority is presented in *Municipal and Regional Planning in Washington State* (Seattle: Bureau of Governmental Research and Services, University of Washington, 1969).

After zoning has been adopted, any amendments or variances must be in accord with the master plan. Thus, significant rezones or variances require changing the master plan first. The process for changing the master plan is similar to the process for adoption: preparation, public hearings, and recommendations by the planning commission on plan changes; hearings and adoption by the governing body. Zoning changes must be considered by the planning commission, hearings held, and recommendations made to the governing body. The governing body must hold hearings on the planning commission recommendations before they can be adopted. If the planning commission recommendations are altered, additional public hearings by the governing body are necessary.

Final decisions on a particular zoning case or the adoption of a master plan rest with the elected legislative bodies of city or county governments. Most consequences of land use are local and are taken into account through market transactions. Yet there are some local effects which may not be reflected in land prices. Recipients of these effects or their representatives may be active in local government planning and zoning decisions. The owner of an existing marina may argue that "sound shoreline development" requires that no new marinas be permitted in the community. A neighborhood association may insist that a high-rise apartment building will impose unacceptable costs upon the public by blocking a view of the Sound from an adjacent park. By having some aspects of land use allocative decisions internalized into the public sector, access to the decision process is open to affected third parties who would not be included in private transactions.

A more complex policy problem is created if the external effects of a land use decision affect third parties beyond the boundaries of the local jurisdiction exercising authority over the land. These effects are more likely to be taken into account if there is an overlap of interests among groups outside and inside the governmental unit. Zoning to permit a port on the Sound to expand into an undeveloped wetland area could affect waterfowl that migrate from Alaska to California. Local and national environmental groups may combine to lobby against a zoning change. Conversely, a community chamber of commerce and an international petroleum corporation may join in support of a permit for locating an oil refinery in a county abutting the Sound. A favorable local decision would represent jobs and economic growth to the former and an efficient location for the production and transportation of fuel to the Midwest and maximizing profit for the latter. If groups concerned with such external effects cannot gain satisfaction at the local decision-making level, they may seek to transfer the issue to a different or larger-scale jurisdiction where they perceive an advantage in additional influence. The following two chapters provide examples of this chain of events.

Municipal and county governments, then, exercise the initial and primary authority in land use planning and zoning. However, permission from local government to utilize land in a particular manner does not automatically mean that the use will be achieved. Even when a proposed use meets zoning requirements additional regulations normally must be met which can involve several public agencies. For example, other local, state, or federal permits may be necessary for such things as building materials, sanitation systems, or dredging in navigable streams. This is especially the case where water law and water regulation provisions must be satisfied. Shoreline land use produces conditions in which concurrent public decisions are needed that involve other forums with boundaries and constituencies that differ in scale from those of local government.

*Water Use Regulation*

In contrast to state and local government regulation of land use, authority concerning navigable waters is primarily federal, or delegated to states by federal legislation (much as states have delegated land use authority to local units). The most important legal provisions relating to navigable waters come under the provisions of the commerce clause of the United States Constitution, where the federal rather than individual state government has primary responsibility. Recent reinterpretations of federal law in light of environmental considerations have supplemented commerce clause authority.

Any use of navigable waters that would interfere with navigation is subject to control by the U.S. Corps of Engineers. Permits must be obtained for piers, bridges, fills, oil platforms—in short, anything that would inhibit the movement of ships or products (e.g., logs) on water. Directly tied to maintenance of navigability is the Refuse Act of 1899, originally designed to control the dumping of solid materials into water —the dumping of liquids was not considered important because they would not interfere with navigation as would solids.

In 1961, as concern for pollution became more widespread, oil pollution from ships engaged in commerce was the object of special federal legislation with the Oil Pollution Act of 1961 (amended in 1965). This brought the discharge of oil from ships, including the pumping of bilges, directly under federal regulation. Shortly thereafter, the Refuse Act of 1899 was reinterpreted to include liquid as well as solid waste, but instead of developing an entire range of water pollution control activities the federal government, in the Water Quality Act of 1970, delegated authority to set water quality standards to state governments.

State governments can also exercise control over oil spills; responsible parties may be liable under both state and federal law concurrently. In Washington the Department of Ecology sets water quality standards and issues permits for discharges into navigable waters. Once the state sets standards satisfactory to the federal Environmental Protection Agency, the EPA recognizes those standards as its own. The Corps of Engineers still must issue a permit for any waste discharge into navigable waters, but it usually will issue a noncontroversial permit after a state government permit has been issued rather than make an independent evaluation of the issues involved.

Under terms of the Fish and Wildlife Act as amended in 1964 and the 1967 Memorandum of Understanding between the Corps and the Department of Interior, the impact of discharges on fish and wildlife must be examined by the U.S. Fish and Wildlife Service, and their advice given to the Corps prior to issuance of a Corps permit. The Corps must also file an environmental impact statement with the Council on Environmental Quality. The Corps of Engineers can withhold a permit even if a state permit has been granted. Thus, requirements of both state and federal authorities must be met before discharges into navigable waters be permitted. State authority in this area, however, is subject to congressional action and thus could be changed in subsequent legislation. The only major exceptions to permit requirements from the Corps of Engineers and state Department of Ecology are discharges of radioactive wastes, which are under exclusive control of the Atomic Energy Commission, and the blockage of navigable rivers for power production, which falls under exclusive control of the Federal Power Commission.

Jurisdiction over lands underlying navigable waters has been troublesome, with both state and federal governments claiming it. These disputes were resolved with the passage of the Submerged Lands Act of 1953, which clarified ownership of submerged lands within the three-mile limit (nine miles in the case of some Gulf Coast states) by declaring ownership and permission to regulate natural resources derived therefrom as residing with state governments. Thus, in Washington any use of submerged lands rquires state permission, which the state Department of Natural Resources grants on a permit or lease basis. If a user wishes to construct an extended pier, permission must be obtained from the Crops of Engineers with respect to navigation, and he must lease or obtain permission to use the bottom lands required from the state Department of Natural Resources. Likewise, the state can lease bottom land for oil exploration or drilling, the undertakers of which would also be subject to the permit requirements of the Corps of Engineers regarding navigation and the Department of Ecology regarding any waste discharges. As an example of the regulatory authority of the Department of Natural Resources, the director declared a moratorium on oil drilling in Puget Sound in 1970 and thus no over-the-water drilling can be undertaken unless DNR changes its current policy.

*Environmental Impact Regulation*

In addition to general land and water law and regulation, the National Environmental Policy Act of 1969 (P.L. 91-190) established the federal Council on Environmental Quality and requirements for environmental impact statements. Any federal agency undertaking, funding, or issuing a permit for a project that might have an impact on the environment must file an environmental impact statement. The statement is prepared by the agency and submitted to the Council on Environmental Quality. Copies are sent to any other federal and state agencies that might have an interest in the effects of the project and copies are made available to environmental groups and interested citizens. Comments are received from all of these sources and public hearings are held by the agency when appropriate during a forty-five-day review period. A final statement is then prepared, and submitted to the council. The council only accepts environmental impact statements when they are complete and accurate—it does not approve the project itself. An accepted statement is a prerequisite, however, for project approval by the federal agency concerned.

Washington state has also established environmental impact statement requirements for activities undertaken by state agencies, regulated by state agencies, or receiving funding from state agencies in the State Environmental Policy Act of 1971. The state act virtually copies the federal act with the state Department of Ecology initially serving as the implementing department. It was unclear whether private developers receiving permits from local government agencies also had to file a statement, but the Department of Ecology interpreted the law as requiring such statements. For example, if a private developer went to a city for a permit to carry on construction, the city had to investigate the environmental significance of his construction. If it would "significantly" affect the environment, a statement had to be filed with Ecology. If the city determined that the environmental impact was insignificant, Ecology requested that that it file a statement indicating it had considered the matter. The enabling legislation, however, was ambiguous about the exact powers of Ecology and the exact requirements for filing environmental impact statements when local government rather than state government agency permits or funding are involved.

In 1974 the legislature changed administration of environmental impact statements from the Department of Ecology to the Pollution

Control Hearings Board. The board is developing a new set of administrative regulations that should resolve some of the unclarity of the initial act.

Acceptance of state environmental impact statements, like federal acceptance, implies no approval of the project itself. The purpose of the impact statement is to make information on environmental consequences available to affected parties at low cost, without any specific requirement that the information itself be taken into account in the decision-making process.

REGULATION AND MANAGEMENT OF PUGET SOUND

The foregoing discussion has indicated that a number of public agencies share responsibility for regulation and management of Puget Sound. No single agency or level of government possesses sufficient scope of territorial boundary or authority to internalize the Sound or the communities of interest related to it. Instead, an array of jurisdictions of various sizes, legal standing, functional specialization, and constituency serves the Sound.

There have been, however, starting places and focal points for conflict resolution and policy making within this complex structure. Land use regulation traditionally begins and normally remains with local governments.

Water use, in contrast, seldom has been a purely local concern. Often such conflicts and policies have involved a number of state and federal agencies. Thus, many levels and units of government might be involved in a chain of events revolving around a given project or policy.

All of the case materials selected in Chapter 7 began as disputes over the land use decisions of localities, but in the process of resolution, the scope of the conflict steadily enlarged until a variety of interests and public authorities were involved.

In addition to issues involving particular projects, there was during the period covered by the cases, 1964-70, a parallel widening of general concern with environmental issues in Washington. As Chapter 8 illustrates, groups concerned with protection of the shorelines moved successively from local government, through the courts, the state legislature, and, finally, the electorate in their attempts to alter the basic structure of government for making general policy and specific decisions affecting the allocation of shoreline resources.

# CHAPTER SEVEN

# Resolving Environmental Conflicts

Conflicts over appropriate allocation and use of the natural resources of Puget Sound are nothing new. Some of the historic conflicts were reviewed in Chapter 4. Most of these concerned varying uses and users of the waters, tidelands, and marine life of the Sound. More recently, major conflicts also have begun to involve the near shorelands. The traditional conflicts remain. The newer ones add another set of public concerns for local, state, and national governments. Thus, the shift to different issues has been additive. Water-oriented land use issues have been added to the long list of water use conflicts such as fishing, dams, and pollution.

During the past several years, these water-oriented land use conflicts have come to be among the most volatile sets of issues under public consideration in the Puget Sound region. Few if any participants in land use policy-making have avoided confrontations with various partisans in these environmental conflicts. Land use decisions which once were nearly pro forma now are certain to be highly controversial. Changes in general plans, alterations in land use zones, approvals of variances from existing zoning ordinances, approval of use permits, development of impact statements, and location decisions are more complex and troublesome in almost every local jurisdiction in Puget Sound.

The case materials selected for this book illustrate some of the more recent water-oriented land use conflicts in the Sound. All four cases concern attempts to develop coastal resources. Each involves proposed location of a major facility in a relatively undeveloped area. The Kayak Point controversy revolved around a proposed Atlantic-Richfield refinery; conflict at Guemes Island centered on possible location of an aluminum reduction plant and supporting facilities initiated by North West Aluminum; Boise Cascade proposed a second home complex and

113

small-boat marina at Anderson Cove; and conflict over the Nisqually delta involved plans by the Port of Tacoma for a deep water port.[1]

Collectively, the histories of these four conflicts parallel state-wide concern with shoreline protection. Details of the development of this concern and the resulting Shoreline Management Act are covered in the next chapter. In a sense, each of the conflicts discussed here is a historical event of considerable importance in the larger political struggle over shoreline protection for the whole state. Naturally, Puget Sound figures greatly in any state-wide conflict dealing with protection of the shoreline. In addition, the specific groups and issues attendant to each successive case discussed here cumulatively affected the outcome of the more inclusive conflict over the Shoreline Management Act.

This developmental aspect of the four cases is their most intriguing characteristic. The cases demonstrate the following key developments in the on-going environmental politics of Puget Sound:

1. Participants learned much about these politics from each successive case; strategies followed in the Nisqually delta controversy reflected considerable adaptive behavior on the part of participants.

2. The scope of the conflicts widened considerably as time progressed; again, the Nisqually delta case involved a larger number of participants and wider range of issues than the first case about Guemes Island.

3. The quality of the functional roles of the state Department of Natural Resources (DNR) and the state Department of Ecology (DOE) changed; by the end, both were active partisans in the conflicts.

4. The environmentalists were able to develop a scale of intervention that began to match that of the "developers"; their final efforts involved political economies of scale (from their point of view) provided by the Shorelines Management Act.

The environmentalists won each contest in two ways. First, they prevented the proposed developments from being located at the chosen site. The projects were either located elsewhere (the oil refinery was placed on another site in the Sound and the aluminum plant was put in Oregon), or abandoned (the deep water port and the marina–summer home complex). Second and much more important are the lasting impacts upon the politics and governments of the Sound. New participants, once relatively poorly organized and under-represented, now are an integral part of the system; environmentalists are here to stay. The system of governments, as discussed at the end of this chapter and in the next chapter, have been significantly altered in practices and in form.

---

1. Information for the case studies was derived from newspaper reports, documents, files, reports, research done by others, and extensive interviews with participants in each controversy.

New and different kinds of issues confront officials responsible for water and land use decisions. Formal and informal requirements constrain public action. Environmental impacts and impact considerations are now part of routine public decision-making.

Conflict resolution, in effect, spills over the traditional boundaries of municipal and county governments. It is no exaggeration to say that recent environmental conflicts, as illustrated by these cases, have pushed the bounds of politics far beyond the scope and means of conventional local governments.

GUEMES ISLAND

Controversy in this case revolved around the proposed location of an aluminum reduction plant on Guemes Island, a relatively undeveloped area characterized by residential and recreational land use. Figure 7-1 shows the location of Guemes Island and the proposed facilities.

North West Aluminum, Inc., took options on several parcels of land on the island in the summer of 1966 and announced its intention to locate an aluminum plant on a 750-acre site. Reactions were mixed. Some local business people, public officials, and landowners favored the proposal. Other local landowners immediately voiced opposition to the project. In time, organized opposition came to include some residents, owners of second homes (mainly from the Seattle area), and environmentalists from around the Puget Sound region. North West, encouraged by support from the local press, labor leaders, the Chamber of Commerce, and officials from Skagit County and the nearby city of Anacortes, pushed for rezoning of the site from residential-recreational to industrial designation.

Thus, the stage was set for the end of conventional land use politics in Puget Sound. Up to the time that environmentalists mobilized effective opposition, this case appeared to be another conventional "zoning game" decision. North West, with the blessing and support of local interest groups, could be expected to gain the proposed change in land use zoning. Things, however, turned out differently. In the end, North West was forced to select another site, a leading court case strengthened the potential role of environmental groups, and "politics as usual" was changed.

*Background*

During the 1960s, the Board of Commissioners of Skagit County established a land use and zoning system in compliance with state enabling legislation. A Planning Department and Planning Commission were created in 1961. The Planning Commission hired a counsulting firm, M. G. Poole and Associates, to prepare a report with the develop-

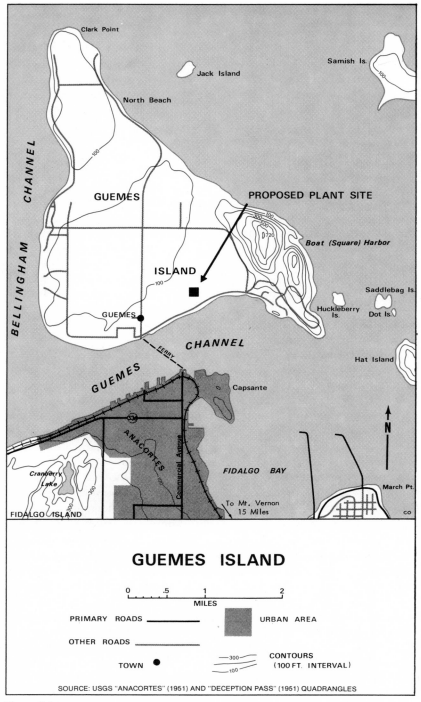

# GUEMES ISLAND

```
0        .5         1                    2
|··|··|··|··|··|·········|··········|·····|
              MILES
```

PRIMARY ROADS ─────────────            ▓ URBAN AREA

OTHER ROADS ──────────

TOWN ●            ─300─── CONTOURS
                 ───100── (100 FT. INTERVAL)

SOURCE: USGS "ANACORTES" (1951) AND "DECEPTION PASS" (1951) QUADRANGLES

Figure 7-1

ment of a comprehensive plan in mind. Between 1962 and 1965, the firm conducted studies, issued preliminary reports, and presented a comprehensive zoning plan for the county to consider. Hearings were held in 1966 before the county Board of Commissioners to consider adoption of the plan. Questions relating to industrial development were discussed at these hearings, with concern expressed over the lack of sufficient industrial sites and over the possible negative impact of industrial locations upon nearby residential and recreational areas. Assurances were given that residential property would be protected. The plan was adopted in April 1966 and appropriate zoning ordinances enacted.[2]

The comprehensive plan designated the area in which the proposed aluminum plant would be located as residential-recreational. Since little of Guemes Island was developed and the particular area is lightly settled coastal lands, the designation makes sense. The San Juan Islands represent some of the best prime residential, second home, and recreational resources in Puget Sound. Many of the islands, including Guemes, already had developed vacation, tourist, summer home, and residential sites. Much of the land is owned and prized by people whose main residences and places of business are in the greater Seattle or other urban areas.

Guemes Island is likely to receive considerable population pressure, particularly for second home development. It is within driving distance of Seattle, seventy-five miles, and lies just across the channel to the north of the city of Anacortes, which is the jumping-off place for tourists, vacationers, and weekenders making use of the San Juan system. Anacortes is one of the main ports of the Washington State Ferry System, which serves the islands and is a natural point of departure for people from nearby urban areas.

Guemes also is well located for industrial development. Bellingham lies twenty miles to the northeast and Everett is forty-eight miles to the south. Thus, industrial and dockage facilities would have easy access to major port and other transportation systems. In addition, major electric power lines were available nearby, a crucial consideration for the location of an aluminum reduction plant. The water near the proposed dockage facilities is sheltered and the channel is deep enough to handle most vessels. Given the relative low cost of the land, the site appeared nearly ideal from the point of view of North West Aluminum officials.

An important part in the planning of North West was the cordial reception afforded by local officials and businesses. The regional

2. Resolution, Board of Commissioners, Skagit County, April 5, 1966. Interim Zoning Ordinance No. 4081, April 12, 1966.

economy was slightly depressed and Skagit County officials and the Chamber of Commerce were anxious to attract new industry to the area. Many of the preliminary contacts between North West representatives and local people centered on the possible economic impact of the project. While the details were and are not clear, the prospect of hundreds of new jobs, thousands of dollars in property taxes, and possible spinoff effects for the lagging county economy was very tempting. It is not surprising that the local press, businesses, and some officials had high regard for North West and the project. No North West official, and not many local people, actually expected the hot controversy that followed. From the point of view of the corporation, they had covered all the bases and expected quick and uncontroversial approval of their project.

## Hearings and Litigation

Unprepared for the up-coming confrontation, although there were already signs of opposition, North West proceeded to follow convention. During the summer of 1966, the company began to consolidate its holdings and to make preparations for dealing with the county officials. News releases given to the press stressed the approximate site of the plant, the probable number of employees, and the time actual operations would begin. Local officials including the city manager of Anacortes, the general manager of the Port of Anacortes, a city councilman from Anacortes, and the president of the Chamber of Commerce publicly supported the proposed project. Newspaper reports estimated that the plant would bring upwards of four thousand people and additional tax revenues of about $200,000 to Anacortes and nearby areas. At this time the only open opposition came from three local landowners who announced they would fight any attempt to change land zoning on the island.

On September 14, 1966, a member of the Planning Commission requested reclassification of the property for the company.[3] The Skagit County Planning Commission ordered a hearing for the purpose of amending the county comprehensive plan.[4] At the same time, the commission approved a plan offered by N. L. Smith, a property owner, for a residential plat known as "Driftwood Shores," located immediately adjacent to the proposed site of the aluminum plant.

This action set the stage for crucial litigation before the Planning Commission's hearing could take place. Smith, with the backing of

3. "Application and Petition for Reclassification of Zoning District," September 14, 1966.
4. Many of the details of subsequent events come from the transcript of the Washington Supreme Court decision on *N. L. Smith* v. *Skagit County*, 76 Wn. 2d 729 (1969).

some local landowners and environmentalists, sought an injunction blocking the hearing, contending that the Planning Commission was acting illegally. A writ of certiorari was issued by the Superior Court of Snohomish County requiring the Skagit County officials to show cause why the proposed hearing should not be prohibited. Hearings on the writ before the superior court and later before a special three-judge panel provided an opportunity for the opponents to the proposed plant to outline what they saw to be the environmental threat of the project and to set the foundation for future litigation in the controversy.

Smith's attorneys argued that the proposed rezoning was not in compliance with the county plan and that opponents had not been given sufficient opportunity to articulate their position. Representatives for North West described the plant and dockage facilities and the various pollution-control measures which were intended to protect the waters of the Sound. At the end of October, the panel set aside the writ and permitted the Planning Commission to proceed with its hearing.

At that time there was considerable support for the plant among local business, labor, and resident groups. They, with support from the press, stressed expected economic return for the county, and characterized the Smith coalition as a well-financed minority raising environmental issues as scare tactics.

On November 7, 1966, the Planning Commission hearing resumed. Adverse testimony revolved around the alleged effects the plant would have on water and air around the island. Environmentalists claimed that effluent from the plant would seriously damage the local environment; corporate representatives claimed that the safeguards adequately protected water and air quality. After the formal hearings, Planning Commissioners met in executive session with officials and representatives of North West to discuss the project. On November 18, the commission voted 5 to 2 in favor of sending the proposed amendment of the county plan to the Skagit County Board of Commissioners.

A "Save the San Juans Committee," a volunteer group, became the most vocal opponent of the decision, charging that the project would cost the county millions of dollars in costs not covered by the corporation.[5] In the face of growing opposition from local people and regional organizations, the county commissioners voted to adopt the recommendations of the Planning Commission. A series of legal actions followed. A group of local residents and second home owners from Seattle filed suit challenging the decision. North West countered with an action to test the validity of all zoning in Skagit County; this was intended to get a ruling on the legality of county action in setting zones and in re-

5. Seattle *Post Intelligencer,* November 6, 1966.

zoning. On January 6, 1967, the requests for trial were united into one action.

At the end of February, North West announced it would not locate a plant on Guemes Island, but that it did intend to continue the suit concerning the county zoning ordinances.[6] Trial was held in the Superior Court of King County (Skagit judges disqualified themselves from the case to avoid possible charges of bias). The North West suit was dismissed, thus indicating the general county zoning was legal.

The court held, additionally, that the industral rezoning was valid and that it was done properly. The charges that the rezone was out of line with nearby uses, and that it was arbitrary, were rejected. More important, the charges involving due process—lack of proper notice, secret meetings, and illegal amending of the interim plan—were all found invalid.

Opponents of the rezone had hoped to show that the county officials had not permitted them proper opportunity and that the processing of the request had been done without following proper procedures. The superior court had rejected all their claims, but they could still appeal.

Appeal was made to the Washington Supreme Court. The original suit of N. L. Smith et al. and a concurrent suit of Evan Nelsen, Harriet Adams, and Clair Heilman were united. The case was heard on April 17, 1969. The decision overturned the rezoning of the site on Guemes Island on the grounds that all potential participants in the hearing processes of the county Planning Commission had not been granted due process. In addition, the court ruled that the rezoning constituted "spot zoning" and was out of step with nearby uses of land.[7]

*Observations*

This important case altered the style of intervention of environmen-

6. Seattle *Times,* February 26, 1967. Even if North West had ultimately won the appropriate county rezoning, before it could proceed with the aluminum reduction plant it would have had to seek permits from the Corps of Engineers (dock facilities and waste water discharge), the state Department of Natural Resources (leasing tidelands and bottom lands for dock facilities), and the Pollution Control Board (air and water waste discharges). North West evidently anticipated controversy in obtaining these permits and thus made their decision to locate in Oregon prior to resolution of the zoning issue.

7. *Smith* v. *Skagit County.* The decision raises questions about the fairness of the hearings. The court questioned the appropriateness of the closed executive session on November 14, 1966, at which North West officials were present but not opponents of the project. The court said: "When pursuant to this announcement of a closed session, it [the commission] invited the representatives of the aluminum company and other powerful advocates of the zoning changes to attend and be heard, but deliberately excluded opponents of the proposed rezoning, the hearing lost one of its most basic requisites—the appearance of fairness. Deprived of this essential appearance of fairness, the hearing failed to meet statutory tests."

talists in the land use decision process. It made it possible to attack land use decisions on *procedural grounds*. Up to this point, most county land use decisions were very loose in terms of procedures. "Zoning game" politics had permitted developers many advantages in the hearings. In effect, they could provide information to decision makers under informal circumstances. Further, opponents to proposed developments could be ignored or reduced to ineffectiveness in the hearing processes. The *Smith* case nearly reversed roles in the hearings. It forced county officials to tighten up procedural aspects of the hearing processes for land use decisions. More formal rules and more orderly processes were to be instituted. All sides must have an opportunity to be heard. Informal relationships with developers were severely constrained. Those wishing to fight proposed developments were provided legally sanctioned wedges into a basically "closed" decision process.

The Guemes Island controversy and the resulting state supreme court decision, *Smith* v. *Skagit County* (1969) may be viewed as the first stage in the chain of events which made environmentalists a major force in Washington politics and which widened the scope of conflict over the resources of Puget Sound to include more participants and issues. In the end, the case contributed to the adoption of the Shorelines Management Act; although the environmentalists won, they found the fight very expensive and were forced to seek other avenues to protect the state's shorelines. While at the same time they continued the efforts to stop individual projects, they began to turn to the state legislature to seek redress.

KAYAK POINT

This case concerns confrontation between property owners with different views of how the area around Kayak Point on Port Susan Bay should be developed.[8] Figure 7-2 shows the location of the proposed refinery on Kayak Point.

The Atlantic-Richfield Company announced in the spring of 1967 that it planned to construct and operate an oil refinery on the twenty-one hundred acres of coastal land it owned. There was immediate negative response from nearby property owners, including local residents and owners of second homes, who wanted the land to remain in recreational and residential use. In the face of this vocal opposition, the company proceeded to ask Snohomish County to amend its comprehensive plan to permit rezoning of the site from rural-residential designation to heavy industrial classification. Soon a "Save Port Susan Commit-

8. Background material about ARCO actions came from transcripts of the Washington Supreme Court decision on *J. T. Chrobuck* v. *Snohomish County,* 78 Wn. 2d 884 (1971).

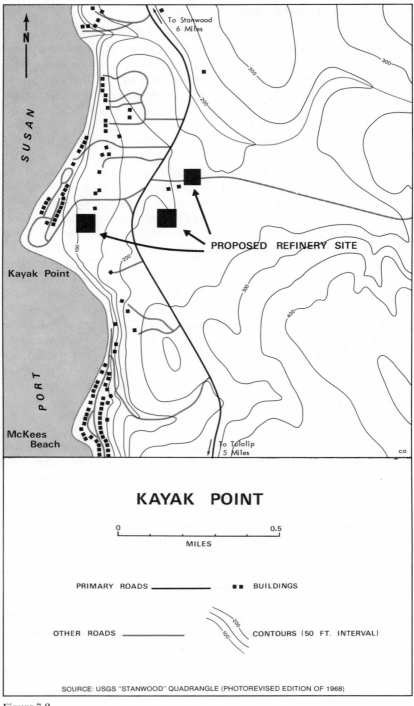

Figure 7-2

tee" was formed under the leadership of Seattle people who owned second homes in the area. The objective of the group, which included local residents although a majority were second home owners, was to retain the county comprehensive plan in its original form. This committee formed the core of opposition to the ARCO project which ultimately led to the state supreme court decision favorable to their position in 1971.

*Background*

The ARCO property is located within the Stanwood Planning Area of the Snohomish County Comprehensive Plan. The plan for the Stanwood area, adopted in 1964, designated this property and the surrounding area as rural and residential. The zoning ordinance classified it as "Rural Use," a residential and agricultural type zone established by the Snohomish County Board of Commissioners upon recommendation of the county Planning Commission.

Port Susan Bay is typical of the many sparsely settled and relatively undeveloped bays, inlets, coves, and other shoreline areas in upper Puget Sound. Near the town of Stanwood, about twenty miles north of Everett and fifty-five miles north of Seattle on the eastern shore of Puget Sound, the area is characterized by very sparse second home, recreational, and country-type residential development. Since the 1964 zoning, the waterfront areas north and south of the ARCO holdings at Kayak Point have been developed, as access became available, as prime residential and recreational sites. The lakes adjacent to the ARCO property—Howard, Goodwin, Shoecraft, and Ki—have experienced considerable development, including many permanent residences. Camano Island, the east side of which faces the ARCO site, also has become a choice residential, second home, and recreational area. Most of the rest of the Stanwood Planning Area is less settled, with some possibility of population pressure from the Everett area.

It is not surprising, therefore, that owners of residences, second homes, and undeveloped sites objected to the proposed oil refinery. Local residents and outsiders with property interests apparently felt that the adoption of the comprehensive plan in 1964 guaranteed the residential and recreational character of the area and protected their holdings. In the meantime, ARCO continued to purchase property on the assumption, based upon a 1956 report of the county Planning Commission, that the rural use designation was for holding purposes and would be changed when application for rezone was made. The company, according to some of the people who sold plots to ARCO as well as other landowners, used pressure tactics in gathering holdings. The acquisition of the acreage took several years and was not complete at the time the application for rezone was submitted to the Snohomish Planning Commission.

The confrontation pitted ARCO against most other landowners of the Stanwood area, who felt that the comprehensive plan protected their interests by excluding industrial zoning in the district. The 1964 version of the plan leaves the question open, but leaning toward ARCO's interpretation:

> It should be noted at this time that Figure 2 [a zoning map] in the appendix does not indicate the Richfield owned land at Kayak Point as a future industrial site. It is the opinion of the staff that this land would be very inadequate for most types of *industry other than a refinery* [emphasis added]. . . . If and when Richfield decides to establish a refinery here the Comprehensive Plan will have to be amended to show this industrial area. Until that time the entire site should be designated as residential since it is felt that this use would be the best for the area from the standpoint of compatibility and practicability.[9]

Thus, the planning document provided support and expectations for both sides.

## Hearings and Litigation

The ARCO application for rezone of the site was received by the Snohomish Planning Commission and referred to the county Planning Department for review and evaluation. A public hearing before the commission was planned for November 30 and December 1, 1967. The hearing notice produced mixed reactions, but mainly outcry from local residents and landowners. The Stillaguamish Tribal Council, which owned land near the proposed site, voted to oppose the refinery. The Save Port Susan Committee was established in October to consolidate opposition to ARCO's proposal. Support, however, came from the Stanwood City Council which took the position that it had been understood for years that the refinery would be located at Kayak Point, and passed a resolution to the county in favor of ARCO's project. Some members of the Planning Commission openly supported the project, but the Planning Department was opposed to it. By the time hearings took place in December, there was considerable organized opposition to the project and pressure was upon the Planning Commission to deny the application for rezone.[10]

9. Snohomish County, "Comprehensive Plan for the Stanwood Area," December 1964, p. 10.

10. It is interesting to note that the planning staff report, "The Stanwood Area Comprehensive Plan Review," November 24, 1967, stated: "A refinery or other heavy industry on Port Susan Bay would not be in the long-run interest of the people of either

Possible negative impacts upon the local environment were discussed at this and a subsequent hearing. Testimony by ARCO officials described the proposed refinery and dockage facilities, projected economic value of the project to the county, and measures which would be taken to minimize visual impact, noise, odor, oil spillage, and water pollution. The Planning Department and representatives of Save Port Susan opposed the application for amendment of the plan at both hearings. The Planning Department study argued that the area was topographically unsuitable for heavy industry and that the proposed use was incompatible with the present and future residential and recreational uses of the area. It recommended denial of the application and against rezoning. Landowner opponents argued that the proposed facilities would harm the Port Susan Bay fisheries, that oil spillage was a grave danger, that large amounts of effluent would be discharged into the bay, and that a refinery would seriously damage the residential and recreational character of the area.[11]

The Planning Commission recommended granting of the application after the first hearing and rezoning of 635 acres for industrial use after the second hearing. It is important to note that this second decision was contingent upon agreement between the county and ARCO about measures to protect the quality of the local environment. These involved set back, buffer zones, and water pollution measures. Although not very stringent, these measures served notice that environmental quality restrictions might be included in approval of a project. As we will see in the next case, such qualifications and requirements can be very restrictive. In a sense, the nominal constraints required in the ARCO case served as a prototype in the Anderson Cove case which followed.

The county Board of Commissioners, perhaps reflecting upon the recent Guemes Island controversy, adopted these recommendations before passing the necessary resolutions to rezone the property. It is also worth noting that the commissioners' hearing was much more formal and careful than in the case of Guemes Island. Local officials were learning to deal with the new requirements of environmental politics.

Local landowners (not all of them local residents) who opposed the rezone filed suit in the superior court seeking to set aside the decision of the Board of Commissioners. ARCO at the same time decided to pursue

Island or Snohomish Counties. We feel that the best long-run use of Port Susan Bay would be to recognize it as an invaluable natural resource area to be preserved for recreational and residential uses."

11. Based upon extensive notes taken from minutes of the Snohomish County Planning Commission meetings, November 30 and December 1, 1967.

ARCO officials, attempting to push their proposal through, flatly stated that if the refinery was not built on Kayak Point, it would not be located in Snohomish County—a threat, of course, carried out when the Cherry Point site was chosen.

an alternative strategy during the litigation. It decided to develop the
refinery at an existing industrial tract with other refineries at Cherry
Point in Whatcom County, some forty-five miles to the north on Puget
Sound.[12]

In the meantime the superior court set aside the decision of the
county Board of Commissioners on the grounds that there might have
been conflict of interest and that the environmentalists had not been
accorded due process before the Planning Commission. Further, it held
that the rezone constituted spot zoning out of character with nearby
land uses. In most respects, the decision is similar to the Smith case. In
one regard, however, it is different. The question of conflict of interest
was raised because a county official had accepted some free travel arrangements provided by ARCO. This aspect of the case further eroded
the informal relations among officials and developers. It served notice
that the courts would look closely at such favors. Upon appeal by Snohomish County, the Washington Supreme Court affirmed the superior
court decision in February 1971.[13]

*Observations*

The entire controversy lasted over four years. The main consequences
are mixed. Some local residents and landowners (excluding ARCO,
which of course had been a local landowner for many years) were able
to protect their interpretation of the future of Kayak Point. They were
able to do this in spite of the actions of their local county officials by
careful work in the hearings and by appeal to judicial processes. The
net result for the region, however, is open. While the localized environment is protected in the sense that industrial development (but not recreational or residential development) is deferred, Puget Sound has another refinery at the Cherry Point industrial tract. It is ironic that the
environmental protection measures at this site are at least equal to or

12. ARCO, like North West on Guemes Island, chose to relocate prior to resolution of
the zoning issue. ARCO would have also had to obtain permits from the Corps of Engineers, state Department of Natural Resources, and Pollution Control Board. ARCO
would have also had to obtain permission to use large quantities of fresh water, possibly from nearby lakes, from the Department of Water Resources. All of these additional permit requirements provided opponents of the refinery with forums for delaying and perhaps defeating the refinery proposal.

13. *Chrobuck* v. *Snohomish County.* Again, the court raised questions about the fairness of the hearings. It supported the superior court findings that opponents had not
been accorded due process of law before the Planning Commission. Part of the finding
involved the refusal of the head of the Planning Commission to permit discussion of
relationships between one of the commission members and ARCO. This member had
served as attorney for ARCO in this matter, but the Planning Commission would not
entertain discussion of possible conflict of interests even though the member, Mr. Lewis
A. Bell, resigned from the commission after the hearings.

superior to those imposed for the Kayak Point development by the original Board of Commissioners decision.

The Kayak Point controversy, and resulting litigation, is the second stage in our study of events reshaping environmental politics in Washington. The opponents of the refinery obviously learned a great deal from the on-going conflict over the aluminum plant proposed for Guemes Island. The two cases overlapped, but decisive steps in the litigation in *Smith* v. *Skagit County* (1969) had taken place before the final rounds in the struggle over Kayak Point. In fact, much of the legal argument was based upon the *Smith* decision. Thus, environmentalists built upon the previous events and legal action to confront ARCO and Snohomish officials in the hearing processes and in the courts.

ANDERSON COVE

This case involves attempts by Boise Cascade Recreational Communities Group to develop a 6,295-acre second home and recreational community, "Nettleton Lakes On-the-Canal," in Kitsap and Mason counties.[14] Figure 7-3 shows the location of Anderson Cove on Hood Canal. Included in the project was a small-boat marina at Anderson Cove on Hood Canal directly adjacent to the residential development. Boise Cascade's efforts produced considerable controversy, particularly in Kitsap County where the bulk of the project, 4,017 acres, and the marina were to be developed. It was before Kitsap County agencies that the application for rezoning and the use permits for the project were first publicly considered.

This case provides the first direct evidence that an "environmental ethic" had become part of the local politics. Much of the opposition to the project was built upon information about other Boise projects and upon information provided from other areas of the country. In addition, local officials were supportive of environmental concerns and questioned the project and the Boise Corporation closely. In this case, the scope of conflict was widened to include many participants not directly connected with the county or the Boise Corporation. Many outsiders provided information, including representatives from regional and national environmental groups, public officials of state agencies, and officials from out of state who had dealt with Boise before. This controversy involved a large network of nonlocal participants and issues. For the first time, the scale of environmentalists in Puget Sound began to match that of the developer.

14. Major sources for discussion of the Anderson Cove controversy are a dissertation, Herman L. Boschken, "Mismarketing in Urban Development"; and a smaller paper, Mitchell Moss, "Environmental Decision Making, 1971."

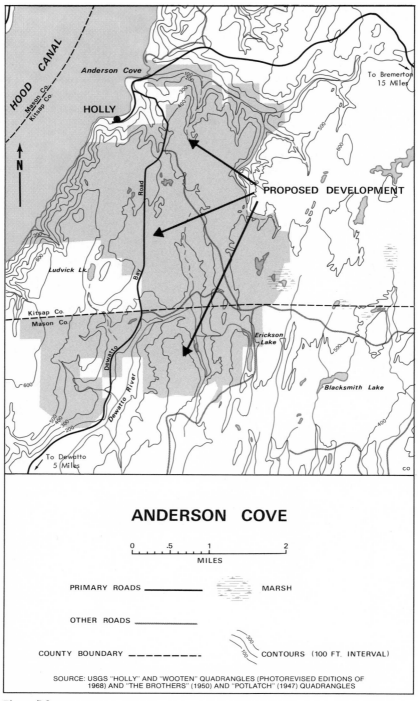

# ANDERSON COVE

```
0        .5        1                    2
|----|----|----|----|--------------------|
              MILES
```

PRIMARY ROADS ————————    ≈≈≈≈≈  MARSH

OTHER ROADS ————————

COUNTY BOUNDARY — — — — — — —    ⌇⌇⌇ CONTOURS (100 FT. INTERVAL)

SOURCE: USGS "HOLLY" AND "WOOTEN" QUADRANGLES (PHOTOREVISED EDITIONS OF 1968) AND "THE BROTHERS" (1950) AND "POTLATCH" (1947) QUADRANGLES

**Figure 7-3**

*Background*

About one third of the population of Kitsap County is concentrated in Bremerton, where the Navy, the county's largest industry, employs half the total labor force. Most of the rest of the county is devoted to agriculture, recreation, and residential development. It is the recreational and residential potential that attracted Boise Cascade and that has long attracted people from the metropolitan Seattle area. One can reach the heart of Kitsap recreational opportunities, Hood Canal, from Seattle by a fifteen-mile, one-hour ferry ride or an hour-and-a-half auto trip via Tacoma.

Kitsap County has extensive shoreline. It borders the west side of Puget Sound and most of Hood Canal is within the county. Within this area are some of the best recreational home sites in the Sound and opportunities for well-protected water sports and fisheries. The confining boundaries of Hood Canal limit its capacity to handle wastes; its waters, shallow by Puget Sound standards, are replenished only every two years.

Anderson Cove is one of many similar, attractive sites in the canal. The cove, like most of the rest, supports a large shellfish population, serves as a nursery for sea life, and contains much food for waterfowl. In all, Anderson Cove, the site of the proposed marina, is a pleasant, undeveloped fish, plant, and water fowl resource, almost an ideal place for the location of a second or vacation home.

The Nettleton Lakes are a series of four larger and several smaller lakes located just adjacent to Hood Canal. Most of the terrain slopes gently toward the Sound, with the steepest and most difficult land (from the point of view of the developer) directly on the canal and Anderson Creek at the point it enters the canal. Much of this undevelopable land (about 25 percent of the total) was designated "open space" in Boise plans.

Nettleton Lakes-on-the-Canal project consisted of 6,295 acres of which 4,017 were in Kitsap County.[15] As proposed, it surrounded not only the lakes but the local town of Holly (population 130). The projected number of dwellings was 6,478, of which 70 percent would be single-family units. In addition, Boise plans included roads, parking, parks, open space, lakes, a golf course, a small commercial reserve, and the marina. As in the case of most Boise proposals, this was proclaimed as a total recreational community.

---

15. Kitsap County, "Public Hearings on Boise Cascade's Nettleton Lakes-on-the-Canal Planned Unit Development," Port Orchard, Washington, April 28, 1970. Also see Boschken, "Mismarketing in Urban Development," pp. 115–34, for details of the proposed project.

Like other rural counties in the Puget Sound region, most of the land in Kitsap County is zoned agricultural, recreational, or residential. Originally, much of the land adjacent to Hood Canal was zoned for high-density development, but a number of disputes, notably one concerning Alderbrook, a vacation area, brought about major changes in the zoning. Under pressure from environmental and landowner organizations, the Kitsap and Mason County officials rezoned most of Hood Canal lands for low-density residential and/or recreational uses between 1965 and 1969. The Boise project would have required rezoning the area for high-density recreational and for marina related uses.

Boise Cascade faced additional constraints which helped foster the ultimate defeat of their project.[16] First, as indicated in the previous case materials, environmental concerns and environmental politics had become topical and important parts of local and state politics. Second, local residents, second home owners, environmentalists, and others had already formed two powerful organizations: the state-wide Washington Environmental Council and the regional Hood Canal Environmental Council. HCEC, dominated by second home owners, represented a formidable force in Kitsap County politics. It had been involved in a number of prior controversies; its most successful efforts involved the rezoning of the land adjacent to Hood Canal to low-density residential classification. Other important activities of HCEC included support for the formation of a tri-county Hood Canal Advisory Commission, successful opposition to a high-rise project at Alderbrook, and cooperation with other organizations in lobbying for the creation of the state Department of Ecology and for the shorelines management legislation. Third, public officials were becoming more cautious in dealing with developers and more concerned with the environmental impact of proposed projects. Local officials were beginning to adjust to the new environmental politics; at the state level, the governor and several department heads were stressing environmental concerns. Fourth, Boise Cascade had developed a questionable reputation in other states, in particular Calfornia, in which second home communities were developed by the corporation.[17] An unfavorable press, much of it well founded, preceded Boise's efforts on Hood Canal.

Boise requested that Harstad and Associates, a Seattle engineering and planning firm, do a confidential study of possible second home sites in the Northwest. The site owned by the Nettleton Company in Kitsap and Mason counties, however, was not designated originally as a suitable property. Only after negotiations on another property in Whatcom

16. Moss, "Environmental Decision Making," pp. 5–8.
17. Ibid., p. 1–2, 5–8; Boschken, "Mismarketing in Urban Development," pp. 141–46.

County were unsuccessful did Boise purchase the holdings of the Nettleton Company, retaining Harstad to begin work on plans for a second home and recreational community there. The consulting company carefully followed Kitsap County planning guidelines and zoning ordinances in preparing a "Planned-Unit-Development" community.

*Hearings*

Although Boise attempted to keep its plans and its relations with public officials orderly to avoid controversy, local residents, nonlocal landowners, and environmental groups soon made difficulties for the company. A first brush came when plans for a small-boat marina at Anderson Cove were submitted to the state Department of Natural Resources for necessary approval of the design. By the time the DNR ordered a public hearing to consider the preliminary proposal in November 1969, powerful opposition to the marina and to the general Boise plans had developed. The DNR never did approve the original design. By the time a second hearing before the DNR was held in November 1970, Boise was confronted by vigorous opposition from HCEC and from a small number of local residents from the little town of Holly.

Criticism of the Boise plans took two tracks. The first argued that proper environmental planning and analysis had not been done, and that the impact of the project (containing plans for a new town of twenty thousand persons) on Holly with a population of a few families would be disastrous. The second track pointed to Boise's alleged pattern of damaging the environment in its land developments elsewhere.

Boise's poor reputation for environmental impact was well known by 1970. HCEC developed contacts with officials and organizations in other localities and states, including Connecticut, New Hampshire, Hawaii, and California. The county prosecutor of Nevada County, California, who had handled suits against Boise in his county, attended the hearings at his own cost. The Center for Environmental Action, a national information and lobby group located in California, provided useful information about Boise efforts elsewhere. Several governmental organizations in Washington also provided opposition at the hearings. Included were the state Departments of Ecology, Natural Resources, Water Resources, Fisheries, Game, and Health; the State Planning and Community Affairs Commission; the State Oceanographic Commission; the State Water Pollution Control Commission; the Hood Canal Advisory Commission; and the Kitsap and Mason County Health Departments. In addition, a number of private groups joined in, including the Seattle Audubon Society; the Washington State Sportsmen's Council; the Daughters of the Pioneers; the Kitsap Rifle and Revolver Club; and the

Mountaineers. By the time of the hearing, a substantial local, regional, and national opposition to the Boise project had been formed.[18]

This array of groups provided an important development in Puget Sound environmental politics. Boise represents a vast package of organizational resources which can be focused on a given project. The coalition of environmental groups and supportive public agencies provides a set of resources which could compete with the corporate resources of Boise. For the first time in the sequence of case studies, people opposing the development had the range of resources needed to confront the developer.

In the subsequent hearings at the county level, this array of groups was very successful in going beyond what had been done before. They actually were successful in securing constraints upon the development in the hearing processes rather than through the courts.

The Kitsap Planning Commission considered Boise's application for a rezone (from low to high density residential), plans for a planned-unit-development, and a preliminary plat for the site. Two public hearings were held, at which all of the aforementioned public and private organizations testified, as well as representatives of Boise Cascade. Usually, Kitsap Planning Commission meetings are very informal and poorly attended. In this case, however, the room was filled and the hearings took on more than usual formality. Boise made a very professional, mixed media presentation which stressed the corporation's concern for environmental issues, the comprehensive study made of the area, feasibility and impact analysis already done, and the careful effort put into the community plans.

After the initial forty-minute presentation by Harstad and Associates for Boise, a series of environmentalists, landowners and public officials testified against the project. They stressed the poor record of Boise Cascade in other areas; they questioned the thoroughness and validity of the preliminary studies and plans; they attacked the lack of environmental impact analysis; they suggested that the project would be an environmental and economic disaster; they challenged specific design features such as the sewage and road systems; they stressed potential negative impacts, especially at Anderson Cove. By midnight of the first day, opposition had wrecked Boise's highly polished presentation and the corporation's reputation had been successfully challenged. Although more public hearings would be held, the initial confrontation was crucial and the other hearings would basically cover the same ground.

Kitsap officials provided a new governmental response. They were

18. Boschken, "Mismarketing in Urban Development," pp. 141–46.

concerned that the project be given careful scrutiny. After very careful consideration of the testimony and consultation with state officials, the Kitsap Planning Commission approved the rezone and the planned-unit-development, rejected the marina plans, and imposed substantial conditions for improving specifications of water quality, sewage systems, roads, density and land use. The County Board of Commissioners reviewed the Planning Commission's findings. After a visit of Boise projects in California and extensive public hearings, the Board of Commissioners upheld the recommendations and passed the necessary resolutions, which contained even more restrictive conditions for the second home development.[19] These restrictions, mainly dealing with increased sewer capacity, improved treatment facilities, lesser density in residential units, and grading and surfacing of roads to reduce runoff and silting, proved to be a major restraint on Boise. Here, for the second time in the case materials, the Board of Commissioners placed restrictions upon the developer for the sake of environmental quality considerations. These Kitsap restrictions were much more stringent than those placed upon ARCO at Kayak Point. This was a clear shift in the view and behavior of public officials toward constraining development in terms of environmental considerations. In the few short years since the Guemes Island case, officials had moved toward imposition of environmental concerns.

Boise Cascade was less than happy with its "victory." While much of the project was left intact, the restrictions placed on it by county decisions made the development uneconomical for the corporation. Boise was already having financial and administrative difficulties, and on June 30, 1971, announced it was re-evaluating its plans for Nettleton Lakes-on-the-Canal because declining economic conditions in the greater Seattle area had adversely affected the potential market for recreational lots on Hood Canal. In effect, the development has been postponed indefinitely.

*Observations*

This controversy illustrates a marked change in environmental politics in Puget Sound. Previously, as shown in the Guemes Island and Kayak Point cases, county officials were able and willing to go along with the proposed developers. In this case, however, county planners, Planning Commission, and Board of Commissioners all had reservations about the project and approved it with crucial environmentally

19. Moss, "Environmental Decision Making," p. 30–35; Boschken, "Mismarketing in Urban Development," pp. 168–71. See also Kitsap County Commissioners, "Decision regarding Boise Cascade Recreation Communities, Inc., Application," Port Orchard, January 5, 1971.

oriented restrictions. Thus, opposition was not pushed toward the courts to seek a legal remedy. Of course, HCEC was prepared to go to court and would have, if Boise had not dropped the project. Although internal problems in Boise Cascade contributed to its decision not to pursue the Nettleton Lakes-on-the-Canal development, the actions of public officials in response to corporate action (both in Washington and elsewhere) and to information and pressure provided by environmentalists was probably commanding. Thus, local governments are shown to be responsive and vulnerable to well-organized environmental groups.

A second important aspect of this case concerned the active involvement of state officials. The DNR was directly involved because of the marina. State contribution, however, went beyond review of an application. Officials provided important information to the county officials, openly opposed the project, and were crucial in the settlement of the controversy. There was virtually none of this in the previous cases. Before this case, the role of state officials in local conflicts was not taken for granted as it is now.[20] The interest and importance of state officials in environmental affairs is now obvious in Washington, but just a few years back, there was much less inclination toward intervention in local decisions.

NISQUALLY DELTA

This case presents the culmination of the widening of the scope of local conflicts and shows the strongest display of political power of environmentalists *before* the passage of the Shoreline Management Act. In this case, the hearing process itself is the scene of defeat for the developers. Interestingly, the developers were not private entreprenuers, but other public agencies trying to carry out what they felt were their public responsibilities. The ports of Olympia and Tacoma proposed to develop a 65-million-dollar combined industrial park and superport complex on the lands of the Nisqually delta (see Fig. 7-4).

Officials of the two ports, anticipating increased demand on the West Coast for superports to handle the huge vessels of the present and near future, were trying to plan and implement new facilities with which to capture some of that expected new business. This kind of entrepreneurial behavior by large-scale public authorities is not unusual. One

20. It is interesting to note that U.S. Corps of Engineers and state officials (especially from the Department of Natural Resources, the Pollution Control Hearings Board, and the Department of Water Resources) could have been brought into earlier conflicts if this had received county approval. By participating in county hearings the state officials could have their views taken into account without being put in the politically controversial position of refusing a necessary permit for a project already approved by local elected officials.

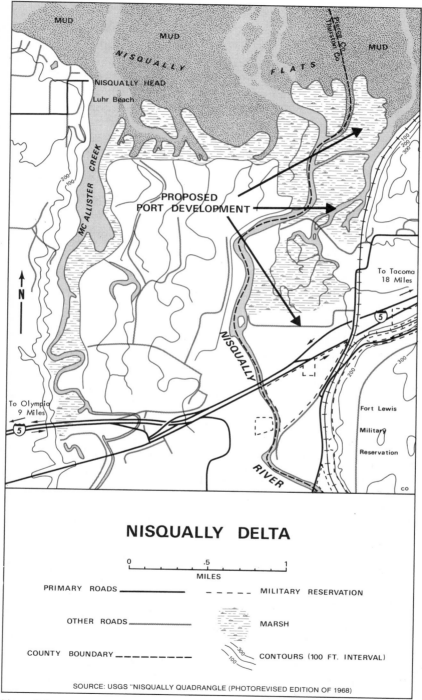

MUD

MUD

NISQUALLY

FLATS

MUD

Pierce Co.
Thurston Co.

NISQUALLY HEAD

Luhr Beach

MC ALLISTER CREEK

PROPOSED
PORT DEVELOPMENT

To Tacoma
18 Miles

5

N

NISQUALLY

To Olympia
9 Miles

5

Fort Lewis

Military

Reservation

RIVER

co

# NISQUALLY DELTA

0       .5       1
MILES

PRIMARY ROADS ————————    — — — — MILITARY RESERVATION

OTHER ROADS ———————     MARSH

COUNTY BOUNDARY — — — — —     CONTOURS (100 FT. INTERVAL)

SOURCE: USGS "NISQUALLY QUADRANGLE (PHOTOREVISED EDITION OF 1968)

Figure 7-4

might say it is expected and that in the recent past such a project would not have been controversial at all. In fact, local business, labor, and public officials could be expected to provide enthusiastic support, which they did. Once more, however, environmentalists provided effective opposition and the proposed superport and much of the industrial development were abandoned by the port authorities. Instead of developing the Nisqually delta, they have concentrated on upgrading their existing facilities. Opponents of the proposed port have continued to push efforts to preserve the delta for open space, recreational, and other environmentally appealing uses.

*Background*

The Nisqually delta is the largest undeveloped estuarine area in Puget Sound. This fact alone makes it an unusual resource system. Its location between Olympia and Tacoma adds to its importance and makes its undeveloped state surprising. Its natural character attracted environmentalists and sports people as well as potential developers.

The delta appeared to be an ideal site for the location of major port facilities. Surface transportation is convenient; Interstate 5 and railway lines cross the plain. There is plenty of land available for support facilities and industrial tracts. And most important, a deep channel lies between the tidal flats and Anderson Island. Drop-off in the tidal area is very rapid: from six to ninety feet in less than one hundred yards. At midchannel, the depth reaches two hundred feet. Such depth can accept the formidable draw of modern bulk cargo carriers and, particularly for this case, super tankers.

It was anticipation of a need for one or more ports on the West Coast which could accept the super tankers that prompted port authorities to push the project. In the mid-sixties, there was much talk of impending need for such facilities to handle the oil expected from the North Slope fields of Alaska where development was expected momentarily. Hardly anyone expected the delays which have slowed exploitation and delivery of oil from the North Slope area. People throughout the Northwest expected fast completion of the Alaska Pipeline. Officials in British Columbia, Washington, and California were planning ways to get some of the expected business. The Nisqually delta was a prime candidate among the undeveloped sites.

There are four major local public jurisdictions involved in the controversy over Nisqually: Thurston and Pierce counties and Olympia and Tacoma port authorities. Typical but confusing boundary designations account for this. The Nisqually River, which flows seventy-five miles toward Puget Sound from the Nisqually Glacier on the southern slope of Mount Rainier, serves as the county boundary for its entire length. Thus, portions of the delta are in both counties: to the west, Thurston, and to the east, Pierce. The river also divides the two port authorities: Olympia to the west and Tacoma to the east.

As we have seen, basic land use zoning decision-making outside municipal boundaries rests with county governments in Washington. Any zoning decision which dealt with the delta would be considered by either Thurston or Pierce County or both if the project crossed county lines. In addition, however, the port authorities were involved in this case. The lands of the delta all are within the boundaries of one or the other. Port authorities have broad powers to acquire, construct, maintain, and condemn land for support of all forms of land, air, and water transportation, including necessary facilities, industrial tracts, transport systems, navigation and harbor improvements, and utilities. They have the power to extend their own boundaries and are governed by an elected board of commissioners. They have limited taxing powers, but may issue revenue bonds upon authorization of the Port Commission, and general obligation bonds upon approval of the voters within the district. In general, they are important and powerful special district governments administered by expert administrators with very proficient support staffs.

The ports of Olympia and Tacoma long have considered the Nisqually delta a desirable area for expansion and development.[21] Since 1949 Olympia has included its portions of the delta in the port comprehensive plan. Since the mid-1960s it has been trying to develop a major industrial park at Hawks Prairie, located on the western edge of the delta. During the period covered by the case, the Port of Olympia was less interested in the delta and more interested in developing the industrial tract. The Port of Tacoma, on the other hand, was the main proponent of developing a superport on a fifteen-hundred-acre tract on its side of the river. Tacoma had been considering the proposed port since 1965 and by 1969 was actively pursuing plans. At this time, port officials felt that its four-thousand-acre facility on Commencement Bay could not be sufficiently modified to handle large bulk carriers. Port studies also forecast that all available land within its holdings for terminal development would have been utilized by 1980. Although the plans and projections are open to question, it was upon estimates of the need for improved port facilities and additional terminal space that the Port of Tacoma proceeded to push for development of a superport in the Nisqually delta.

21. Major sources of information for details concerning the background of the Nisqually conflict are James J. Kyle, "The Nisqually Delta Controversy" (M.A. thesis, University of Washington, 1970), and Puget Sound, League of Women Voters, *Nisqually in Conflict* (Seattle, Wash., 1970).

Continuous opposition to attempts to develop the delta and adjacent lands dates from 1965 when the Port of Tacoma held public hearings to consider inclusion of the Pierce County side in their comprehensive plan. A group of citizens attempted to block the port's proposal. Although they forced the hearings to be extended, the newly founded Washington Citizens Committee for Outdoor Resources failed to deter the Port Authority. The committee then tried to get the U.S. Department of Interior to consider reserving the delta as a national bird refuge, but failed because the area was considered not large enough (members of the group feel the Interior Department has changed its position since then).[22]

The committee's next major concern was information that North West Aluminum was considering the Hawks Prairie site for their plant in 1965-66. As we have seen, North West decided to locate at Guemes Island. Members of the group apparently feel that they had influenced North West considerations. From 1966 to 1970, the group continued to be active in protecting the delta by contacting public officials and by supporting efforts of the Washington State Department of Game in its efforts to develop a wildlife preserve. The Department of Game proposed to provide public access to Nisqually delta resources for streambank fishing, waterfowl habitat and shooting, and natural history education. At the time of the 1965 hearings held by the Port of Tacoma, the department joined with the Committee for Outdoor Resources, the Audubon Society, the Mountaineers, the Sierra Club, and delta farmers in opposing the port's efforts. Three months after the hearings, the Port Authority announced its intentions to conduct feasibility studies and that construction of major port facilities in the delta was ten or fifteen years away.

The Department of Game reacted quickly to the port's announcement.[23] Using plans developed in the late 1940s, the department voted to exercise options to buy 283 acres of delta land. Officials from both port authorities appealed to the Department of Game on the grounds that the purchase would jeopardize their plans, but to no avail. They then asked the governor, Daniel Evans, to establish a two-year moratorium while feasibility studies for terminal facilities could be done. The governor brought the parties together with the state Department of Commerce and Economic Development, which appeared to side with the ports. The Department of Game did not change its position, but agreed to inform the port authorities in case further purchases were

22. Interview with Mrs. Flo Brodie, President, Nisqually Delta Association, August 16, 1972.

23. Kyle, "Nisqually Delta Controversy," pp. 45–47.

forthcoming. The Department of Game made a second purchase in August 1967 despite objections from the two port commissions. Controversy between the department and the ports simmered down until 1969, when renewed controversy developed over plans of the two ports for possible development of delta and adjacent lands. The Department of Game, owner of 630 acres of delta land, became an active participant in the discussions, generally opposing industrial and port development in the Nisqually delta.

The Nisqually delta presented a policy problem in which there was no chance of a mutually satisfactory solution. Any industrial and/or port development was considered unacceptable to environmentalists, most local landowners, state agencies such as the Department of Game and the state Interagency Committee for Outdoor Recreation, and sports-recreation groups. On the other hand, port officials tended to view the delta as the most important consideration facing them. This antagonism laid the foundation for continued hostility in the controversies which would follow. Efforts of the two port authorities in the delta were bound to receive much coordinated opposition.

*State Government Action*

Continuing controversy over the Nisqually delta was one of the events which prompted greatly increased state interest and activity in coastal management. Governor Evans took leadership in state concern with environmental issues, developing a package of proposals and calling a special session of the legislature specifically to consider environmental problems.[24] This 1970 special session created the new Department of Ecology to coordinate state activities in waste management, water resources management, and pollution control. The legislature failed to pass another Evans-sponsored measure, the Seacoast Management Act, but grounds were established for subsequent legislative and citizen action on the Shoreline Management Act in 1971 (discussed in Chapter 8). Foundations had been established for aggressive state action in coastal and shorelines affairs.

During the same special session, the Washington House of Representatives passed a resolution requesting the Legislative Council to conduct a study of possible uses of the Nisqually delta.[25] In addition to a council staff report, the resolution specifically requested that two famous scientists, Gordon Alcorn and Dixy Lee Ray, already on record as supporting preservation of the delta, assist in conducting the study. Drs. Alcorn and Ray prepared a report on the basic ecology of the delta and possible

24. Ibid., pp. 60–62.
25. House Resolution No. 70–41, February 7, 1970; see also Seattle *Times,* November 9, 10, 11, and 12, 1970, and Kyle, "Nisqually Delta Controversy," p. 61.

impacts of alternative developments upon it. Their report did not come out until November 9, 1970, after the basic zoning decisions in Thurston County covering Hawks Prairie had been reached, but it figured prominently in it and in the controversy over the port proposal for the Pierce County portion of the delta.[26]

The report found that the Nisqually delta could not support industrial and port activities and at the same time serve as a natural wildlife preserve and recreation site. Upon the findings of the report, the Legislative Council pushed for legislation in the 1971 session that would have protected the river basin from any sort of major development, but the bill was killed in committee.[27] Nonetheless, the so-called Alcorn Report served to boost environmentalists and to hinder the two port authorities.

Conflict between the port authorities and state officials deepened when Dr. Richard H. Slavin, director of the Planning and Community Affairs Agency, in a speech to the League of Women Voters, proposed the creation of a glacier-to-the-Sound environmental preserve for the Nisqually delta.[28] In October, the league produced a study, "Nisqually in Conflict," which laid out the basic boundaries of the conflict and provided an unbiased evaluation of the various proposals for use of the delta lands, including the port and the environmental preserve. Next Governor Evans announced at his November 19, 1970, news conference that he supported the development of a management system to protect the environmental resources, safeguard the recreational uses, and permit the orderly development of the entire Nisqually River Basin.[29] At the same time he created a task force to study and to recommend to him and to the legislature the best ways to implement the proposed system. The preliminary draft of the task force report, available for review in early 1971, did not support the port authorities' point of view.[30] In fact, Tacoma officials feel that this report seriously undercut their credibility and dealt the last blow to the proposed port complex for the delta.

## Hearings in Thurston County

The land on the Thurston County side of the delta was unzoned in

26. Gordon Alcorn and Dixy Lee Ray, "The Future of the Nisqually Delta Area" (prepared by Gary B. Lewis, Vice President, Innova, Inc., Seattle, Wash.), submitted on November 9, 1970.

27. Seattle *Times,* April 23, 1971.

28. The speech was given at "Nisqually in Conflict," a one-day conference jointly sponsored by the Thurston County and Tacoma–Pierce County League of Women Voters, September 24, 1970, Tacoma Community College, Tacoma, Wash.

29. Seattle *Times,* November 20, 1970.

30. Nisqually River Task Force, "River Basin Study" (preliminary draft).

1968 and 1969 when the Olympia Port Commission was trying to interest buyers in the proposed Hawks Prairie Industrial Park. Attempts to secure interim industrial zoning produced additional controversy over the future of the Nisqually delta. In 1969 the Great Northern Railway (now merged with Burlington) purchased land in the tract and requested in 1970 that it be zoned for industrial use. Some local landowners, alarmed over this, in turn requested that Thurston County prepare interim zoning for the delta and nearby areas in an effort to clarify their position and protect their holdings. The applications were sent by the Planning Commission to the Planning Department for study and recommendations. Amid charges (never proven) that the county and the railroad had a prior agreement about the zoning, the old Committee for Outdoor Resources changed its name to the Nisqually Delta Association (NDA) and led the fight against the proposed industrial zoning. The first hearings before the Thurston Planning Commission were scheduled for July 21-24, 1970. These and subsequent hearings before the county Board of Commissioners served to put the Nisqually conflict in focus.[31]

The planning hearings were extensive, involving three days in all, and were unusually tense. County officials, sensitive to the charges that there may have been prior commitment to Great Northern, and aware of the implications of the *Smith* decision and related litigation, made every effort to make sure that the hearings met the letter of the law. On the other side, the NDA attempted to make the hearings more formal in the hope that the commission would make procedural errors that might serve as the base for litigation.

The Planning Department supported the zoning proposal, stressing the separation of the site from the main part of the delta and the various measures which would be taken to minimize adverse effects upon the local environment. Railroad representatives also discussed the environmental protection measures that would accompany development of the site, the need for additional industrial development, and the contribution the industrial park would make to the local economy. Both planning and railway spokesmen repeatedly emphasized that the site was not really part of the delta and would not adversely affect other uses of the area. The Planning Commission agreed, and on July 24, 1970, approved the interim zoning and recommended that the county Board of Commissioners enact the necessary ordinances.[32]

The strategy of the NDA was to attempt to get the commission to postpone the hearings until after the upcoming Alcorn-Ray report

31. Seattle *Times,* July 23, 24, 1970.
32. Ibid., July 24, 1970.

(made public in November). The commission rejected this ploy on the grounds that the Hawks Prairie development was removed from the delta proper and would not materially affect delta resources. Next, NDA, working in close cooperation with the Audubon Society (which owned a small portion of the wildlife preserve administered by the state Department of Game), the Sierra Club, and the Mountaineers, produced expert testimony, notably from faculty from the University of Washington, that the proposed industrial park would have detrimental effects on the nearby delta area (about three miles away). Each person was given four minutes to testify, hardly sufficient from the point of view of the environmentalists, but apparently enough to satisfy legal requirements.

Hearings were held before the county Board of Commissioners in September and October. The September 25, 1970, hearings found the same opponents confronting each other during the three-hour session. NDA and the Audubon Society had more support this time from a state official. As previously mentioned, it was on September 24, the day before the hearings, that Richard Slavin had made his proposal for Nisqually River park at a conference sponsored by the Thurston County and Tacoma–Pierce County Leagues of Women Voters. The opposition was very effective and the environmentalists won a deferment. The victory, however, was short-lived. On October 27, 1970, the Board of Commissioners approved an interim zoning ordinance including the nearly twelve-thousand-acre Hawks Prairie Industrial Park.[33] This action was opposed by the state Departments of Game and Fisheries, which requested delay in approval pending the Alcorn-Ray report on the delta ecology, but two members of the three-person board felt that there was insufficient evidence to show that the proposed industrial zoning would be materially detrimental to the environment of Thurston County. The decision required that the park be set back one thousand feet from the water, provided a transportation route through a large buffer zone, and made certain noise, air, and water pollution considerations binding.

The NDA at first decided to challenge the zoning decisions in the superior court, charging that the Olympia Port Authority, the county Planning Commission, and the railroad had developed an agreement favorable to Burlington Northern interests *before* the planning hearings. Attorneys hoped to prove that the hearings were a sham, maintaining that they were illegal, arbitrary, and capricious. During pre-trial conferences attorneys for NDA came to believe that their case was weak and there was little chance of winning. NDA decided to in-

33. Ibid., September 9, Octover 27, 1970.

vest its time and funds in other matters rather than pursue litigation.[34]

Failure to pursue legal action did not mean, however, that things had completely cooled down for Thurston County, Olympia Port Authority, or Burlington Northern. In November, during controversy over the Tacoma plans for port development in the delta, railway officials once more were moved to publicly defend their plans for the Hawks Prairie tract. Again they stressed the efforts being made to shield the delta from the industrial park and the measures taken to prevent water and air pollution from facilities to be located there.

The experience and events surrounding the zoning controversy fueled the opposition to any kind of development of the delta. Publicity contributed to adverse image problems for the Port of Tacoma. Negative response to the Thurston County actions from state officials and environmentalist groups rubbed off onto Tacoma and Pierce County. Timing for consideration of the proposed port was bad from the point of view of Tacoma port officials, but they were trapped in a sequence of events, only partly of their own making. In the end, adverse reaction and strong opposition from state officials and environmentalists caused the Port Commission to drop plans for the superport.

## Port of Tacoma Activities

Port officials like to say that they did not actually have plans for the delta, but a three-stage planning effort was begun in 1968.[35] It was in the early portions of Phase 1, the feasibility study, that serious public concern began to develop about possible location of a superport in the Nisqually delta. A report to the National Council on Marine Resources and Engineering Development in January 1968 mentions possible joint development of port facilities in the delta by Port of Tacoma and Port of Olympia. This was reported in the Seattle *Times* and public response began to develop.[36]

Port officials have not progressed beyond Phase 1. Phase 2, Preliminary Exploration and Development, and Phase 3, Acquisition and Design, have not and perhaps never will be carried out. Opposition from the NDA and state officials during the work on the feasibility studies and a series of public hearings held by the legislature proved sufficient to derail Tacoma plans. Much of the conflict parallels that in the Thurston County hearings in time and style. More important here were the direct intervention of the governor and top state officials from the De-

34. Interview with Mrs. Flo Brodie, August 16, 1972.
35. Kyle, "Nisqually Delta Controversy," pp. 53–55.
36. A. E. Hall et al., "Shoreline Utilization in the Greater Seattle Area; A Case Study," prepared for the National Council on Marine Resources and Engineering Development, MERI Project No. 1083, January, 1968, Management and Economics Research, Inc., Palo Alto, California; Seattle *Times*, June 6, 1970.

partments of Ecology, Natural Resources, and Planning and Community Affairs. A task force set up by the governor to study the feasibility of management of the Nisqually River Basin proved instrumental in convincing the Port Authority to withdraw its plans for the delta. The heavy involvement of the governor and high administration officials distinguishes this case from the others reported in this book. The Nisqually conflict marks the watershed of basically unrestrained local control of land use in Puget Sound.

As indicated earlier, the Port Authority was concerned over the actions of the Department of Game in securing land on the Thurston side of the delta. The department wanted to secure parcels on the other side, but shortage of funds and lack of willing sellers retarded its efforts. The extended controversy over Hawks Prairie did little to comfort the Tacoma Port Authority, even though the Port of Olympia won out. The general environmental movement in Washington was at the peak of its power and port officials were cautious about their dealings with these groups. All of these things impressed upon the Port Commission the need for extreme care in pursuing the preliminary portions of its plans for Nisqually delta.

Hearings before the Puget Sound Task Force of the Pacific Northwest River Basins Commission in early June 1970 provided the first head-on confrontation between NDA and Port of Tacoma. NDA representatives and some scientists opposed both the superport in Pierce County and the industrial tract in Thurston County. Port officials spoke of the need for expanded port facilities, in particular facilities to handle large bulk carriers and supertankers. They argued that multiple use of the delta including the eleven-hundred-acre proposed port would be possible and that port facilities would actually improve recreational use of the delta. The general manager of the Tacoma Port Authority urged joint study by the ports and recreational agencies to develop a master plan. Environmentalists countered by stating that such multiple use was unfeasible and port development would destroy the delta as a wildlife and recreation area.

The next major round of the fight between environmentalists and port authorities took place during legislative interim hearings on the Alcorn-Ray report. The report was presented on November 9, 1970, at the public hearing attended by more than two hundred persons.[37] As indicated before, the report questioned the probable impact of the port project and went on to suggest that a full-scale study of the Nisqually River system be undertaken. In general, the scientists felt that it was not possible to have a clean port and a wildlife preserve side by side on

37. Seattle *Times,* November 10 and 11, 1970.

the delta; the fuller study recommended would examine appropriate and complementary uses of the delta. Within ten days, Governor Evans proposed a task force to study the Nisqually River; its specific charge was to evaluate the feasibility of developing a seventy-five-mile park along the entire river. The governor strongly backed the proposal, saying, "Until that goal [establishment of the park] is realized, the environment of the Nisqually River system must be maintained through such means as the many federal and state programs and funding sources currently available."[38] The governor's position, according to port officials, more or less doomed the project.

By December it was open season on the Port of Tacoma's plans. For example, the director of the newly created Department of Ecology, John A. Biggs, told port authorities on December 4, 1970, that a superport on the Nisqually delta was no longer a real possibility. In a speech before the Washington Public Ports Association meeting in Tacoma he said, "Ten years ago, Tacoma could have built about anything it wanted in the Nisqually area . . . but I doubt that it could be done today. I feel that the people who want the delta retained in its natural state now represent the majority of public thinking."[39] The next blow came when Governor Evans appointed his task force to study the river basin in January 1971. The thirty-four-member group was headed by Richard Slavin, director of the Department of Planning and Community Affairs, who was one of the originators of the idea and one of the early outspoken critics of the port plans. Although Tacoma port officials clung to their plans through the winter months, by spring when the first preliminary report of the task force was available for review, the conflict was about over. In the end, the task force never really considered the delta as a site for a superport. Tacoma port officials are bitter about the actions of the governor and the task force, but publicly have said the port plan is a dead issue.[40]

*Observations*

Port of Tacoma officials probably are correct. Their timing was bad and the intervention of state officials ruined their chances of successful use of delta lands in the near future. If the Port Commission and its staff had been able to contain the conflict within the bounds of Pierce County, there are few participants who doubt that the plans would have continued (given cooperation from the U.S. Congress and the Corps of Engineers). As this case shows, however, it has become increasingly difficult for agencies to contain environmental disputes. Private

38. Ibid., November 20, 1970.
39. Ibid., December 5, 1970.
40. Interview with James J. Peterson, Engineer, Port of Tacoma, August 14, 1972.

groups such as the Nisqually Delta Association have contacts with other local, regional, and national groups which provide outside resources. People living in other areas have vital interests which transcend local boundaries; much of the opposition to Tacoma's attempts came from King County sources. Intervention of state agencies put local authorities and interests to great disadvantage. The Port of Tacoma would be hard pressed to take on the governor and his high administrators. In short, the boundaries of the conflict, once defined in environmental terms, passed beyond the capabilities of the powerful, but territorially limited, Port Authority.

Redefinition of the issues did as much as anything to trouble the port officials. As Mr. Biggs said, in the early or middle sixties, little effective opposition could have been mounted against such a proposal. Economic growth and monetary return would have been overwhelming arguments. Claims of environmental destruction would have proven useless. By 1970–71, however, the ecology idiom and its supporters had become engrained in the politics of Puget Sound. Appeals to environmental values can muster considerable support from a variety of private and public people and organizations. Ecological awareness makes location decisions, whether for superports, nuclear power plants, refineries, highways, or residential developments, open to effective challenge at the local level, in state politics, among federal agencies and Congress, as well as in the courts.

CONCLUSIONS

The inherent complexity of the issues is the most vexing aspect of environmental politics. Introduction of ecology into ordinary politics has expanded the boundaries of conflict and conflict resolution so that the issues exceed the boundaries of the agencies responsible for planning for and allocation of the resources of Puget Sound. Few if any agencies are able to encompass the vast range of participants, information, organizations, and values involved in the production of a fair impact statement, locational decision, or planning document. The range and number of variables involved in a single proposal often exceed the capabilities of most municipal, county, regional, or state agencies and departments in Washington.

*Environmental Quality as an Issue*

In all four cases, opponents of the proposed projects were more or less successful in raising environmental issues during the controversies. Environmental quality became a very useful means of gathering support. Yet, it was not always true that environmental quality was the key point of the conflicts. In the Guemes Island, Kayak Point, and Anderson Cove cases, the initial conflicts were about different perceptions of how the areas ought to be developed. Life-style rather than ecology was the crucial point of conflict. In the Guemes conflict, initial controversy centered on the possible impact of the plant upon land use and land value in an area already basically given to light residential and recreational uses. Opponents to the refinery planned for Kayak Point were similarly concerned; many local and outside landowners had vested interests in maintaining established land use patterns. In Anderson Cove, environmental issues were discussed from the beginning, but the backbone of the environmental organization, the Hood Canal Environmental Council, was local and nonresident landowners who wished to preserve the low-density residential character of the area. Even in the Nisqually delta conflict, where environmental issues were always part of the dispute, much of the conflict centered on different points of view of landowners.

Thus, underneath concern for preservation of the environment were more narrowly defined, self-interest values. This is not to say that the environmentalists and others were not really interested in the ecology; they were. Rather, it is to point out that much of the conflict was based upon mutually exclusive interpretations of how the land and water resources should be *developed*.

Fortunately for the organized opponents of the several projects—Save the San Juans, Save Port Susan Committee, Hood Canal Environmental Council, Committee for Holly Environment, and Nisqually Delta Association—there was close fit between the interests of those favoring light residential and recreational development and those concerned with environmental quality. It is obvious that light use is much less threatening to the local ecology than industrial and high-density development. Once environmental issues are introduced, there is a natural bias against the large-scale projects and toward residential-recreational uses.

Defining controversy in environmentalist terms widens the scope of conflict, introduces popular and government support systems otherwise unavailable, and puts the proponents of the project on the defensive. The Anderson Cove and Nisqually cases illustrate how effective the use of environmentalist terms and strategies have become. Kitsap officials acknowledge that the efforts of the environmentalists alerted them to considerations, interpretations, and information they might not have considered. There is little doubt that the already poor image of Boise Cascade suffered under environmentalists' attack. Olympia and Tacoma port officials are certain that casting the Nisqually conflict in environmental terms contributed much to their difficulty and eventually led to the withdrawal of the superport plans. They feel, correctly, that defining the conflict as a struggle to save the environment automatically made them the "bad guys" and cast suspicion upon their plans. It certainly brought the state government fully into the fight; the early intervention of the Department of Game helped define the issues in terms of environmental compatibility and later state involvement was based upon the premise that the river basin is a unique system that must be preserved.

Successful introduction of environmental issues into Puget Sound politics has altered the places of conflict resolution, widened the conflicts so that traditional local politics can no longer contain the controversies, put any kind of development on the defensive, and brought the state government directly into basic land use decisions. Land use decisions which were pro forma in the early sixties are certain now to be highly controversial. Environmentalists have redefined land use politics in Puget Sound and Washington.

### Vulnerability of Local Governments

Local governments and politics are very vulnerable to outside interests and organizations. Regional, state, national, and international interests and organizations are able to determine to a large degree what at first appears to be a local dispute. The scope of operations and the array of resources of many of the contending parties tend to exceed the capabilities of local officials and agencies. In the past, this worked to the advantage of developers. Corporate practices and resources often overwhelmed local officials. More recently, however, opponents of developers have developed organizational scale and resources which not only are able to confront and match those of private and public large scale organizations, but in the process overrun local residents, officials, and agencies much in the same manner as the developers have. In impact upon local decision processes, it is often difficult to distinguish among private giants such as ARCO and Boise Cascade, public agencies such as the Department of Game and the Tacoma Port Authority, and ecology groups such as the Hood Canal Environmental Council and the Sierra Club. Values and intentions aside, such organizations present problems for local interests and governments.

The Guemes and Kayak cases illustrate how outside economic interests in effect develop "joint ventures" with local interests and officials. North West and ARCO were nearly able to play conventional zoning politics in which their interests would be indistinguishable from those of the local business community. In both cases, the developers touched bases and expected little if any opposition. It is clear in the initial stages —remember that the lands held by ARCO had been purchased many years before—both corporations expected full cooperation from local officials. They were successful even in the face of opposition, and the environmentalists (in this case, self-interested property owners) were forced to seek litigation to overcome corporation impacts on local processes. In both cases, the litigants were successful in charging denial of due process and in suggesting conflict of interest. The arbitrary handling of the Planning Commission hearings was the key issue in the litigation which upset the rezoning decisions.

The *Smith* case forced local officials to be less accommodating to developers and to provide an arena for other views and considerations. The hearing processes were formalized and made open so that those opposing the development might have their say. As we saw in the Anderson Cove conflict, the changes in planning processes encouraged local officials to be more prudent. In the Anderson and Kayak cases the Board of Commissioners placed constraints upon the developer in the name of environmental quality. Thus, not only the environmental participants but also their values were made part of the decision process. Officials were motivated to question the developer carefully and to make room for divergent views.

In the Thurston County decisions in the Nisqually case, county and port officials were very careful to permit their opponents at least nominal oportunities to present their points of view. While litigation served to cut down unrestrained influence by developers, it also served to open up the process to other inputs. The net result is a much more broad operation, but much more complex and costly for all participants. This cost factor should be kept in mind. The increasing cost associated with dealing with the cases one by one was a prime motivation for the environmentalists seeking a state-wide authority system for shorelines protection. Confronting the developers in case after case at the local level would have been much too expensive for such groups. The state-wide system permits a more economical expenditure of resources.

*Political Learning*

The cases provide evidence that all participants in water-oriented land use decisions are learning to cope with each other and with institutional constraints. It is apparent that environmentalists in Puget Sound learned much from each of the four cases. There are threads of information, tactics, and personnel which flow from one to another. Further, there is the suggestion of a national information network. Much of the opposition to Boise and to the Port Authority was based upon information and experience elsewhere. As suggested above, the costs of maintaining effective scanning, information exchange, and mobilization are high. Nonetheless, coalition behavior was effective in the short run.

Political learning appears to be taking place among the developers as well. There is probably less concert (or need for it), but collective learning and behavior is apparent in all four cases. Successively, the developers became attuned to the new dimensions of land use politics. It is apparent that in these conflicts, the developers anticipated opposition; much of the initial planning for Anderson Cove, Hawks Prairie, and the superport was kept secret as long as possible. Both port authorities were aware that environmental issues would be a major concern and made plans to account for environmental quality concerns (e.g., buffer strips, pollution-control measures). Their public presentations stressed minor impact upon and/or compatibility with other uses.

The intelligence network of the environmentalists, however, proved to be formidable. In the Anderson Cove case, experts and other witnesses from all over Washington and other states were brought to the hearings. In the Thurston hearings, officials were confronted by a coalition of seven organizations as well as scientists. In the Port of Tacoma experiences, many of the same organizations and people appeared at hearings and gave public statements and produced reports. More than one public official voiced concern over what was sometimes viewed as an environmentalist conspiracy.

In the earlier cases, the industry was located in areas which would accept them: the aluminum plant in Astoria, Oregon, and the refinery at Cherry Point, Washington. In both cases, the corporate planners simply sought out areas already zoned for industrial use and/or where there would be less controversy over possible impacts upon local ecology. The opposition at Cherry Point used hearings for permits from the Corps of Engineers and the Department of Natural Resources as forums to voice their concern, and even in industrially zoned areas, environmental constraints were imposed upon refinery operators as a condition of the permits issued.

### Boundary Problems

As stated in the beginning of this book, fitting different boundaries accounts for much of the problem of management of the resources of Puget Sound. This is an age-old problem, but it takes on fresh significance in the light of ecological awareness. As it stands now, the governmental and market structures that account for much of the information exchange and collective decision-making for the planning and allocation of natural resources in the Sound inadequately fit the boundaries of the natural phenomena, the distribution of uses, the definitions of common and individual good, the emerging conflict patterns, and the distribution of influence.

The case materials show that outsiders played a crucial role in the outcome of each. Much of the support for and the organization of the major environmental groups came from people who lived elsewhere. These outsiders were motivated by self-interest (e.g., as owners of recreational and second homes), concern for the environment of Puget Sound (e.g., possible negative impacts upon the regional as well as the local ecology), or commitment to environmental goals (e.g., keep the developers from destroying the world), or a combination of all three. Whatever the motives, in the Anderson Cove, Kayak Point, and Guemes cases, the respective organizations opposing the development were dominated by people from Seattle or other urban centers.

Thus, there was a poor fit between local government (the arena in which land use decisions legally were made) and the actual distribution of support and influence of environmentalist groups. Local officials often were dismayed by what they considered outside interference. Local proponents felt that outsiders were unjustly involved in their affairs. Local opponents of the projects welcomed such outside support and resources; their efforts would have been less effective without it.

The intervention of state government into the controversies blew apart capacity of local governments to control the conflicts. In fact, many local officials in the Nisqually conflict bitterly resented state intervention, especially from Governor Evans. Shifting the controversy to state agencies and state hearings radically altered the capacity of the Port of Tacoma to fight. In the end, it will alter future environmental controversies.

Environmental politics in Puget Sound have become nonterritorial in the sense that there are no geographical boundaries which can contain the controversies. Many local governments lack personnel, information resources, and power to handle such conflicts. The quick development of regional and national environmentalist groups has pushed conventional land use decision-making out of shape. The aggressive stand, policies, and organizational developments at the state level in Washington have shifted some of the responsibility to higher levels. The widespread use of litigation to protest local and state decisions and the resulting changes in decision-making procedures have added new dimensions to environmental politics. The state is going through a period of adjustment while local, regional, and state interests and governments are sorting out the complexities of environmental politics.

This sorting out of responsibilities and relationships now is focused on the shorelines management system set up by the legislation whose development paralleled the foregoing cases. The Shorelines Management Act developed out of much the same concerns which underly the four cases. For whatever personal and self-interested reasons, many people of the Puget Sound region and elsewhere felt that the on-going conflicts about appropriate use of the near shorelands could only be resolved through the establishment of a state-wide system of management. Such a system was established in basic form in 1972.

At least for the near future, much of the conflict resolution concerning land use on the Sound will involve sorting out the roles of local and state agencies and interests. Many cases such as the ones discussed here are sure to appear. Their resolution, however, is likely to be much different. Local zoning politics is forever altered. The future is unclear, but it will involve continued adjustment among various levels and agencies of government attempting to make the shorelines management system function. Our next chapter examines the basic legislation. In effect, it provides a case study of the development of the legislation and its requirements.

# CHAPTER EIGHT

# The Washington Shoreline Management Act

During the late 1960s a series of conflicts over environmental issues erupted in the state of Washington. Most of these concerned the use and condition of bodies of fresh and salt water and their shoreline areas. Thermal and industrial waste pollution, depletion of fisheries, offshore oil drilling, residential and commercial development over and adjacent to water, and oil spill prevention and control all became the focus of intense and often protracted controversies. These involved a range of citizens, interest groups, and private and public organizations. While many of the issues related directly to Puget Sound (some of which were reviewed in detail in the preceding chapter), the ocean beaches, the Columbia, and other rivers and lakes in the state were also included.

As the number and variety of incidents accumulated, the nature of the solutions sought by interested parties changed. Initially, the public conflicts occurred in the form of *ad hoc* controversies with changing mixes of interest groups, city and county governments, port authorities, state and federal agencies, and courts. Then they gradually evolved into a concerted effort by environmentalists to create a centralized authority and uniform set of rules to govern the development and management of shorelines throughout the state.

While concern for the protection of Puget Sound's physical, biological, and aesthetic features was a major motivation in much of the effort to achieve shoreline management legislation, there were never serious demands for a resource management system that would have a primary responsibility for some or all of the Sound. Thus, events between 1966 and 1972 produced state-wide regulation for shorelines which will substantially affect future resource allocation in the Sound without providing any mechanism for developing policies for the Sound as a whole. The nature of the decision process which led to the approval of a Shoreline Management Act by Washington state voters in 1972 and the ways in which it does and does not affect Puget Sound offer a useful illustration of the use of the political process to resolve conflicts over allocation of estuarine resources.

THE SETTING

Three of the case studies discussed in Chapter 7 involved conflicts over the conversion of basically undeveloped coastal areas to industrial or residential use. Each controversy centered on a land use decision by a county government. Each was characterized by a strong belief on the part of the opponents of development that the responsible county officials would not give adequate weight to environmental values and, in some instances, lacked the technical support to evaluate properly the implications of the proposed land use changes. Thus, while a number of other resource issues involving relation to Puget Sound and the rest of the state were at issue, it was the controversy over what development, if any, should occur in shoreline areas and who should make the decisions that came to be a dominant political question before the state legislature for a period of four years. Further, the groups seeking to transfer control of shoreline development from the local to the state level ultimately were forced to bypass the legislature as well and go directly to the electorate through the initiative process.

To understand the circumstances which culminated in the Shoreline Management Act of 1971 several distinct but interacting sets of events should be identified. One concerns decisions that were made at the county level of government. The Guemes Island, Kayak Point, Anderson Cove, and Nisqually delta conflicts were widely publicized in 1966, 1967, 1969, and 1970, respectively. These cases were important in creating wide-spread public concern over shoreline areas among environmentalists and in influencing the types of solutions they would seek to implement. A parallel series of events took place in the legislative arena. The lack of success of conservationists in obtaining action on proposals concerning rivers and shorelines in 1967 and 1969 sessions of the state legislature also played a major part in defining the controversies that would arise in the 1970 and 1971 sessions.

A third series of events of quite different nature were important in creating strategic opportunities and setting of legal parameters for a shoreline management system. These included judicial decisions, legislative activity in other states and nationally, and events that raised environmental consciousness such as the discovery of vast oil reserves in Alaska in the late 1960s and the Santa Barbara oil blowout in 1969.

The formal rules and informal processes of the Washington political system constitute a final background element in the formulation of shoreline policy. Washington politics have traditionally emphasized citizen and interest group access to policy making and constrained the development of cohesive and disciplined political parties. The size of its population and the economic and social dominance of the Seattle–King County area in the state also provided a powerful political base for influencing state legislation. These factors help to explain how a relatively small group of people, largely from the Seattle and Puget Sound region, were able to have access to the governor, state administrative agencies, the legislature, and the electorate and strongly influence the passage and content of a highly controversial environmental bill.

In broad terms, efforts to impose more environmentally oriented values upon shoreline development moved successively from the county level to the courts, the governor's office and legislature, and then the electorate. As indicated in Chapter 7, in two major initial encounters at the local level, opponents of the aluminum reduction plant on Guemes Island and the oil refinery at Kayak Point failed to stop approval of the projects by the Skagit and Snohomish county governments. However, they were successful in challenges to both decisions in the state courts.

The Anderson Cove case followed a different path. Citizen opposition to the Boise-Cascade recreational community on Hood Canal undoubtedly influenced the Department of Natural Resource's decision to withhold approval for a marina on state-owned tide lands at Anderson Cove. Further, well-organized groups of local residents were able to marshall testimony against the project by experts from outside and inside the state in local hearings. The extensive public hearings and the decision by the county commissioners to impose a stringent set of conditions on the development were influenced by the experience in the other two cases. The demonstrated ability of environmentalists to challenge local land use decisions in the courts again contributed to the blocking of local plans for port expansion in the Nisqually Delta.

After moving between local government and the courts for several years, environmental interests, particularly the Washington Environmental Council (WEC), began to work seriously for state legislative action in the late 1960s. While statutes were proposed in 1967 and 1969, it was not until the special sessions of 1970 that a major legislative push occurred. At that time, a court case, *Wilbour* v. *Gallagher,* arising independently of the environmental movement, created a situation in which state legislation was necessary to remove a legal cloud from all shoreline development that required landfill. As a consequence, a number of important interest groups that were hostile to the WEC bill wound up supporting a substantially amended version. Indeed, it was amended to the point that the WEC successfully opposed its final version and no legislation was passed during the session.

On the basis of this experience, the WEC decided to draft a regulatory measure itself and have it submitted to the legislature as an initiative proposal. The necessary number of signatures was obtained on initiative petitions and the legislature, in its 1971 regular sessions, was faced with a number of choices. It could enact the WEC initiative bill without amendment and have it become law; act favorably but still submit the matter to the electorate; or reject the initiative or take no action and have it automatically placed on the ballot at the next general election. In the case of no action or rejection the legislature could approve an alternative measure and have it put on the same ballot with the initiative to allow the voters to choose one or the other or neither. This last option was chosen by the legislature and the final decisions on whether there would be shoreline regulation at all and which of two proposed statutes would prevail were made by the voters in approving the legislature's alternative bill in November 1972.

### 1970 SPECIAL LEGISLATIVE SESSION

Legislation to control the use of a resource requires that a number of specific questions be answered, each of which may involve its own set of complex policy issues. Regulation of shoreline areas is no exception. There is, for example, no widely accepted definition of the landside boundary of a shoreline area. A basic question, then, is what is to be controlled—what constitutes the shoreline area? Similarly, there is no convention for including fresh- as well as saltwater bodies in the same management system. A second major issue is to decide how much of "it" should be controlled—all bodies of water or only those of certain size, flow, or other selected characteristics? The criteria upon which the control system is based must also be spelled out. The values to be reflected must be made operational in some form. Finally, decisions must be made as to where public authority to administer the system should be placed. The state, a regional agency, local governments, or some mix are all potential candidates.

Each of these issues was built into the legislative debates in the state of Washington: what was to be controlled; how much of it; by whom; and according to what criteria. The Washington Environmental Council played a major role, along with Governor Daniel J. Evans, initiating consideration of these matters and defining the framework of shoreline control to which the legislature was forced to respond. Consequently, a review of how the Washington Environmental Council developed and pursued its own position on shoreline management is necessary to an understanding of the policies that were ultimately adopted.

The WEC was established largely in response to the failure of a bill of relatively limited scope in the 1967 legislative session. The Scenic

Rivers Act (HB-234) would have identified wild and scenic rivers in the state and recommended procedures for their management. After the session, a number of conservationists and outdoor sports enthusiasts who had backed the bill joined together to create the WEC as a state-wide lobbying organization to "encourage citizen, legislative and administrative action toward the protection and restoration of our natural and historic heritage and the creation of an urban environment which reflects those values."

At the 1969 regular session EHB-567 was introduced at the governor's request and passed in the house of representatives with WEC support. It did not receive approval in the senate. This legislation was concerned with the preservation of the state's Pacific Ocean beaches which stretch from the Columbia River to the mouth of Puget Sound. A court ruling in 1967 had been a factor in efforts to pass the act. In the *Hughes* v. *Washington* 1967 case the United States Supreme Court overturned a decision by the Washington Supreme Court and ruled that coastal property owners rather than the state acquired ownership of lands accreted to their property.[1] In recognizing that the decision had important implications for the future of the state's coastline, the court pointed out that there was a need for state guidelines to control development on accreted land under private ownership. Another bill was introduced in the 1969 session which constituted the first comprehensive proposal to regulate the uses of both the tidelands and shoreland of the state (HB-787). The bill was not acted upon by either chamber and no public hearings were held on it.

The lack of support in the legislature for these bills, the *Hughes* decision, and the accumulating controversies at the county level over shoreline development reinforced the determination of the WEC to place a high priority on gaining approval of a state-wide shoreline management system. The next opportunity for action was provided when Governor Evans announced in 1969 that he would call a special session of the legislature in January 1970 to consider a number of pressing environmental problems in the state, including shoreline management. The governor planned to use the special session as a vehicle for a broad package of environmental protection measures. The creation of a Department of Environmental Quality, legislation to regulate surface min-

1. *Hughes* v. *Washington*, 389 U.S. 290 (1967). State of Washington had claimed under Article 17 of the state constitution it had ownership of "accreted lands" on property owned by Mr. Hughes. Washington Supreme Court agreed, but was overturned by U.S. Supreme Court. It ruled that the question was governed by federal law when uplands had been conveyed by U.S. prior to Washington statehood. The Hughes decision took all accretions on upland from the state and placed it in the hands of upland property owners. It pointed out, however, the need for state guidelines and for controlled development.

ing, and an inventory of scenic rivers and shorelines were also part of his agenda. The proposal for a new agency to centralize state regulation of air and water pollution and solid waste disposal reflected the growing importance of environmental policies in Washington politics.

Initial drafting of the shoreline proposal for the special session took place during the summer of 1969 and involved close communication between the governor's office and the WEC's newly formed Ocean Beaches Committee (OBC). The thinking of the OBC was influenced by several actions that had been taken in the neighboring state of Oregon. In 1967 the Oregon Beach Law was passed (Act 601-1967, Sections 390.605 *et seq.* of the Oregon Statutes). It provided that beach areas below the vegetation line had received uninterrupted public use for so long as to establish a legal right of access for the public. The Oregon Highway Department was given authority to administer the act and regulate any construction on private as well as public beaches below the vegetation line. Another Oregon statute enacted in early 1969 which also was considered important by the OBC required that all counties in the state adopt land use zoning ordinances that would meet state determined minimum standards. Counties which did not presently have acceptable provisions were given two years to comply. In cases where the deadline was not met, the governor was required to establish zoning regulations for the county. The OBC forwarded a copy of this law to Governor Evans in July.

An intern in the Governor's Office was assigned the responsibility of putting together a draft shoreline proposal. The California Mc-Ateer-Petris Act, as amended in 1969, which established the San Francisco Bay Conservation and Development Commission, and the Shorelands Zoning provisions of the Wisconsin Water Resources Act of 1965 were drawn upon for ideas here. Consequently, a number of drafts shuttled between the governor's staff and the OBC during the summer and fall of 1969.

The first proposals were limited to salt water and covered only the Pacific Ocean beaches. The governor favored the inclusion of Hood Canal, but there was a general feeling that any effort to include coverage of Puget Sound in the act would insure its defeat in the legislature. After considerable discussion, however, the WEC's executive board, at the request of the OBC, voted in early December to back legislation that would cover the entire saltwater coast line of the state, including Puget Sound. The governor's immediate response was to stay with the original boundaries. Within a week, however, on December 4, a decision was announced by the Washington Supreme Court which signficantly affected the ensuing legislative deliberations.

The *Wilbour* v. *Gallagher* ruling required that serious consideration be given to alternative ways to organize a coastline management system, particularly from a development-oriented perspective, rather than have the WEC proposal treated as a yes or no question.[2] The court made it quite explicit that the public interest must be represented in shoreline developments and that a political rather than judicial solution was needed. There were now potential costs attached to a failure to enact some form of control, and environmentalists were provided with a lever that had not existed before. In addition, the decision made it almost certain that Puget Sound would be included in any coastline control measure. Thus, the nature of the legislative conflict over the seacoast management act was substantially changed from what either its supporters or opponents had anticipated by adjudication of a conflict among private parties that originated nearly a decade before.

Lake Chelan is a fifty-five-mile-long scenic body of water in Chelan County on the eastern slopes of the Cascade Range. The case involved a controversy between neighboring landowners which began in 1961 when one of the parties started to fill in a portion of the lake to build a trailer park. The owners of adjacent lots, Wilbour and Green, brought a class action asking that the fill be removed on the grounds that it reduced the value of their property by blocking their view of the water and also by denying access to an area that had previously been covered by water and used for recreational purposes by the applicants and the public.

The lake was subject to seasonal variations in its water level due to a dam constructed by the Chelan Electric Company in 1927. The company was authorized to raise the lake above its natural level from 1,079 to 1,100 feet between late spring and September each year. The action by Gallagher would prevent the yearly flooding of the area by filling it to a height of 1,105 feet above sea level. The trial court awarded the plaintiffs damages but refused to abate the fill. On appeal, the supreme court reversed, basing its decision on the proposition that the fill by Gallagher constituted an obstruction to navigation. It stated:

When the circumstances of an artificial raising of navigable waters to a temporary higher level is synthesized with the law dealing with navigable waters having a naturally fluctuating level, the logically resulting rule for the protection of the public interest is that, where the waters of a navigable body are periodically raised and lowered by artificial means, the artificial fluctuation should be considered the same as a natural fluctuation and the right to go where the navigable waters go, even though the navigable waters lie over privately owned lands.

On this basis, the court concluded that when the level of Lake

2. *Wilbour* v. *Gallagher*, 77 Wash. Dec. 2d, 307 (1969). This is widely known as the "Lake Chelan Case."

Chelan is raised to 1,100 feet, the submerged land is subject to the rights of navigation, together with its incidental rights of fishing, boating, swimming, water skiing, and other recreational purposes. Consequently, the fill in question was found to obstruct the submergence of navigable waters and ordered removed.

The decision clearly jeopardized the legal status of any future shoreline development on navigable water which required fill. The first direct impact of the ruling was felt before the year ended. Governor Evans announced on December 30 that he had written to the Corps of Engineers stating that the issuance of a permit for the planned construction of a highrise hotel over water at Alderbrook on Hood Canal would be contrary to the law of the state on the basis of the Lake Chelan decision by the supreme court.[3] At the same time, the governor stated that the Chelan case now made the inclusion of Puget Sound in a seacoast management act a necessity, regardless of the political difficulty, if the legal cloud over shoreline development was to be removed.[4]

By the time the legislative session was under way in mid-January, the possibility that the Chelan precedent could lead to the abatement of all fills in navigable waters had become an increasingly serious matter of concern.[5] The court itself had anticipated this problem and suggested a method of resolving it in footnote 13 in the decision. The court's majority expressed concern over the lack of any representation of relevant public agencies—the town or county of Chelan or the State of Washington—which should have an interest in "what, if any, and where, if at all, fills and structures are to be permitted (and under what conditions) between the upper and lower levels of Lake Chelan."

The court went on to note that there were undoubtedly places on the lake where developments requiring fill would be desirable and went on to say that perhaps interested public authorities could solve the dilemma by "establishment of harbor lines in certain areas within which fills could be made, together with carefully planned zoning by appropriate authorities to preserve for the people of this state the lake's navigational and recreational possibilities. Otherwise there exists a new type of privately owned shorelands of little value except as a place to pitch a tent when the lands are not submerged."

Governor Evans and environmentalists had taken the position that the decision would apply to all navigable waters in the state and that a seacoast management system had been mandated by the court. Development-oriented groups that otherwise would have opposed any substan-

3. The Corps of Engineers is vested with the power to enforce federal jurisdiction over navigable waterways and issues necessary permits for dredging and fills.
4. Seattle *Times*, December 30, 1969.
5. Charles E. Corker, "Thou Shall Not Fill Public Waters without Public Permission: Washington's Lake Chelan Decision," *Washington Law Review*, 45 (1970): 65-93.

tive legislation and, in particular the WEC bill, were put in the position of having any major coastline development potentially challengeable in the courts if no action was taken during the 1970 session. The Guemes Island and Kayak Point cases had already shown that environmentalists would utilize the opportunity if they failed to obtain a state-wide regulatory system. Thus developers, land speculators, and homeowners in the coastal zone and public agencies such as port authorities and the Department of Natural Resources began to press for legislation that would satisfy the court but would also (1) forestall state zoning to which local governments objected; (2) provide alternatives to the WEC proposal; (3) allay the apprehension of major port authorities that state control over the seacoast would be used to favor one port at the expense of others; and (4) appease the general desire of developers and land speculators that there be no more controls than presently existed over coastal construction.[6] The WEC-proposed seacoast management act which was introduced into the House of Representatives as HB-58 early in the session met none of these conditions.

In general terms, the WEC's bill directed the anticipated new Department of Environmental Quality to adopt a set of guidelines for optimal state-wide use of seacoast resources with standards for protecting, preserving, and, where possible, restoring the seacoast. In case of conflicting uses, those to be preferred would be consistent with pollution control and the prevention of irreversible damage to the ecology and environment of the seacoast.

Once the guidelines were adopted, comprehensive plans and zoning ordinances of local governments would be required to comply with them. If, within a year after such guidelines were promulgated, any local government was not in compliance, the department would issue planning and zoning regulations for the area. This special seacoast zoning would extend at least one thousand feet inland from the line of vegetation and such other land areas on or offshore that were reasonably necessary to accomplish the stated policy of the act.

The legislation also gave the department the authority to acquire real property through purchase, lease, or condemnation if such action was determined necessary to further the policy of the act. In addition, the department's approval was required for the sale or lease of any coastal property owned by the state or local governments. The state would reimburse local governments for 75 percent of the costs incurred in preparing plans and zoning ordinances in accordance with the act. Finally, during the interim period between the adoption of the statute and the

6. Interview with Representative Alex Julin, chairman of the House Natural Resources Committee, by Susan M. Finney, June 1970.

approval of local plans and zoning actions by the department, a permit system would be utilized. No construction of a permanent nature, or activity such as filling, dredging, or the discharge or accumulation of sewage, could take place without a permit issued by the department.

Initial hearings on HB-58 brought opposition from local governments, port authorities, land developers, business associations, and the state Department of Natural Resources (DNR).[7] An effort was made, however, to negotiate a compromise bill in the House once the implications of the Chelan decision became more apparent. In late January, DNR presented a substitute bill to the House Committee on Natural Resources, and its representatives later met with WEC leaders and agreed to a series of compromise amendments. Even so, it was not possible to gain enough support in the committee to pass the proposal on for a vote of the House before a January 30 cut-off date for new legislation.

Both the House and Senate had agreed on a rule that only bills already approved by one would be considered by the other after that date. The possibility existed, however, to revive the seacoast management act by amending it to make it legislation still eligible for consideration. This option caused the governor to exert tremendous pressure for action during the first week of February.

On February 2, Governor Evans publicly called for a seacoast bill to be amended to pending legislation. The following day he announced in a television broadcast that the state was holding up fifty shoreline construction applications because of the Chelan ruling, and urged the public to back a seacoast management act. Finally, on February 5, the governor made an unprecedented appearance before the House Natural Resources Committee to appeal for the enactment of coastal legislation, without which, he forecast, there would be endless litigation and hardships for the public and private property owners.[8]

Under mounting pressure, the House Natural Resources Committee produced a new version of the seacoast management act on February 7 by adding it to Senate Bill 58 after eliminating all but the first sentence of the Senate's original draft. The next day the WEC Executive Board voiced strong and unanimous opposition to the revised act. On February 10, House and Senate leaders, uncertain of being able to produce a majority vote, initiated discussion with representatives of the WEC

7. Prior to the session, the independently elected commissioner of Public Lands, who heads the Department of Natural Resources, let it be known that he believed the DNR should be the administering agency for any seacoast legislation. A representative of the department testified against the WEC proposal, in part, on the grounds that it was too restrictive on development. Seattle *Times*, January 1970.

8. *Daily Olympian*, February 5, 1970.

and DNR to seek amendments that would gain their support for the bill. After reaching agreement on certain changes, the bill went to the floor of the House on February 11. The negotiated amendments were not accepted, however, and others were added which made the bill even less acceptable from an environmental point of view. The governor was less than satisfied with the new draft but made it clear that he felt that this version was a first step and was preferable to no action.[9]

The House approved the measure on February 11. The bill was taken up by the Senate on the next day, the last day of the session but, in spite of a series of complex parliamentary maneuvers, it died in committee.

The full circle had been turned between January 12 and February 12. After the failure of the compromise amendments to the DNR substitute bill, the WEC put all of its resources into efforts to prevent the passage of the House-approved version. It is worthwhile at this point to review the major differences between the WEC-backed HB-58 and the bill passed by the House, EHB-58. The 1970 conflict constituted the first serious legislative consideration of a coastal management system, and the two proposals reflect basic policy divisions between conservation and development-oriented management models which sparked a controversy that would span two more years.

EHB-58 affirmed the need for control of shoreline development and the coordination of planning but at the same time called for the state to observe and protect private property rights. No mention was made of seacoast restoration, nor was there a clear priority for protection and preservation of shorelines and for nonpolluting uses. EHB-58 states that seacoast tidal beaches should be managed so as to plan and foster all reasonable and appropriate uses. Such plans should be designed to "minimize" both any resultant damage to the ecology and environment and also any interference with public use of waters over such tidelands.

A major deviation from the WEC bill concerned administration of the act. All state agencies, such as DNR or Department of Parks and Recreation, and local governments would assume administrative responsibility for the act in public shoreline areas that they controlled at that time. The anticipated Department of Environmental Quality would administer controls over privately held beach lands. Rather than a single point of authority at the state level, enforcement of the provisions of EHB-58 would be the responsibility of a number of state as well as local agencies. An equally serious difference between the two bills concerned the amount of land that would come under control of the act. Both proposals covered the same linear shoreline from the Co-

9. Seattle *Times,* February 9, 1970.

lumbia River through Puget Sound. EHB-58, however, dropped the
one-thousand-foot upland planning zone and provided no specific landside boundary. Apparently the provisions would have applied only to
beaches proper. The thousand-foot line had been strongly opposed by
local governments in general and particularly by officials from counties
with seacoasts.

The strategic as well as the legal position of the Department of Environmental Quality was also weakened in the engrossed bill. Under
HB-58 the department would draft state-wide guidelines and then hold
hearings in Olympia before their final adoption by the department. In
EHB-58 hearings were to be held at the county seats of seacoast counties
before the guidelines were drafted. More important, final approval of
the proposed guidelines would be made by the legislature and not the
department. Further, EHB-58 provided the department with no power
of condemnation of property if needed to carry out the provisions of the
act nor with authority to approve the sale or lease of seacoast property
by any public agency in the state.

Two of the differences that most concerned the WEC involved local
compliance with state guidelines in the planning and zoning of the seacoast and the procedures for issuing interim permits. Once guidelines
were adopted under EHB-58, public agencies would be required to
adopt planning and regulations that were "reasonably consistent" with
the guidelines. In contrast, WEC designed provisions would require
local governments to "comply" with the state guidelines in their comprehensive plans and zoning ordinances for the seacoast. Prior to the
adoption of the guidelines both proposals provided that any new construction would require a permit from the administering state agency.
EHB-58 contained detailed discussion of the purposes for which construction might be allowed while HB-58 listed the types of construction
which were proscribed without a permit. Among other provisions,
EHB-58 stated that permits could be issued for construction "that the
public agency determines will be in conformance with both the probable and alternative public planning and regulations for the area," and
consistent with the general goals of the act: "If such construction might
cause *substantial* irreparable damage to the seacoast tidal beaches, the
granting of a permit shall be *discretionary*" (italics added).

From the WEC perspective, the differences between the provisions
necessary for an adequate seacoast management bill and those in
EHB-58 were irreconcilable. WEC leaders viewed the latter as legislation deliberately designed to "give away" the seacoast to developers.
John Miller, speaking for the council on February 9, claimed that the
House bill would do a good deal more to encourage the development of
the seacoast than to protect or restore it and went on:"All references to

pollution control, conservation and wildlife have been eliminated and you have a bill that allows massive construction on tidelands, thus undermining existing public rights in that area."[10] Jack Robertson, then president of the WEC, characterized the 1970 special session as one in which "we saw some real naked political power. The speculators were able to take the moribund Seacoast Management Act, cause it to be gutted of its meaningful features, and substitute giveaway provisions of their own choosing."[11]

The creation of the Department of Ecology (DOE) was a major accomplishment of the 1970 special session of the legislature. Part of the package of proposals from Governor Evans, DOE was designated to give guidance to and to coordinate the state's environmental management activities. It has responsibility for coordination of pollution control programs (Water Pollution Control Commission, Air Pollution Control Board, Department of Health), solid waste disposal (Department of Health), and water resources management (Department of Water Resources). The director is authorized to undertake studies on all aspects of land, air, and water environmental problems. He and DOE consult and cooperate with the federal government as well as other states and Canadian provinces in the study of and the management of environmental problems. Such items as allocation of surface and groundwater, flood control, resources planning, flow requirements, waste discharge, oil spills, and waste management fall under the responsibilities of DOE. In addition, it may engage in surveillance and monitoring to see that state requirements are met and it handles enforcement of environmental laws—regulatory orders, civil penalties. In short, DOE became the state's main research and development, coordinating administration and enforcer for environmental planning, policy, regulations, and procedures.

Development of I-43

There was little question among all major parties to the conflict that the next regular session of the legislature in January 1971 would see an even more intense struggle over coastal regulation. The WEC was expected to introduce a proposal equally strong as the one it had backed in 1970. Governor Evans also was committed to support a shoreline management system that would place controls upon development. State agencies and local governments now managing shoreline areas or responsible for land use zoning would again be faced with the problem of

10. Ibid.
11. Jack B. Robertson, "Why We Had to File Initiative 43," October 8, 1970 (mimeo), p. 1.

influencing the content of any bill that appeared likely to succeed in order to maintain as much of their present power as possible.

From the perspective of development-oriented groups, a stand-off now existed. Unacceptably strong shoreline regulation had been defeated but the weaker bill they had favored had not been approved either. Consequently, the legal status of any future development had not been resolved. Immediately after the special session, a number of groups petitioned the state supreme court to review the Lake Chelan decision. Among those asking for a reversal were the Washington Land Developers Association; the Orion Corporation, which had planned a large-scale residential project on Padilla Bay near Anacortes; the Port of Seattle, concerned about the future of a world trade center it expected to build; and the Department of Natural Resources.[12] No hearing was granted by the court, and the matter was appealed to the U.S. Supreme Court.

Soon after this the implications of the *Wilbour* v. *Gallagher* ruling became more manifest. In April 1970, the Corps of Engineers formally denied a bulkhead permit necessary for the construction of a high-rise resort hotel at Alderbrook on Hood Canal, which Governor Evans had objected to earlier as being contrary to the law of the state under the Chelan ruling. Later, in October, the U.S. Supreme Court also denied a hearing on the Chelan case.

The legislature itself was now far more active on the issue of shoreline management. In contrast to the failure to authorize any studies after the matter had first been seriously raised in the 1969 session, two separate interim groups were directed to investigate the question and report back to the 1971 session. A House resolution referred the unsuccessful seacoast management act to the Legislative Council and charged it with developing a draft statute.[13] The Senate assigned similar responsibilities to its Committee on Governmental Operations.

WEC leaders also set about drafting a new shoreline control act in the spring of 1970. The experience in the special session had several important influences on how the organization proceeded. It reinforced a belief that the ultimate authority for shoreline development must be transferred from local governments to a state agency other than DNR. Further, the successive failures to obtain legislative support for shoreline-related environmental protection proposals in 1967, 1969, and 1970 raised the question as to whether this route would ever be productive.

An alternative method of passing legislation is available in the state

12. *Daily Olympian*, February 18, 1970.
13. The Legislative Council functions as a continuing joint House-Senate Interim Committee with a permanent staff. It conducts studies and issues reports to the legislature. In 1971 its members included sixteen representatives and fifteen senators.

of Washington, as the Constitution provides for popular initiatives. This process allows citizens to directly draft legislation and, if an adequate number of petition signatures is obtained, submit it to the legislature or voters. In this case, if the necessary signatures were obtained prior to the 1971 legislative session, the initiative proposal would first be submitted to that body. The legislature would then have the option of either passing it unamended or placing it on the ballot in a state-wide general election and have the voters decide. (The legislature actually has several options in responding to an initiative petition and these will be discussed in more detail below.) If a majority of the voters approve an initiative it becomes the law of the state and is not subject to amendment for two years except by extraordinary vote of the legislature. As the spring and summer progressed, this option came to be viewed as more and more of a necessity by the WEC.

During April 1970 the WEC's Executive Board delegated the drafting of a new bill to an *ad hoc* committee. The members, for the most part, had been involved in developing and lobbying for HB-58. There was also an overlap in membership between this committee and the Executive Board. No open hearings were held but the views of business, labor, public agencies, and the governor's office were sought. Several meetings took place between the *ad hoc* committee and a subcommittee of the legislature's Joint Committee on Governmental Cooperation which, as events developed, was to undertake the only serious interim study of seacoast control.

The governor also was having a bill drafted in an effort to design a statute that was both effective and acceptable to the legislature. Appearing before a meeting of the WEC in June, Evans stated that he would lead a campaign to get a seacoast management bill approved in the 1971 session. Aware that the WEC was considering use of the initiative, the governor urged working through the legislature again. If this failed, he said, he would give full backing to an initiative measure.[14]

As the new WEC draft took form, several meetings were held between the *ad hoc* committee and a subcommittee of the Joint Committee on Governmental Cooperation. The discussions proved helpful in letting the WEC hear and take into account certain objections of opposing groups. The net effect, however, was to have WEC leaders conclude that they could not support any statute likely to be developed by the joint committee and that the chances of having an environmentally acceptable bill passed in 1971 were no better than in the previous session.[15]

14. Seattle *Times,* June 8, 1970.
15. Robertson, "Why We Had to File I-43," p. 2.

On August 24 the WEC announced that it would undertake an initiative petition to force the legislature either to accept its version of a shoreline protection act or submit it to the voters of the state for their decision. The intiative draft was filed with the secretary of state in early September and a state-wide signature-gathering campaign was begun in October. The WEC had until December 31 to obtain and submit petitions signed by approximately 105,000 registered voters. Over 160,000 people signed by the end of the year, more than enough to validate the proposal as Initiative Measure No. 43.[16]

The content of the initiative was based on the same underlying assumptions that had influenced the drafting of HB-58. One was a belief that local governments did not have the resources, expertise, or, often, the motivation to protect and conserve the shorelines against pressure from developers, especially those with political influence. As one WEC leader put it, "If local governments were doing their job, we wouldn't be in the mess we are in now."

Even if cities and counties had been expected to behave differently, the WEC still preferred a system of regulation centralized at the state level because the cost of developing the necessary expertise in each jurisdiction with responsibility for land use control on the shoreline would be too great; the problem of overall coordination of shoreline regulation would remain; and, if the shoreline were considered a resource belonging to all of the people, a state agency, responsible to the governor, was seen as more likely to represent the interest of the state as a whole in making decisions. It was a prevalent view that a management system based on local control would inevitably ignore "the fact that there are many people in Tacoma who would like to preserve their favorite fishing spots in Eastern Washington, and that there are those in Spokane who much want to protect their summer homes on Whidbey Island or in the San Juans."[17]

From a tactical view, it was felt that placing shoreline authority in a centralized agency would largely eliminate the potential problems and costs of contesting the decisions of the hundreds of local governments that presently had jurisdiction over shoreline land use. Consequently, the newly created Department of Ecology was seen as the ideal agency at that state level 'to administer the WEC drafted act. It had been supported by the WEC during the 1970 session and was considered most responsive to environmental concerns. In addition,

16. Under the Washington Constitution, an initiative measure requires the signatures of a number of registered voters equal to 8 percent of the number who voted in the last gubernatorial election.

17. Dorothy C. Morrell, "Initiative 43 v. ESHB 584: A Thumbnail Comparison," June 7, 1971 (mimeo), p. 5.

it was felt that if shoreline management was added to DOE's existing authority, the agency would be in a position to coordinate its air and water quality responsibilities with the control of land use in coastal areas.

In many ways, Initiative 43 offered a far more systematic and extensive management framework than its predecessor in 1970. The most sweeping change was the inclusion of fresh- as well as saltwater bodies. While the upland area to be zoned was reduced to five hundred feet, the shorelines of lakes of over twenty acres and navigable streams came under regulation. It would establish a number of environmental rights, ban offshore drilling, introduce consumer protection requirements in shoreline land sales, regulate building heights, set stringent standards for timber cutting, and require the Department of Ecology to adopt a state-wide plan for the shoreline zone and directly administer a permit system for all major shoreline development. Thus, virtually all of the basic sources of conflict that flared up over HB-58 were contained in I-43 together with some explosive new ones. Local government control over shorelands would be largely eliminated and conservation values would clearly predominate over development.

The basic values of the initiative were stated in Section 2, its "Declaration of Values," in which it was stipulated that a comprehensive shoreline plan and regulation of development should give preference to:

1. Long-term benefits over short-term benefits;
2. State-wide or regional interests over local interests;
3. Natural environments over man-made environments;
4. The location of industrial and commercial facilities in existing developed industrial or commercial areas over their location in undeveloped, rural or residential areas of the shoreline.

Section 2 also provided that the comprehensive plan and permit system should accomplish the following goals, among others:

1. Protect the natural resources and natural beauty of shoreline areas;
2. Provide adequate locations for aquaculture and commercial and industrial developments requiring location on the shoreline;
3. Provide and protect public access to publicly owned shoreline areas;
4. Minimize interference with view rights, the public's right to navigation, and outdoor recreational opportunities;
5. Regulate signs and illumination in shoreline areas and access to and traffic in the shoreline areas by motor vehicles and motor-craft;
6. Conserve and enhance the natural growth of fish and wildlife;
7. Fulfill the responsibilities of each generation as the trustees of the shoreline areas for succeeding generations.

The act would apply to all saltwater and freshwater bodies of the state and a zone extending for five hundred feet in all directions on a horizontal plane from the line of ordinary high water. The shorelines of lakes of less than twenty acres and along rivers above the upstream limit of navigability for public use would be exempted from state permits. Cities and counties, however, would assume responsibility for managing and protecting these areas in conformity with the policies of Section 2. The construction of a single-family dwelling unit for use by the builder or his family on land purchased prior to the statute-effective date and construction authorized under the Thermal Power Plants Act also would require no state permits.

Responsibility for preparing and administering a comprehensive plan for the shorelines and a permit system in compliance with Section 2 was placed with the Department of Ecology. DOE was directed to establish a shoreline protection division responsible to the director and supervised by an assistant director. A sum of five hundred thousand dollars was to be allocated to the division from the state general fund for the first fiscal biennium of its operation and nine hundred thousand for the second.

The procedures for developing the state comprehensive plan contained a number of provisions to minimize local influences. The state was to be divided into at least seven regions by the director of DOE. Each would establish a regional citizens council composed of at least thirty members, including local governmental representatives and citizens. The citizens were to be appointed by the governor, would constitute a majority of the council, and at least 10 percent of their number must be from outside the region. These councils would meet as needed and advise the DOE in the development of the comprehensive plan but would cease to exist once it was adopted.

DOE was allowed thirty-six months to complete its draft plan. The final adoption was delegated to the Ecological Commission.[18] This body was to hold hearings on the draft in each of the regional areas where citizens councils had been established and ultimately adopt a plan by majority vote.

Once the comprehensive plan was approved, no development could occur in the shoreline areas without a permit issued by the DOE with limited exceptions largely related to property maintenance. Prior to the adoption of the state-wide plan, the DOE would issue permits and base its decisions on compliance of the applicant with the policies stated in Section 2. Appeal to permit decisions could be made to the Pollution

18. The Ecological Commission is composed of seven members appointed by the governor from among those in the population with general knowledge of and interest in environmental matters. It contains one representative of organized business, one from agriculture, one from organized labor, and four from the public at large.

Control Hearing Board which could approve, modify, or reverse the action of DOE.[19]

Local governments could be involved in the administration of certain limited permit authority at the discretion of DOE. The department could delegate to requesting cities and counties all or part of its authority to issue permits for shoreline developments which were "not substantial," which, according to the act, would be those affecting the division of less than ten acres and any development for which either the fair market value or cost was less than fifty thousand dollars in any one-year period.

Several specific restrictions were placed on extraction of resources under the initiative. Section 13 concerned erosion control. It stated that permits would not be issued for commercial harvesting or cutting of timber which would result in openings in the forest canopy within shoreline areas larger in diameter than the average height of the immediately surrounding trees. Such cutting would be authorized only when it was in pursuit of a purpose other than logging for which a permit had been issued, or when the director of DOE determined it was required to avert a threat to public health and safety.

Oil and gas exploration and production were barred from the shoreline areas of Puget Sound, including Hood Canal and the San Juan Islands. The DOE was at the same time directed to undertake a study and report recommendations to the governor within thirty-six months on oil and gas exploration and production from the shoreline areas of the state.

A final restriction was placed on the height of new or expanded buildings in the shoreline. Such structures were limited to thirty-five feet above the average grade level where they would obstruct the view of the shoreline from a substantial number of residences or areas adjoining the shoreline. This limit could be waived only in specifically designated areas in the comprehensive plan.

THE 1971 SESSION

On December 31, 1970, just prior to the opening of the legislative session, the Washington Committee for a Responsible Environmental Policy, which was formed in the fall to oppose the WEC petition campaign, issued a statement concerning I-43. The committee had no wide base of support but it did represent some of the more conservative business and industrial views on shoreline management which had been influential with the legislature in the past. Their statement pointed out

19. The Pollution Control Hearings Board is composed of three members appointed by the governor, with the consent of the Senate, for six-year terms. Members must be experienced or trained in matters pertaining to the environment.

that the committee shared an active concern for the environment with all citizens but was "deeply disturbed" by the "irresponsible . . . let's do something, even if it's wrong philosophy" of the WEC as expressed in its initiative.

In particular, the provisions of I-43 were seen as: (1) hamstringing the economy by delaying and blocking needed construction; (2) preventing the development of a state-wide land use policy through the introduction of a strip zoning provision; (3) threatening the tradition of local control and self-determination; (4) destroying current plans to disperse industrial development to reduce future environmental problems; (5) making it necessary to confront the voting public with a confusing and costly campaign upon a highly technical and complex subject; and (6) assailing fundamental ideas about the integrity of private property.[20]

A somewhat less sweeping but equally negative response to I-43 emerged from the Legislative Council. The council's interim study produced a nine-point set of guidelines for shoreline legislation and a critique of the intiative. It was not a serious study of shoreline management options and contained no alternative proposals. The report, issued in January, informed members of the Forty-second Legislature that the WEC initiative failed to meet any of the council's nine criteria and concluded that "we certainly must present to the citizens a better solution to the problem than the impossible confusion and misdirection of Initiative 43."[21]

The successful petition campaign for Initiative 43 substantially changed the strategic position of both the WEC and its opponents at the beginning of the session from what it had been in 1970. The legislature had several options under the state constitution. It could approve I-43 without amendment, in which case it would become law without being subject to veto by the governor. The measure could also be approved but still submitted to the voters for final action. Conversely, the legislature could reject the statute or take no action on it. In either of these cases, the secretary of state automatically would put the matter on the ballot at the next general election. One other strategy was available to the lawmakers if I-43 was to be put to the voters. The legislature could enact a completely separate bill on shoreline management and

20. Statement by Richard M. Farrow, chairman, Washington Committee for a Responsible Environmental Policy, on the occasion of the filing of Initiative 43 (mimeo).

21. Memorandum to members of the 42nd Washington State Legislature and the governor, from members of the Legislative Council, re Seacoast Management Legislation, January 15, 1971. The much more active interim subcommittee of the Joint Committee on Governmental Cooperation, under Senator R. R. Grieve, did produce a draft bill. It was generally viewed as very development-oriented and was never seriously considered during the session.

have it placed on the same ballot. If both were approved, the one with the higher number of votes would become law. Otherwise, either the one with a majority would be enacted or both would be defeated.

Given this situation, development-oriented groups had an obvious political problem. They could not simply prevent the passage of any shoreline legislation during the session and have the matter end there. At the same time, if an alternative bill to I-43 which did not seriously address the question of environmental protection was enacted, two other types of difficulties could arise. Such a proposal might not pass the legislature if there was strong opposition from the governor and environmentalists. If a token bill was submitted to the electorate, its success was a gamble in competition with I-43.

The WEC found itself in another type of bind. By mid-January it was clear that the initiative measure had no serious support within the legislature. Leaders in the legislature clearly intended to draft an alternative bill to place before the voters. This put the WEC in the position of lobbying for as strong a bill as possible to put on the ballot in competition with its own I-43. Otherwise they faced the possibility of a well-financed campaign for a weak environmental statute winning a majority in the general election.

Only one major proposal was put before the legislature early in the session that could be considered a serious effort to balance environmental values. This was the governor's bill HB-584, which was referred to the House Committee on Natural Resources and Ecology. Drafted by Charles Roe, assistent attorney general, the proposal sought to circumvent the state-local conflict by establishing a shoreline management system to be administered by local governments within guidelines established by DOE, except for certain specified "shorelines of state-wide significance." The latter areas would be the responsibility of DOE. The bill covered the total saltwater shoreline, lakes of three hundred acres and rivers navigable for commerce, and a zone up to five hundred feet above ordinary high water or the vegetation line.

Hearings on HB-584 in February produced opposition from the WEC, particularly in terms of the weakened role of the state in shoreline control. A number of people speaking for local governments expressed reservations for the opposite reason, but tended to hold open the possibility of negotiations. More direct opposition was voiced by representatives of marine-related industries and developers. Shortly thereafter, the chairman of the Natural Resources Committee, Representative Zimmerman, appointed an *ad hoc* special committee with some members from outside the legislature to draft a substitute version of the bill that would be acceptable to major interests. Three legislators, a law professor, representatives from the attorney general's office and the Association of Washington Counties, and a citizen, who also happened to be a member of the WEC, made up the committee. Their work was largely unpublicized. By the end of March, Zimmerman reported that his full committee had reached agreement on a substitute bill and that it would be the only one reported out, thus killing the initiative and the governor's original proposal.

Substitute HB-584 proposed a more limited geographic coverage. Its shoreline zone extended two hundred rather than five hundred feet upland. Controls covered lakes of one thousand acres or more rather than three hundred and rivers were included on the basis of minimum flow requirements rather than navigability. Local governments were given a greater role in planning and administrative control. Of particular importance, the new proposal contained an emergency clause. With this provision, the bill, if passed, would go into effect immediately after the legislature adjourned rather than be held in abeyance until the 1972 general election.[22] While the measure would still have to be voted on by the citizenry, along with I-43, it would have been in operation for over a year by then. The voters would be forced to decide whether or not to dismantle a functioning shoreline program rather than simply making a choice of which one, if any, should be implemented.

House debate on the measure began on April 4. It was further weakened, in terms of environmental protection, by amendments from the floor before its approval two days later. Prior to final action, the governor threatened to shift his support to I-43 if the bill underwent additional changes.[23]

Once the bill moved to the Senate, both the governor and WEC brought strong pressure for revisions which would tighten controls on development. The senate considered the bill for a month and did add stronger environmental protection provisions before approving it. The House concurred in the Senate version and the measure was enacted on May 7 as the Shoreline Management Act. Two weeks later the governor signed the act but exercised his item veto power to eliminate Section 3(c) which provided that the Department of Natural Resources would be granted the same powers, duties, and obligations as local governments under the act over lands under its jurisdiction. The governor took the position that the provision diluted a goal of the act to place

22. Normally a statute goes into effect 90 days after adjournment of the legislature. However, by including an emergency clause stating that the enactment is "necessary for the immediate preservation of the public peace, health and safety, the support of state government and its existing institutions" the ninety-day wait can be waived.

23. Seattle *Times*, April 5, 1971.

administrative authority in a single state agency, DOE, so that a uniform state policy could be developed.

The Shoreline Management Act (SMA) and I-43 both awaited submission to the voters in 1972. From an environmental perspective, the legislature did pass a shoreline measure—something it had refused to do in previous sessions. The extension of control to freshwater bodies had received no serious opposition, in large part because of the Chelan case. Much stronger environmental controls were included in the SMA than had been present in the aborted EHB-58, which seemed to represent the furthest the legislature was willing to go in 1970. On the other hand, the SMA and I-43 still differed greatly on the two basic points that had produced the most controversy in the past—placing controls at the state or local level and the degree of restriction to be placed on shoreline development.

I-43 had been drafted and approved under conditions fully controlled by the WEC. The organization's ability to obtain 160,000 signatures indicated, at a minimum, that a substantial number of citizens wanted a chance to consider shoreline controls if the legislature refused to act. The SMA evolved in a decision structure that was, if anything, biased against strong environmental controls but which included a far greater range of interests than had been represented in the WEC deliberations. As the subsequent election would indicate, the values of the voting public were closer to those of the legislature. At the same time, there is little doubt that without the threat of I-43 and the activity of the WEC at previous legislative sessions, a bill as strong as the SMA would not have been forthcoming. The governor's continuous and increasing pressure on the legislature also played a major role. With only the WEC and allied environmental groups to deal with, the legislature's response to the imperative for action created by the Chelan ruling would have been directed more toward removing a legal barrier to development than toward creation of a sound shoreline management system.

THE SHORELINE MANAGEMENT SYSTEM

The Shoreline Management Act became operative on June 1, 1971, under the emergency clause in the statute. Subsequently, it was approved by the electorate over I-43. A more detailed review of the SMA's content at this point will provide an outline of the present management system and indicate the nature of the choice that was available to voters in November 1972.

*Policy Declarations*

Management goals in the SMA are more generalized than in the initiative and place more emphasis upon a balance between conservation and use of the shorelines. In Section 2, the legislature declares that "unrestricted construction on the privately owned or publicly owned shorelines of the state is not in the best public interest" which should be protected through coordinated planning, while "at the same time, recognizing and protecting private property rights consistent with the public interest."

Section 2 further states that it is the policy of the state to provide for the management of the shorelines by planning for and fostering all reasonable and appropriate uses and that this policy is designed to "insure the development of these shorelines in a manner which, while allowing for limited reduction of rights of the public in the navigable waters, will promote and enhance the public interest. This policy contemplates protecting against adverse effects to the public health, the land and its vegetation and wildlife, and the waters of the state; while protecting generally public rights of navigation and corollary rights incidental thereto."

Stronger regulations and more specific priorities are reserved for a special class of shoreline area "shorelines of state-wide significance." For these areas, the act declares that planning and permit decisions should give preference, in the following order, to uses which:

1. Recognize and protect the state-wide interest over local interest;
2. Preserve the natural character of the shoreline;
3. Result in long-term over short-term benefit;
4. Protect the resources and ecology of the shoreline;
5. Increase public access to publicly owned areas of the shorelines;
6. Increase recreational opportunities for the public in the shoreline

Further, where alterations of the natural condition of such shorelines are permitted, priority should be given to the following uses: (1) single family residences; (2) ports; (3) shoreline recreational uses; (4) industrial and commercial developments that are particularly dependent upon their location on or use of shorelines; (5) other developments which will provide an opportunity for substantial numbers of people to enjoy the shorelines.

*Boundaries*

The area covered by the SMA differs in three ways from I-43. Some sections of the shoreline are completely excluded; the upland zone is narrower; and, as noted, different rules are used for different portions of the shoreline. The act declares that "shoreline," for regulatory purposes, means all water areas of the state, their associated wetlands, and the land underlying them, with the following exceptions: (1) shorelines of state-wide significance; (2) shorelines on segments of streams upstream of a point where the mean annual flow is twenty cubic feet per second or less; (3) shorelines on lakes of less than twenty surface acres in size.

Whereas I-43 placed responsibility on the state for managing and protecting areas of the latter two types, the SMA makes no similar provision. The opposite is true of shorelines of state-wide significance. They are treated as acres of special concern, while no such distinction was made in the initiative.

In the case of both shorelines and shorelines of state-wide significance, their "wetlands" or "wetland areas" are defined as those lands extending landward for two hundred feet (as opposed to five hundred in I-43) in all directions as measured on a horizontal plane from the ordinary high water mark.

Shorelines of state-wide significance were identified by the legislature in the act and not left to administrative discretion. Saltwater areas are specifically named; lakes are defined by surface size; and rivers by flow, as follows:

1. . . . [the Pacific coast or] western boundary of the state from Cape Disappointment in the south to Cape Flattery in the north . . .;

2. Those areas of Puget Sound and adjacent salt waters and the Strait of Juan de Fuca . . . as follows:

    A. Nisqually Delta—from De Wolf Bight to Tatsolo Point;

    B. Birch Bay—from Point Whitehorn to Birch Point;

    C. Hood Canal—from Tala Point to Foulweather Bluff;

    D. Skagit Bay and adjacent area—from Brown Point to Yokeko Point; and

    E. Padilla Bay—from March Point to William Point;

3. Those areas of Puget Sound and the Strait of Juan de Fuca and adjacent salt waters north to the Canadian line and lying seaward from the line of extreme low tide;

4. Those lakes, whether natural, artificial or a combination, with a surface acreage of one thousand acres or more . . . ;

5. Those natural rivers or segments thereof as follows:

A. Any west of the crest of the Cascade range downstream of a point where a mean annual flow is measured at one thousand cubic feet per second or more;

B. Any east of the crest of the Cascade range downstream of a point where the annual flow is measured at two hundred cubic feet per second or more, or . . . [those rivers] downstream from the first three hundred square miles of drainage area, whichever is longer.

The political sensitivity of making these designations is suggested by the procedure contained in the act for expanding such areas. Any additional shorelines of state-wide significance must be acted upon by the legislature. Recommendations may be made for further designations to the legislature by the director of the Department of Ecology when there are special economic, ecological, educational, developmental, recreational, or aesthetic values to be considered. Prior to any recommendation, however, the director must hold a public hearing in the county or counties that would be affected.

*Administrative Structure and Permit System*

A major goal of the backers of the SMA was to vest shoreline regulation basically in local government, with the state setting guidelines and monitoring local decisions. The terms of the act are quite explicit on the subject. Section 5 declares that "local government shall have the primary responsibility for initiating and administering the regulatory program." Conversely, it continues that the Department of Ecology "shall act primarily in a supportive and review capacity with primary emphasis on insuring compliance with the policy and provisions of the law."

The first phase of implementing the act, however, rests primarily with DOE. The department is directed to adopt a set of guidelines for regulating shoreline use in conformity with the SMA. The guidelines, in turn, will be used by local governments to develop "master programs" for the relevant shorelines within their boundaries. The master program is composed of a comprehensive use plan, the use regulations, and a statement of the desired goals and standards of the plan. Before these master plans go into effect, they must be submitted to and approved by the DOE as confirming with the provisions of the SMA. If a local government fails to adopt a master program the department is authorized to devise one which will remain in effect until an acceptable program is forthcoming from the local agency involved. In the case of shorelines of state-wide significance the position of the DOE is stronger. It has the authority to adopt and implement a master plan for the area if the one developed by the local unit is not found to be satisfactory.

There is no state-wide integrated comprehensive plan for shoreline development under the act as provided for in I-43. Rather than an overall plan adopted by DOE, the "state's master program" is defined as the cumulated total of all local master plans approved or adopted by DOE.

As with the development of plans, permits are administered locally. While all shoreline development must be consistent with the policies of the act, not all developments must have a permit. The SMA provides that "substantial developments" will require permits and that they shall be issued by the appropriate local governmental unit. Substantial developments are defined as those in which the total cost or fair market value exceeds one thousand dollars or any development which materially interferes with the normal public use of the water or shoreline. Exemptions are provided for normal maintenance or repairs of existing structures, building of protective bulkheads common to single-family residences, and the like.

The permit requirement is also waived in two other cases. One concerns construction under a certificate obtained in conformity with the state's Thermal Power Plants Act, which is similar to I-43. The second, however, involves utilities and recreation buildings or structures included within a preliminary or final plat approved by the applicable state agency or local government prior to April 1, 1971, provided that certain other related conditions are met. Developments under this exemption must be completed within two years after the effective date of the act. In contrast, I-43 exempted land purchased prior to the statute only for the construction of a single-family residence for the purchaser or his family.

Ultimately, all permit applications must be for uses which conform with the master program of the area. In the interim between the effective date of the act and the approval of the master programs, relevant jurisdictions will issue permits only when the proposed development is consistent with the policies stated in Section 2 of the act, the guidelines and regulations of DOE when adopted, and, as far as can be ascertained, with the master program being adopted for the area.

The monitoring role of DOE is also reflected in the permit process. If, during the interim period, the department believes that any permit has been granted that is inconsistent with the act, it can appeal the local action within thirty days to a shoreline hearings board. Either the department or the attorney general can make such an appeal after the interim. If the department believes that a permit is being used in ways that are inconsistent with the provisions of the act, it can seek to have it rescinded by appeal to the shoreline hearing board.

A six-member hearings board is established by the act to serve as a quasi judicial body. Three of the members are selected from the Pollution Control Hearings Board. One member is appointed by the Association of Washington Cities and another by the Washington Association of Counties. Both serve at the pleasure of the appointing organizations. The commissioner of Public Lands or his designee is the final member. Any decision by the board requires the agreement of at least four members. Local governments can appeal actions of the DOE to the board. Citizens, however, can use the board to appeal permit decisions only if the request is found to be based on valid reasons by the department or attorney general and is certified to the board.

*Resources Extraction and Height Limits*

Provisions on two topics which were highly controversial in the legislature are included in both the act and I-43. In both cases, however, the wording of the SMA is less restrictive. Timber cutting regulations apply only to shorelines of state-wide significance. Within the two-hundred-foot zone of these areas, only selective commercial cutting is allowed so that no more than 20 percent of the saleable trees may be harvested in any ten-year period. Authorization is provided for other harvesting methods when they are necessary for regeneration. Surface drilling for oil or gas is prohibited in the waters of Puget Sound north to the Canadian boundary and the Strait of Juan de Fuca seaward from the ordinary high water mark and all lands within one thousand feet from the mark.

As in I-43 there is a height limit on structures. Permits cannot be issued for any new or expanded building or structure of more than thirty-five feet that will obstruct the view of a substantial number of residences on areas adjoining the shoreline except where a master program does not prohibit such a height and only when overriding considerations of the public interest will be served.

*Time Table*

Two interrelated time schedules were set up in the SMA for the DOE and local governments to establish the framework, guidelines, and plans which will collectively constitute the management system. The DOE was directed to undertake and complete the following no later than the dates indicated:

September 28, 1971—initial draft of the guildelines and submission to local governments for comment
February 26, 1972—completion of a final guideline draft and submission for review
March 26, 1972—completion of public hearings on final draft
June 24, 1972—holding of a public hearing to adopt final guidelines

Local governments were to fulfill basic responsibilities, the completion of an inventory of their shorelines, and the drafting of the master program, on the following schedule:

November 30, 1971—submission of a letter of intent to the DOE indicating that the governmental unit will undertake and complete the shoreline inventory and the master program
January 26, 1972—last date for responses to DOE initial draft of guidelines
November 30, 1972—shoreline inventory to be completed
December 24, 1973—submission of master plan to DOE (at least eighteen months after the effective date of the guidelines)

In general terms, then, the process of creating the system was to be completed within two and a half years. The DOE was directed to cooperate fully with local governments in meeting their responsibilities. In addition, there is a provision in the act which authorizes the DOE to distribute grant funds appropriated by the legislature to assist local governments in the preparation of master programs. The grants, however, may not exceed the amount the local government contributes to the costs of the program.

SHORELINE MANAGEMENT AND PUGET SOUND

The Shoreline Management Act of 1971 is one of the few laws of its type that has been adopted in the United States, particularly in terms of its coverage of both freshwater and saltwater bodies. It clearly affects Puget Sound in special ways through such provisions as the status of shorelines of state-wide significance and oil and gas drilling prohibitions. However, no specific planning or concern for the Sound itself as an integrated resources system is provided.

Initiative No. 43 would have offered the possibility for the DOE, in its comprehensive plan, to treat Puget Sound as an identifiable subregion. Under the present system, as with the state as a whole, the master program for Puget Sound will be the cumulated master plans of the twelve counties and their cities. These jurisdictions still differ substantially in their existing expertise and fiscal resources for shoreline planning and management.

Most land use conflicts over shoreline use will still arise at the local level and it can be expected that there will be substantial variations in views toward development among the officials and citizens of the various units exercising shoreline regulation around the Sound. The wide social, demographic, and economic differences among the counties were outlined earlier in this study. In the 1972 election on I-43 and the SMA, voters were asked to make two decisions. First they voted on the question of whether to have either of the statutes or none. Then a decision was made on which of the two was preferred. If the vote on the first was negative, the second would be academic. In responding to these choices, six of the twelve counties on Puget Sound preferred neither act: Island, Jefferson, Kitsap, Mason, Pierce, and Skagit (see Table 8-1). These counties contain only one third of the total population and, with the exception of Pierce, have limited development. However, without the King County ninety-two thousand majority for some action, the vote of the remaining eleven counties would have rejected any shoreline legislation by a slight margin (this would have also been true for the state as a whole without the King County vote). As with the rest of the state, which cast 68 percent of its vote for the SMA over I-43, Puget Sound counties decisively favored the law which quite explicitly left more flexibility for shoreline development and retained basic authority at the local level. Further, the planning zone of the act extends only two hundred feet upland and will not directly affect all shore-related development for the Sound.

TABLE 8-1

THE 1972 VOTE FROM PUGET SOUND ON INITIATIVE NO. 43 AND ALTERNATIVE NO. 43-B (SHORELINE MANAGEMENT ACT)

| County | Total Vote | For Either | | Against Both | | Total Vote | Prefer 43 | | Prefer 43B | |
|---|---|---|---|---|---|---|---|---|---|---|
| | | No. | % | No. | % | | No. | % | No. | % |
| Whatcom | 29,096 | 17,109 | 58.8 | 11,987 | 41.2 | 25,254 | 9,665 | 38.3 | 15,589 | 61.7 |
| Skagit | 21,464 | 10,105 | 47.1 | 11,359 | 52.9 | 15,903 | 3,866 | 24.3 | 12,037 | 75.6 |
| Island | 9,534 | 4,702 | 49.3 | 4,832 | 50.7 | 6,808 | 2,035 | 29.9 | 4,773 | 70.1 |
| San Juan | 2,518 | 1,346 | 53.5 | 1,172 | 46.5 | 1,976 | 543 | 27.5 | 1,433 | 72.5 |
| Snohomish | 84,609 | 42,830 | 50.6 | 41,779 | 49.4 | 62,837 | 18,302 | 29.1 | 44,535 | 70.9 |
| King | 394,051 | 243,101 | 61.7 | 150,950 | 38.3 | 329,036 | 115,395 | 35.1 | 213,641 | 64.9 |
| Pierce | 115,019 | 54,225 | 47.1 | 60,794 | 52.9 | 88,738 | 33,794 | 38.1 | 54,944 | 61.9 |
| Thurston | 31,213 | 16,192 | 51.9 | 15,021 | 48.1 | 24,576 | 7,182 | 29.2 | 17,394 | 70.8 |
| Mason | 8,866 | 3,649 | 41.2 | 5,217 | 58.8 | 6,254 | 1,386 | 22.2 | 4,868 | 77.8 |
| Kitsap | 37,815 | 17,431 | 46.1 | 20,384 | 53.9 | 27,656 | 7,835 | 28.3 | 19,821 | 71.7 |
| Jefferson | 4,168 | 1,734 | 41.6 | 2,434 | 58.4 | 3,052 | 956 | 31.3 | 2,096 | 68.7 |
| Clallam | 14,254 | 7,287 | 51.1 | 6,967 | 48.9 | 10,491 | 2,714 | 25.9 | 7,777 | 74.1 |
| Puget Sound Total | 752,607 | 419,711 | 55.8 | 332,896 | 44.2 | 602,581 | 203,673 | 33.8 | 398,908 | 66.2 |
| Puget Sound less King County | 358,556 | 176,610 | 49.3 | 181,946 | 50.7 | 273,545 | 88,278 | 32.3 | 185,267 | 67.7 |
| State-Wide | 1,154,299 | 603,167 | 52.3 | 551,132 | 47.7 | 897,469 | 285,721 | 31.8 | 611,748 | 68.2 |
| State less King County | 760,248 | 360,066 | 47.4 | 400,182 | 52.6 | 568,433 | 170,326 | 30.0 | 398,107 | 70.0 |
| State less Puget Sound Counties | 401,692 | 183,456 | 45.7 | 218,236 | 54.3 | 294,888 | 82,048 | 27.8 | 212,840 | 72.2 |

While not a management or planning system for the Sound as such, the SMA does change criteria and rules for some but not all resource policy questions concerning the area. The distribution of authority between the state and local governments basically structures a role of *ad hoc* involvement for the DOE in issues that arise out of the provisions in or application of local master programs with one exception. In the case of shorelines of state-wide significance, the DOE is authorized to adopt its own master program if program of local jurisdiction is not in conformity with the act. Under these circumstances, the balance in state-local roles will only evolve out of interaction over a period of time.

The governance of Puget Sound is still conducted through a substantially decentralized system in which the rules, relative status of parties, and policy outcomes are subject to influences from a variety of sources: state statutes; federal actions; court decisions; location choices in the private sector; and the amount and intensity of resources interest groups are willing to expend. A question that remains is to what extent the SMA will effect the behavior and performance of this system.

# CHAPTER NINE

# Governing Puget Sound in the Future

## INTRODUCTION

Puget Sound is a dominant physical feature of the state of Washington. Its water surface and shoreline constitute a resources system for the major urban-industrial center in the state and its less developed periphery. The Sound is commonly treated as an identifiable subregion by people outside its boundaries. People living in proximity to its shores are well aware that they are residents of the Puget Sound region. Yet, in spite of numerous legislative, administrative, and interest group activities aimed at regulating the condition and use of a variety of the Sound's resources, there has been no well-articulated demand for a regional agency to manage this extensive and rich resources system. This phenomenon is not limited to Puget Sound. The same can be said for other estuarine areas of the United States.

A variety of governmental units of varying size and authority make and administer policies and regulations affecting the Sound. There has been a general pattern of public responses to Sound-related issues which has evolved into an increasingly complex set of separate, but interdependent, subsystems for internalizing both publicly and privately produced externalities affecting the shoreline resources of the region and the state as a whole. The history and characteristics of the Shoreline Management Act (SMA) provide a good picture of these dynamics.

Passage of the SMA was a major policy action that culminated one phase of a continuing political conflict over developmental and conservation values. Much of the debate over the statute concerned the future of Puget Sound. However, the act set up a state-wide system of shoreline regulation. The Sound is subject to the law as part of the state's shoreline rather than because there are any specific provisions relating

184

to it as an entity. Further, the act deals only with a portion of the total range of policy issues about resources allocation relevant to the Sound. The legislation also involved a conflict over the scale of government that should administer the regulations and engage in shoreline planning. A compromise resulted which created a system of shared control over shoreline development between state government and cities and counties.

The evidence indicates that this variegated system through which the Sound's resources are managed is a reasonably accurate reflection of the particular social, economic, and physical attributes of the region itself and the political style of decision-making and administration within the state. It also conforms to a more general pattern of "governance" for large bay and estuarine bodies in the United States. The remainder of this chapter will review the nature and capacity of the vertically and horizontally divided governing structure in the Sound region. As initial steps, a look will be taken at the general experience in the country with governments for large sheltered bodies of water and, then, the characteristics of the twelve-county Sound area will be re-examined.

ESTUARINE GOVERNMENT

A very common and almost reflexive response to complex urban-resources problems in this country has been to propose that a new and larger governmental unit be created with boundaries that match the physical scale of the problems. The literature concerning metropolitan areas, river basins, air and water pollution, and air transportation abounds with recommendations for regional agencies of one type or another. There is virtually no precedent, however, for efforts to establish resources-oriented governmental units to manage estuarine systems. Apart from the merits of creating regional agencies to solve public problems, it is useful to consider the absence of this tradition in the case of estuarine waters.

In the United States, even in bay or Sound areas with extensive urban development, the bodies of water have not been used as the basis for determining the boundaries of a multipurpose marine resources management agency. Long Island Sound, as well as Puget Sound, and Cheasepeake, Delaware, Narragansett, and San Francisco bays are examples. San Francisco Bay does have a bay-oriented special authority. The Bay Area Conservation and Development Commission was established in 1965 by state legislation. Its powers, however, relate only to regulating fill and diking within a one-hundred-foot zone from the shoreline.

Environmentalists, civic activists, and academics who have been involved at the national level in formulating the current modes of thinking about coastal zones and associated wetlands have been concerned with state and national systems of regulation rather than the management of marine resources at specific locations. In this framework the shoreline has been treated as a linear resource which could be administered from a state or national level. Consequently, there have been no calls for the establishment of agencies which internalize large sheltered bodies of water and their periphery as a means of resolving coastal zone problems.

Another factor has also inhibited support for a regional marine resources agency. By far the most active movement to extablish a new scale of government is this country has been at the metropolitan level. Normally these efforts have been directed toward centralizing some or all of the powers of existing cities, districts, and counties in a region into a single area-wide government. It is assumed that such action will facilitate rational land use development and the more efficient production of municipal public services. These thrusts for metropolitan reorganization affect estuarine areas in two ways. Even though many large population centers are located on many major estuaries in the nation, proposals for metropolitan governments have almost never included shoreline or marine resources management as part of their functions. In a more indirect way, land-oriented metropolitan reform efforts have tended to pre-empt community agendas in the field of governmental reorganization and to monopolize civic activity.

Even if there were a well-developed national movement and rationale for a regional solution to estuarine management, a number of factors concerning the Sound itself would have inhibited the establishment of any such agency. While residents of the region identify with the Sound as a physical system and a symbol, social, economic, and political variables sharply separate communities around the shoreline from one another. The size and complexity of the Sound create numerous resource and policy systems which have differing boundary scales and call for different public intervention strategies.

SOCIOECONOMIC AND POLITICAL REALMS

The distribution of people and activities around the Sound is tremendously varied. Neither socioeconomic homogeneity nor region-wide spillover effects are present to act as a catalyst for demands for some type of authority for governing Puget Sound as a resources system. The predominant demographic feature of the area is the extremely high percentage of the total population located in a relatively small portion of the region. The economy is similarly concentrated. King County and Pierce and Snohomish counties, neighboring to the south and north, constitute the metropolitan core and the economic and political

center of the region. Yet even Pierce County indicated different preferences on shoreline management with its negative vote on the Shoreline
Management Act.

In combination, the three metropolitan counties have 1,832,896 residents or 81.6 percent of the twelve-county total. More than one half are
in King County. King, Pierce, and Snohomish have 92.5, 82.4, and 71.6
percent respectively of their populations living in urban areas. The
next highest county, Whatcom, drops to 51.5 percent. There is a parallel concentration of cities and towns in terms of size and numbers.
The core counties have two thirds or sixty-four of the ninety-nine incorporated places in the region. They contain fourteen of eighteen municipalities with over 10,000 people and all cities over 50,000.

Economic variables are equally skewed. King County has 56.2, Pierce
15.1, and Snohomish 11.6 percent of the total employment of the region
or 82.9 percent together. The percentage of employees in manufacturing for King, Pierce, and Snohomish is even greater—92.3 per cent.
To sample other economic indicators, the three metropolitan counties
have 84.2 percent of retail sales; 95.9 percent of wholesale sales; 88 percent of bank deposits; and 90.1 percent of new reported capital expenditures. The figures for local government revenue, 83.1 percent; local government expenditures, 84.0 percent; and local government employment,
83.0 percent more closely approximate the three counties' proportion of
the regional population but still reflect an overwhelming majority of
local public resources.

The second level of population and economic concentration can be
found in four other counties—Skagit, Whatcom, Thurston, and Kitsap.
These units account for from 5 to 15 percent of the regional totals in the
above categories. The third realm, including the other three counties
on the east side and Island and San Juan, account for less than 5 percent
of virtually all of the demographic and economic indicators that have
been discussed.

In addition to the social and economic distances between the metropolitan core and the rest of the Sound, there is also significant geographic space separating the highly urban, three-county tier, from the
rest of the region (see Table 9-1).

Thus, apart from Tacoma and Everett within the metropolitan core,
no other major city in the region is less than fifty miles from Seattle by
highway or less than an hour by combination of highway and ferry.

The spatial distances of communities from one another around the
Sound and the great differences in population size, economic scale, and
life-style have been barriers to the development of a sense of common
identity for governing purposes. As is evident from the case studies reported in Chapter 7, these differences can be translated into substantial

TABLE 9–1
DISTANCES FROM SEATTLE TO LARGEST CITY IN EACH OF THE OTHER COUNTIES

| County | Largest City | Distance and Ferry-Time from Seattle |
| --- | --- | --- |
| Snohomish | Everett | 29 miles |
| Skagit | Mt. Vernon | 61 miles |
| Whatcom | Bellingham | 89 miles |
| Pierce | Tacoma | 33 miles |
| Thurston | Olympia | 60 miles |
| Island | Oak Harbor | 70 miles plus 10-minute ferry ride* |
| San Juan | Friday Harbor | 76 miles plus 2-hour ferry ride* |
| Mason | Shelton | 81 miles |
| Kitsap | Bremerton | 1-hour ferry ride* |
| Jefferson | Port Townsend | 50 miles plus 30-minute ferry ride* |
| Clallam | Port Angeles | 74 miles plus 30-minute ferry ride* |

* Part of most direct route requires ferry ride.

political and economic conflicts over the type and rate of shoreline development various groups prefer to have take place outside the urbanized core. In three of the case studies, environmentalists from the Seattle–King County area were aligned with local groups in other counties to fight industrial or residential complexes on previously undeveloped land. Further, as indicated in Chapter 8, the King County area also provided the major organizational and voting strength for the Washington Environmental Council's efforts to obtain a state-wide shoreline management statute through lobbying before the legislature and citizens' Initiative 43. The explicit purpose of the urban-based WEC was to slow down and change the nature of shoreline development for the state as a whole.

If the results of the referendum on the Shoreline Management Act and Initiative 43 in 1972 are analyzed on a county-by-county basis, significant differences in attitude toward governmental regulation of the shoreline appear around the Sound. The political weight of King County's voting power clearly shows. Before making a choice between the WEC's and the legislature's management proposals, voters had to make a decision on whether they wanted the option of approving either of the two. A no vote here would have defeated any state-wide system of regulation. On this question, 55.8 percent of all ballots cast in the region were favorable. However, if the King County vote is not included, the remaining eleven counties would have narrowly rejected any type of regulation by 50.7 percent. Skagit, Island, Pierce, Mason, Kitsap, and Jefferson counties all produced negative majorities ranging from 50.7 to 58.8 percent.

In the future, as King, Pierce, and Snohomish counties continue to grow and maintain their massive population and economic dominance, residents from the core will make increasing demands upon the other counties for fishing, park and recreation facilities, boat moorages and rendezvous sites, and second homes. These are all direct-consumption activities which tend to be incompatible with the type of development that would generate more balanced internal economies for the non-metropolitan sections of the region.

The physical size and character of the Sound also have inhibited the identification of communities around the rim of the Sound with common resource problems. There are substantial differences among the five sections of the Sound discussed in Chapter 2—Northern and Southern Puget Sound, Hood Canal, the waterways east of Whidbey Island, and the Straits and San Juans. Variations in the depth of water, tidal patterns, seasonal differences in freshwater runoffs and water exchange, the physical obstruction of sills and differing coastal topology result in considerable changes in the marine environment from one section to another. For example, the relative shallowness of Hood Canal and limited mixing during tidal movements make the canal more vulnerable to pollution and other human activities than the southern or northern sections of the Sound, which have far deeper water and greater tidal and mixing action. Further, the spillover effects of such things as shoreline development, municipal or industrial waste, or oil spillage tend to be relatively localized in relation to the total area of the region as a whole.

SUBAREA INFRASTRUCTURE

The Sound as a whole, because of its vastness and physical and social heterogeneity, has not produced a governmental infrastructure around its boundaries. It is possible, however, that more homogeneous sections have fostered some level of multicounty organization. This does not mean simply marine-related agencies. The question, rather, is whether any section of the Sound has developed a high enough level of internal interaction to produce any type of public organization with boundaries that include more than one county. Such an infrastructure could facilitate the evolution of a marine resources–related component. San Francisco Bay, for example, is substantially more homogeneous than the Sound. All but one of the nine Bay Area counties have at least two hundred thousand residents and two thirds have populations of over five hundred thousand. Since the 1920s an elaborate set of multicounty districts, authorities, and governmental councils have been created to deal with such things as transportation, water and air quality, parks and recreation, and planning. All of this was prior to the formation of the Bay Area Conservation and Development Council in 1965.

In the case of Puget Sound, the beginnings of a governmental infrastructure are found in the one section, the metropolitan core. The Municipality of Metropolitan Seattle covers all of King County for sewage disposal and public mass transportation services. It also collects and disposes of sewage from portions of southern Snohomish County by contract. The origins of this agency involved an effort by civic leaders to create a metropolitan type of government for the immediate Seattle area and solve a water pollution problem affecting a number of suburban communities. The increasing pollution of Lake Washington in the 1950s by untreated sewage from Seattle and the rapidly growing suburban population around its shores provided the occasion for obtaining authorization from the legislature for a new type of multipurpose municipal district and the opportunity to have it approved by the voters in the Greater Seattle area. While the law permits these governmental units to provide up to six urban functions, voters only sanctioned sewage disposal when the agency was formed in 1958. It was not until 1972 that a combination of legislative acts and voter approval of a bond issue provided the base for Metro to effectively add mass public transportation as a function.

Two other units do exist which include all of the metropolitan core as well as Kitsap County. The Puget Sound Air Pollution Control District is one. King, Pierce, Snohomish, and Kitsap counties, plus a number of cities within their boundaries, also comprise the membership of the Puget Sound Governmental Conference. This metropolitan council of governments, as noted in Chapter 6, has authority only to recommend to its component parts and not to directly enact regional policies. It has engaged in extensive work in developing information and plans for such things as regional transportation, open spaces, recreation, water, and sewage services. The conference also offers a forum for local governmental officials and administrators to consider and interact on regional questions. However, there has been substantial and successful opposition to various suggestions that the conference be given limited powers to act as a regional government for the area.

Beyond these counties, which are the four largest in population, there are no other subareas of the Sound which have become centers for similar clusters of multicounty local governmental agencies. Neither functional needs, such as transportation, nor common pool resource management problems have precipitated the evolution of multicounty units elsewhere. The infrastructure that has developed in the King, Pierce, and Snohomish core largely involves traditional land-related municipal problems of metropolitan areas and is not marine oriented.

## THE GOVERNING PATTERN

It is clear from the earlier chapters of this study that the absence of a formally integrated resource management system does not mean that policies are not made and administered or have coherence in relation to one another. Nor does it mean that market transactions are not regulated or their externalities internalized into the public sector. It does mean that a single regional government model of resources management has not been adopted.

Political processes in Washington have produced a system in which marine-related resource utilization is controlled by both private market transactions and a number of state and local legislative and administrative bodies. Federal departments and bureaus also comprise a part of the system. The scope, structure, and relationships of these units have shifted over time toward greater interdependency and more explicit and mandated interaction. Policies are most commonly made and implemented in this framework for particular geographic subareas of the Sound or for the Sound as a segment of a larger resources system such as the shoreline, fisheries, or recreation, rather than for the Sound per se.

The trend in Washington over the last decade has been toward an increasing role for the public sector in regulating the use of and enhancing resources generally. The same is true in relation to the Sound. Much of this occurred as part of, and drew support from, a nation-wide popular movement to protect the environment and require that conservation values be given greater weight in decisions affecting resource utilization. Further, a number of specific events external to the state, such as the 1969 Santa Barbara oil spill, the behavior of the Boise-Cascade Corporation in building recreational communities elsewhere, or the creation of the Bay Area Conservation and Development Commission in California, all had effects on the course of events in Puget Sound.

This national backdrop combined with factors within Washington to make environmental protection a significant issue on the agenda of many localities and the state as a whole. The direct accessibility of interest groups to the legislature in the absence of strong political party organization, the availability of the initiative process to citizens, and the role of the governor as a major public figure in the state all contributed to the emergence of a new type of environmental politics.

These conditions facilitated various combinations of Seattle–King County–based and local environmental groups in other parts of the Sound region in overturning or influencing decisions by county officials on shoreline development and in literally forcing the legislature to enact a state-wide coastal management bill. The same circumstances provided support for the governor to secure legislation to change and strengthen both the state's policies and its administrative structure for dealing with resource utilization.

The overall effect upon politics in the state has been two-fold: expansion of the scale of conflict and increase in the role of state government. Traditionally conflicts over shoreline development were resolved at the city or county level as a local zoning issue. This is no longer true. Recent environmental controversies centering on land use decisions have pushed the scale of politics far beyond local boundaries. Environmental groups have shown that it is possible to intervene in local decision-making processes; overturn local action in the courts; and reorganize and enlarge the formal scale of shoreline policy making through political activity at the state level. A concommitant effect of this increase in scale has been to increase the costs of participating in issues that relate to the shoreline. A substantially greater investment of money, time, and other resources is required for local interests to match those of metropolitan-based or state-wide groups attempting to intervene in a county-level zoning decision. To go to court and pursue appeals is even more costly.

The time required for litigation can force a developer, even though the case is won, to turn to a new site before the issue is resolved in court. Effective lobbying before the legislature or contesting or pushing a state-wide initiative or referendum takes a state-wide organization and the resources to maintain it.

As the scale of politics has increased, so has the role of state government in environmental questions. The state has expanded its authority in controlling the utilization of Puget Sound resources in relation to local government and the private sector. State departments and agencies which produce goods and services relevant to the Sound, such as recreation, the ferry system, and fisheries enhancement, have substantially increased their programs and levels of public investment to meet consumer demands. Finally, in several instances, there have been steps to produce better coordination among state resources agencies.

These developments at the state level have not lessened the complexity of the governing system for the Sound. They have resulted, however, in more explicit recognition of the interdependencies of the component units and in attention being given to efforts to rationalize their relationships as new programs are established, existing ones increased, and authority redistributed among levels of government.

Events leading to the passage of the Shoreline Management Act, for example, involved quite explicit conflicts over whether public controls should be increased over the development of shoreline lands and, if so, at what governmental level they should be placed. When the Washington Environmental Council undertook a campaign for new shoreline controls, it insisted that a state agency exercise the primary regulatory power. After a series of sharp conflicts in the legislature in 1970 and 1971, both the legislature and subsequently the voters of the state in 1972 chose a statute which created state authority over shoreline development but left the basic planning and decision-making at the local level. The role of the state, through the Department of Ecology, is largely one of setting general guidelines and monitoring the decisions of cities and counties and hearing appeals from local decisions. The act does establish a new distribution of authority and specify a new set of decision rules which give greater weight to conservation values in the utilization of the shoreline. In practice, however, the law leaves the force of the state's involvement pretty much an open-ended question to be worked out over time. In other new areas of state activity, especially for power plant siting and outdoor recreation planning, more clear-cut roles have emerged for the state.

State agencies producing final-consumption goods and services relating to the Sound have had steady expansions in their output and diversification of activities. Since acquisition of the ferry system in 1951, the legislature, for example, has authorized the purchase of new vessels in 1965 and 1971 for amounts of $24 million and $19 million respectively. Even though one ferry line carrying five hundred thousand passengers in 1960 was replaced by a bridge, the total passengers serviced by the ferry system grew by over one million between 1960 and 1970. The Department of Fisheries has continuously increased the number of hatchery salmon planted in Washington waters. The total rose from 78.8 to 176.7 million between 1960 and 1971. Over 76 million of the latter figure were released into Puget Sound. In addition, Fisheries set up a Sport Salmon Enhancement Program in Puget Sound in 1971, which included such projects as bait fish studies and dogfish shark removal.

Both Fisheries and the Department of Natural Resources are engaged in support of acquaculture projects in the Sound. In 1971 Fisheries had cooperative fish rearing agreements with one private firm, the Small Tribes of Washington, and the National Marine Fisheries Service. At the same time, Natural Resources was undertaking studies of the potential of underwater resources such as seaweed and the engineering feasibility of underwater structures for future production of oysters and clams.

The Park and Recreation Commission has also greatly expanded its water-related activities, and the planning and development of underwater parks and boat launching and destination facilities in the Puget Sound region have become growing elements in the overall park and recreation program at the state level.

Beyond sheer expansion of activities, the state has moved toward creating mechanisms to provide a higher level of conscious interaction among its administrative agencies. The histories of the Thermal

Power Plant Site Evaluation Council and the Interagency Committee for Outdoor Recreation both reflect this trend as well as a move toward the inclusion of other levels of government in state resource allocation decisions. The way in which these units relate to the Sound is also typical for state agencies. They have substantial impacts but are not organized to deal with the Sound per se.

Public concern over the development of nuclear energy dates back to the 1950s. By the mid-1960s two different types of concerns produced an initial step toward a new state role in this field. Conservationist groups were increasingly troubled by the potentially negative effects of nuclear power plants upon the environment. At the same time, utilities, anticipating demands for greater production of energy, felt that they were beginning to face excessive delays and uncertainty in developing new plants because of the number of governmental units from which one type of approval or another was required. The state also had a growing interest in balancing environmental considerations and energy needs as well as one in providing for a more systematic coordination of state agencies with authority on plant siting.

These concerns resulted in recommendations to the governor (at his invitation) from the legislature's Joint Committee on Nuclear Energy and the governor's Advisory Council on Nuclear Energy and Radiation that a council be established to evaluate power plant sites. The new unit, composed of relevant state agencies, was created by executive order of the governor in 1969. It was given statutory authority by the legislature in 1970 at the request of the governor.

The Thermal Power Plant Site Evaluation Council is charged with weighing the state's need for abundant low-cost electrical energy with protection against potentially adverse effects of power plants upon the environment, including the state's waters and their acquatic life. The heads of the departments of Ecology, Fisheries, Game, and Natural Resources and the Interagency Committee for Outdoor Recreation and the Parks and Recreation Commission, as well as seven other agencies, sit on the council. Local government is also represented. One additional member is appointed by the legislative authority of the county in which the proposed site is located. This person serves during the life of the particular application. The council holds hearings on site applications. During the hearings it determines whether the location and plant design conform to local zoning and land use and will satisfy environmental standards. Upon completion of the hearings a recommendation is made to the governor, who has the final authority to grant a certificate of approval.

Two aspects of the council's activities are particularly relevant to the shoreline of Puget Sound. In view of the concentration of population and industry and the natural advantages of coastal locations, the Sound's shore will be preferred for siting plants to meet future electrical energy needs in the region. Final decisions, however, rest with the council and governor and do not come under the Shoreline Management Act. The council preceeded the SMA by one year in legislative approval. Consequently, the SMA specifically exempted power plants which have obtained certificates of approval from the governor.

Coordination in the field of recreation developed in a quite different way. Public demands for outdoor recreational facilities increased significantly during the 1960s, along with urban population and general economic growth in the state. As a result, there were both widespread popular support for expanded governmental programs at the state and local levels and a willingness on the part of voters to approve bond issues for recreational purposes. A state-wide Citizens' Conference on Open Space and Recreation Development held in 1962 made a number of proposals to enhance recreation, including the establishment of an Interagency Committee on Outdoor Recreation. A report of this new committee, composed of representatives of state agencies, to a Governor's Conference on Outdoor Recreation in late 1962 contained a set of recommendations which laid the groundwork for future developments.

In 1964, the legislature successfully submitted an $11 million bond issue to the voters for the acquisition of land for outdoor recreation facilities. At the same time, a citizens' initiative, the Marine Recreation Land Act of 1964, authorized unclaimed taxes on fuel used in water craft to be used for the acquisition or improvement of land on fresh and salt water for marine recreation purposes. This runs to over one million dollars a year. More important, however, the initiative gave the Interagency Committee for Outdoor Recreation (IAC) statutory authority to administer and allocate funds from an Outdoor Recreation Account. The account included unclaimed monies from marine fuel taxes and the 1964 and subsequent bond issue of $40 million approved by the voters in 1968. The IAC was formally designated by the legislature in 1967 as the state agency for outdoor recreation planning.

The IAC's membership includes five citizens appointed by the governor for three years and the directors of the departments of Commerce and Economic Development, Ecology, Fisheries, Game, Highways, Natural Resources and the Park and Recreation Commission. This body has become the central focus in the state for cities, towns, counties, and park districts which have recreation programs and for federal agencies providing grant funds within the state. Any state or local unit can apply for funds from the Outdoor Recreation Account and federal matching grants through the IAC. To be eligible, the proposed project must generally conform to local and state-wide outdoor recreation plans.

Again, as in the case of the Thermal Power Plant Site Evaluation Council, the authority of the IAC covers the state as a whole and there are no special provisions for dealing with the Sound as a region. Yet, the Sound area has received substantial benefits from the funding priorities of the committee, which has made allocation roughly on the basis of the distribution of recreation consumers. Between 1965 and 1972, the IAC granted funds to three state agencies and ninety different units of local government. Approximately 35 percent have been for water oriented projects within short travel-time of most state residents. As noted in Chapter 6, over 55 percent of the local government projects approved during the life of the IAC have been in King, Pierce, and Snohomish counties and 65 percent of the total in the twelve-county region.

This set of institutional arrangements and the public authorization of funds to meet a rising demand for outdoor recreation facilities have emerged over a relatively short period of time—six years. Fiscal incentives through the control of state funds and access to federal grants have allowed a degree of planning and coordination to occur while still having outdoor recreation directly produced by a large number of governmental units within the state and the Sound region. In addition, voter willingness to authorize bonds and the major portion of funds granted for projects in the Sound region reflects a high level of demand by urban residents for final-consumption use of the shoreline for recreation.

THE FUTURE

The rapid increase in the role of the state government in the allocation of Puget Sound resources is the major change that has occured over the last decade. Yet, this also reflects the more general dynamic and evolving character of the Sound's governing structure. In the future, as in the past, the disposition of resources and the development of the shoreline will depend upon the behavior of a combination of groups and governmental agencies and contextual factors rather than on policies issued from a hierarchically organized decision-making structure.

In summarizing the processes which govern the allocation of Puget Sound resources, the following attributes can be identified. First, control of the water surface, seabed, shoreline, and wetlands is distributed among and, in some cases, shared by, local, state, and federal legislative, administrative, and judicial bodies. Second, while there is no governing unit for the Sound as such, there are a number of subsystems of differing scale—sometimes separate, sometimes interleaved—which provide structure, authority, and rules for making and implementing policies for particular geographic subareas of the region or segments of larger resources systems. Third, the scale of environmental politics has grown. Participants in conflicts in local communities must be prepared to face the intervention of external groups and see the scale of the conflict substantially enlarged. The increase in scale has been accompanied by an increase in the cost of contesting resources-related issues in the political, administrative, and judicial arenas. Fourth, the direction of change in resources allocation decisions has been from the private to the public sector. This is true in terms of regulating levels of intermediate and final consumption, intervention to control spillover effects, and public investment to maintain and enhance the stock of particular resources. Fifth and finally, even though the trend has been from individual to collective decision-making, there is no value concensus within the region on such issues as the appropriate balance between development and conservation or at what governmental level particular types of controls should be placed. The outcome of changes over the last decade has been to create an increasingly complex infrastructure for public decision-making which is composed of multiple subsystems of varying scale, exercising differing types of authority and providing different access patterns for individuals and private and public groups.

A variety of policy issues and conflicts can be expected to arise in the future. Some, such as a generalized controversy over the rate and type of shoreline development that should occur outside the metropolitan core, have been noted. Most of the issues in this case will be played out through the administration of the Shoreline Management Act at both local and state levels. The nature of the act, however, does not present a clear picture of what development patterns can be expected. Asssuming that the provisions of the law will remain basically the same for the immediate future, a number of factors will affect the actual power of the state and local units over shoreline land use and the relative strength of developmental and conservation proponents in influencing use patterns.

How well the Department of Ecology is funded for the administration of SMA; whether any special effort is made by the state to deal with the Sound or its subareas as resources systems; the investment level of local governments in planning and administering their shorelines; the viability of the national environmental protection movement; the state of the economy; and the resources that private land holders are willing to commit to putting their property to the highest economic use will all affect how the shoreline of the Sound as a whole and its subareas evolve under the new legislation.

Other issues relating to the Sound: the siting and regulation of power plants; oil spill regulations and precautionary measures; new federal shoreline military installations; offshore oil drilling; construction of super-tanker port facilities; and responses to new marine technology all have a high probability of arising in some form. Public responses will grow out of the most relevant subsystem or subsystems. The ultimate test will be whether impasses can be avoided and new policies and configurations of public organizations can be created.

The physical, social, economic, and political systems that relate to resource policy questions found within and overlapping the Sound region do not fit a single boundary. The range of resources, their users and methods of utilization are so varied that they could not be administered by one public agency, even of regional scale, unless its own authority was divided among a myriad of subunits. To remain viable, this variegated governing structure must allow for learning to go on within and among its subsystems and new public arrangements to evolve.

Uncertainty in future development patterns on Puget Sound is not undesirable, particularly given the lack of a strong value consensus among citizens of different parts of the region. The governing structure, with its range of participating units and access points, provides citizens with a reasonable expectation that their preferences will be taken into account in the overall decision-making process. Those who advocate particular "solutions" for the future management of the Sound's resources may find such an open-ended system unsettling; however, uncertainty with regard to specific outcomes where there is no concensus, combined with wide access to decision-making, are characteristics of a fair governing system.

It is common for studies of environmental policy to end with either a plea for a radically reformed governing structure—usually organized on a hierarchical basis—or a new morality. In contrast, the conclusions here must be that humans, whatever their values and preferences, have done a reasonable job in creating an institutional structure for the governance of Puget Sound's resources that matches the diversity and complexity of the Sound's resource system and the uses people make of it. This does not mean that the system is perfect or that it can or should stabilize in a static form. Citizen access is extensive but participation is becoming more costly. Various subsystems have become more sophisticated in resource management and in recognizing their interdependencies but there is certainly more to be done. State and local governments tend to underinvest in relation to the Sound in management and regulatory functions in contrast to directly consumable public goods and services. Even so, the system has demonstrated a capacity for learning and continued evolution as new resource use preferences and conflicts have emerged.

# Bibliography

Avery, Mary W. *Government of Washington State*. Seattle: University of Washington Press, 1966.

Bish, Robert L. *The Public Economy of Metropolitan Areas*. Chicago: Markham Publishing Co., 1971.

————, and Robert Warren. "Scale and Monopoly Problems in Urban Government services." *Urban Affairs Quarterly* 8 (September 1972): 97-122.

Bish, Robert L., and Vincent Ostrom. *Understanding Urban Government: Metropolitan Reform Reconsidered*. Washington, D.C.: American Enterprise Institute, 1973.

Bone, Hugh A. "Washington State: Free Style Politics." Pp. 380-415 in Frank H. Jonas, ed., *Politics in the American West*. Salt Lake: University of Utah Press, 1969.

Borland, Stewart, and Martha Oliver. *Port Expansion in the Puget Sound Region*. Seattle: Division of Marine Resources, University of Washington, WSG-MP 72-1, October 1972.

Boschken, Herman L. "Mismarketing in Urban Development: A Case Study of Boise Cascade Recreation Communities." Ph.D. dissertation, University of Washington, 1972.

Bradley, Earl H., Jr., and John M. Armstrong. *A Description and Analysis of Coastal Zone and Shorelands Management Programs in the United States*. Ann Arbor: University of Michigan Sea Grant Program, March 1972.

Buchanan, James M., and Gordon Tullock. *The Calculus of Consent: The Logical Foundations of Constitutional Democracy*. Ann Arbor: University of Michigan Press, 1962.

Campbell, D.C. *Introduction to Washington Geology and Resources*. Olympia: State of Washington Department of Conservation, Division of Mines and Geology, Information Circular no. 22R, 1962.

Cheung, Stephen N. S. "The Structure of a Contract and the Theory of a Non-exclusive Resource." *Journal of Law and Economics* 13 (April 1970): 49-70.

Collias, E. E., and A. C. Duxbury. *Bibliography of Literature: Puget Sound Marine Environment.* Seattle: Division of Marine Resources, University of Washington, December 1971.

Commission on Marine Science, Engineering, and Resources. *Our Nation and the Sea.* Washington, D.C.: U.S. Government Printing Office, January 1969.

————. *Marine Resources and Legal-Political Arrangements for Their Development,* vol. 3. Panel Reports, Washington, D.C.: U.S. Government Printing Office, January 1969.

Corker, Charles E. "Thou Shall Not Fill Public Waters without Public Permission: Washington's Lake Chelan Decision." *Washington Law Review* 45 (1970): 65-93.

Crutchfield, James A., and Giulio Pontecorvo. *The Pacific Salmon Fisheries: A Study of Irrational Conservation.* Baltimore, Md.: John Hopkins Press, 1969.

Dicken, S. N. "Western Oregon and Washington." Pp. 54-64 in O. W. Freeman and H. H. Martin, eds., *The Pacific Northwest.* New York: John Wiley and Sons, 1954.

Gordon, H. Scott. "The Economic Theory of a Common-Property Resource: The Fishery." *Journal of Political Economy* 62 (April 1954): 124-42.

Harrison, Peter. "The Land Water Interface in an Urban Region: A Spatial and Temporal Analysis of the Nature and Significance of Conflicts between Coastal Uses." Ph.D. dissertation, University of Washington, 1973.

Haskell, E. H., and V. S. Price. *State Environmental Management: Case Studies of Nine States.* New York: Praeger, 1973.

Hayek, F. A. "The Use of Knowledge in Society." *American Economic Review* 35 (September 1946); 519-30.

Ketchum, Bostwick, ed. *The Water's Edge: Critical Problems of the Coastal Zone.* Cambridge: Massachusetts Institute of Technology Press, 1972.

Lindblom, Charles. *The Intelligence of Democracy: Decision-Making through Mutual Adjustment.* New York: Free Press, 1965.

Morry, Susan F. *1970 Seacoast Management Bill: Background and Analysis.* Seattle: Division of Marine Resources, University of Washington, October 1971.

Nathan, Harriet, and Stanley Scott, eds. *Towards a Bay Area Regional Organization.* Berkeley: Institute of Governmental Studies, University of California, 1969.

Olson, Mancur, Jr. *The Logic of Collective Action: Public Goods and the Theory of Groups.* Cambridge, Mass.: Harvard University Press, 1965.

Ostrom, Vincent. "Operational Federalism: Organization for the Provision of Public Services in the American Federal System." *Public Choice* 6 (Spring 1969): 1-18.

————. *The Intellectual Crisis in American Public Administration.* University: University of Alabama Press, 1973.

Pacific Northwest River Basins Commission, Puget Sound Task Force. *Puget Sound and Adjacent Waters.* Vancouver, Wash.: 1970. This is a multivolume study with appendixes on navigation, fish and wildlife, water related land resources, pleasure boating, water quality control, power, and other resources of the Puget Sound Region.

Rauscher, E.A. "The Lake Chelan Case: Another View." *Washington Law Review* 45 (1970): 523-33.

*Shorelines Management: The Washington Experience.* Proceedings of a Symposium, Environmental Quality Committee, Young Lawyers Section, American Bar Association, Washington Sea Grant Program, University of Washington, Seattle, 1972.

Spangler, Miller N. *New Technology and Marine Resource Development.* New York: Praeger, 1970.

Spencer, Wallace H. *Environmental Management for Puget Sound: Certain Problems of Political Organization and Alternative Approaches.* Seattle: Division of Marine Resources, University of Washington, November 1971.

Sweet, David. *The Economic and Social Importance of Estuaries.* Columbus, Ohio: Batelle Institute, 1971.

Tullock, Gordon. *The Politics of Bureaucracy.* Washington, D.C.: Public Affairs Press, 1965.

U.S. Bureau of the Census. *Census of Population 1970, General Social and Economic Characteristics,* vol. 49, *Washington State.* Washington, D.C.: Government Printing Office, 1972.

U.S. Department of the Interior, Bureau of Fish and Wildlife Service. *National Estuary Study,* vols. 1-7. Washington, D.C.: U.S. Government Printing Office, 1970.

Washington State Research Council. *The Research Council's Handbook.* Olympia: 1973.

# Index